Young Citizens of the World

- What really counts as social studies?
- What does good social studies teaching look like?

Young Citizens of the World takes a clear stance: social studies is about citizenship education that is informed, deliberative, and activist – citizenship not only as a noun, something one studies, but as a verb, something one DOES. The holistic, multicultural approach is based on this clear curricular and pedagogical purpose.

Straightforward, engaging, and highly interactive, the text lays out a three-part process for civic preparation that helps students understand their world and their place, as citizens, in it: becoming informed, thinking it through, and taking action. Six outstanding teaching strategies bring this framework to life. Social studies for young learners is treated as constructive, dramatic, deliberative, conceptual, literature-based, and inquiry-oriented.

Each chapter is written as a civic engagement. Teaching/learning projects throughout are invitations to learn through intensive, integrated meaningful studies of special places, important people, and significant times. These civic engagements are teacher-ready for use in elementary classrooms. Readers are encouraged to rehearse the projects in their social studies education courses and then to reinterpret them for their classrooms.

Providing a powerful alternative to the Expanding Horizons social studies curriculum, *Young Citizens of the World* is a compelling choice for elementary social studies education courses, as well as for practicing teachers who wish to enhance their social studies instruction.

Marilynne Boyle-Baise is Professor, Department of Curriculum and Instruction, Indiana University, Bloomington.

Jack Zevin is Professor of Social Studies Education, Queens College, City University of New York.

Young Citizens of the World

Teaching Elementary Social Studies through Civic Engagement

MARILYNNE BOYLE-BAISE
INDIANA UNIVERSITY, BLOOMINGTON

JACK ZEVIN
QUEENS COLLEGE, CITY UNIVERSITY OF NEW YORK

Routledge
Taylor & Francis Group

NEW YORK AND LONDON

First published 2009
by Routledge
270 Madison Ave, New York, NY 10016

Simultaneously published in the UK
by Routledge
2 Park Square, Milton Park, Abingdon,
Oxon OX14 4RN

Routledge is an imprint of the Taylor & Francis Group, an informa business

© 2009 Taylor and Francis

Typeset in Minion Pro by Prepress Projects Ltd, Perth, UK
Printed and bound in the United States of America on acid-free paper by Edward Brothers, Inc

Library of Congress Cataloging in Publication Data
A catalog record has been requested for this book

British Library Cataloguing in Publication Data
A catalogue record for this book is available from the British Library

ISBN 10: 0–8058–8042–9 (hbk)
ISBN 10: 0–415–99941–3 (pbk)
ISBN 10: 0–203–88060–9 (ebk)

ISBN 13: 978–0–8058–8042–7 (hbk)
ISBN 13: 978–0–415–99941–0 (pbk)
ISBN 13: 978–0–203–88060–9 (ebk)

This book is dedicated to our families, especially to Michael Baise and Iris Zevin, for their unstinting support, over the years, with our many hours of academic research and writing.

Contents

Preface
Why this book?

We've been teaching elementary social studies to prospective teachers for a long time. Over the years we have used a range of texts to center our courses. Most texts, even very good ones, tend to present social studies as a series of discrete parts: aims and standards, social science content, map and globe skills, instructional approaches, and assessment strategies. Future teachers struggle to grasp the essence of social studies; it seems so broad and abstract. What, they ask, really counts as social studies? They want to know, what does good social studies teaching look like?

Taking a Stance

In this book, we take a clear, unequivocal stance toward these questions. From our perspective, social studies is about citizenship education, not social science acquisition. It is about citizenship, not only as a noun, as something one studies, but also as a verb, as something one DOES. For young learners, it is developmental, constructive, dramatic, deliberative, conceptual, and inquiry-oriented. Social studies should help youth understand their world and their place, as citizens, in it. We define citizenship-as-a-verb and provide a three-part process for civic preparation: become informed, think it through, and take action. This framework is not new, but, rather, revitalized. As we discuss later in detail, it harks back to the scholarship of an icon in social studies, Harold O. Rugg, who proposed that citizenship education is the "democratic-method-in-action" (1936, p. viii)—it is a rehearsal of civic engagement.

Each chapter is written as a civic engagement, and this term carries a double meaning: projects are intended as engagements, or invitations to learn, and they are presented as demonstrations of democracy-in-action. We think that civic engagements tap into ways elementary youth actually learn: through intensive, integrated, meaningful studies of special places, important people, and significant times. Moreover, such studies are, at heart, what social studies is meant to be: interesting, holistic, cross-disciplinary investigations of social/cultural/political/economic ideas, trends, and events. We offer these civic engagements fully wrought, as teachers might utilize them in elementary classrooms. Our prospective teachers practice the projects, as part of our collegiate courses, then reinterpret them for their classrooms.

Another reason for this book: there is a tendency among social studies educators of all stripes to be ahistorical. We simply do not know the historical roots for our field. We are unaware of the definitions, purposes, experiments, and biases built into the field from its earliest days. Thus we tend to mix and match all sorts of carefully delineated schools of thought, or invent our own renditions of social studies. In this book, to counter this tendency we ground the field, linking the past to the present with trends that span curricular time.

And, just one more thing: talk abounds about research-based practice, but few educators actually do it. Instead, we often bemoan the gap between theory and practice. In this book we include a section on "Learning from Research" in each chapter, then we link investigative insights to instructional suggestions. In this way, we hope to foster outstanding, powerful social studies teaching and learning.

Chapter by Chapter

In each chapter, we try to tap into the essence, vitality, and verve of social study. We aim to make each chapter an exemplar for living, breathing, robust social studies; there is nothing dull or tedious about it. Instead, we dare teachers to be different, to challenge customary social studies, making business-as-usual—unusual.

- Chapter 1: **Social Studies as Citizenship Education** describes the historic roots of the field.
- Chapter 2: **Citizenship as a Verb** defines the conceptual framework for the book.
- Chapter 3: **Democracy Project I** and Chapter 4: **Democracy Project II** focus on learning democratic principles and talking democratically.
- Chapter 5: **Worldview** demonstrates the development of world-mindedness.
- Chapter 6: **History Mystery** takes an investigative slant on rediscovering our past.
- Chapter 7: **Biography Workshop** provides a means to teach civic history through the composition of citizen's life stories.
- Chapter 8: **Store** focuses on economic decision-making.

- Chapter 9: **Explore** investigates place and space.
- Chapter 10: **Engage** returns to historic roots for the field, updating the early call to teach social studies as "living one's civics."

You can envision the chapters as linking to, yet *contrasting* with, the normal course of events in elementary schools. Chapters do not have to be used in the order they appear in the book. Thus, for example, *Democracy Project* I (Chapter 3) teaches about the Constitution, offering a deliberative alternative to a Constitution Day party. *Worldview* (Chapter 5) provides an option to the Columbus story, challenging the myth of discovery and investigating the Columbian Exchange. *History Mystery* (Chapter 6) can be utilized anytime, but, in November, it can foster inquiry into the lives and concerns of indigenous peoples. *Newlandia*, an engagement in *Explore* (Chapter 9), is another good fit for November, when pilgrims and pilgrimage are a focus, offering a deliberative simulation of human settlement. *Store* (Chapter 8) helps youth grasp the economic culture of which they are a part, offering food for thought during seasons of giving. *Biography Workshop* (Chapter 7) is a perfect way to bring lives of outstanding citizens to light, especially during months devoted to particular groups. *Engage* (Chapter 10) can be taught all year, as an ongoing impetus to serve and learn.

Civic Engagements

Each chapter presents a civic engagement that is structured in the following way.

- *What and Why?*: In this section, we introduce the project and suggest its worth.
- *Learning from Research*: In this section, we connect the project to research about how children learn social studies.
- *Teacher's Scholarly Knowledge*: In this section, we outline the background knowledge needed to introduce big ideas, frame historic events, mount relevant inquiries, guide decision-making, and take community action related to the topic at hand.
- *Teaching Resources*: In this section, we provide resources for teaching, including children's literature, primary documents, films, visuals, music, and role plays.
- *Teach!*: In this section, we draw upon six outstanding teaching strategies to promote powerful citizenship education.
- *Teacher Review*: In this section, we invite teacher reflection. We encourage readers to look back on the chapter, rethinking its main points and contemplating what they have learned.
- *Making Connections*: In this final section, we make linkages from the present chapter to earlier ones. We attempt to create interweavings that permeate conventional chapter boundaries.

Outstanding Teaching Strategies and Forms of Engagement

In our quest to teach citizenship-as-a-verb, in the **"Teach!"** sections within the chapters we utilize six outstanding teaching strategies and two forms of engagements. These strategies enact aspects of our civic framework—*Become Informed, Think it Through, Take Action*—as outlined below. We see these strategies as sequential, building children's knowledge from one activity to the next; however, not neatly so. Students might read a little, write a little, role play a character, then read some more. In each chapter we utilize some, but not all, of the strategies—as pertinent to the topic of focus. The graphic organizer on page xv illustrates the usage of these strategies across chapters.

Become Informed

- **Teaching Strategy: Focus In**: A strategy to focus children's attention on the subject at hand, usually through a selection of quality children's literature.
- **Teaching Strategy: Teach for Ideas**: A strategy that helps youth form ideas through studying multiple examples.
- **Teaching Strategy: Teach for Inquiry**: An investigative strategy that helps youth discover information.

Think It Through

- **Teaching Strategy: Teach through Drama**: A strategy that gives children a sense of "being there" in a place or time.
- **Teaching Strategy: Write to Learn**: An expressive strategy that helps students recall and write about what they have learned, creatively, taking on a role of someone pertinent to the time or topic.

Take Action

- **Teaching Strategy: Teach for Deliberation**: The use of a discussion web to assist youth in their consideration of multiple points of view.
- **Engagement: Civic Action**: An engagement in civic affairs, teaching others, working with others, for the benefit of all. These endeavors develop civic skills, such as letter-writing or conducting a meeting.
- **Engagement: Service Learning**: An engagement in which there is a relationship between classrooms and communities as children work with and learn from local mentors. These efforts develop an ethic of service: tolerance, humanism, open-mindedness, and communal spirit.

Pedagogical Pauses

We invite teachers to pause and think creatively throughout the text. We utilize several icons to raise special attention.

TABLE 0.1 Young Citizens of the World: Structure of the Book

Teaching Strategies; Forms of Engagement	Focus In	Teach for Ideas	Teach for Inquiry	Teach through Drama	Write to Learn	Teach for Deliberation	Civic Action	Service Learning
Chapter 1								
Chapter 2	Aunt Flossie's Hats	What is Oral History?	What was the 92nd Division?	Ruby Bridges	Oral Histories	Greensboro Sit-ins		Publishing Oral Histories
Chapter 3	A More Perfect Union	What is the Constitution?	• Who is Qualified to be President? • What do Members of Congress Do?	Constitutional Convention		Count Me In	Make a Classroom Constitution	
Chapter 4	Horton Hears a Who					• Making a Democratic Classroom • What did we Learn? • What's the Problem? • Getting Ready for Discussion • Holding a Discussion	High (Town) Council	
Chapter 5	• Encounter • The Biography of Chocolate	• What is the Columbian Exchange? • What is the History of Chocolate?	• Who was Christopher Columbus • Did Slaves Make Chocolate?	From Bean to Bar: How Chocolate Gets Here	• Encounter with Christopher Columbus • Chocolate Making: What's Your Role?	Was the Columbian Exchange a Good or Bad Thing?	Share your Knowledge	
Chapter 6	The Ballot Box Battle	What is Women's Suffrage?	• Learning to do History • Why did Suffragists Use Protests?	Susan B. Anthony Trial			Demonstrating the Women's Suffrage Movement	
Chapter 7	Mighty Times	What Makes a Biography?	Who was Rosa Parks?	Refusing to Give Up her Seat	Composing the Biography		Teach about Rosa Parks	
Chapter 8	The Story of Money	• What is Money? • What is Scarcity?	What Should I Do with my Money?	• Store • Mini-economy		Saving or Spending?	Organize a Buy Nothing Day	Raise Funds for a Good Cause
Chapter 9	• Me on the Map • Emeka's Gift	• What is an Explorer? • M&M's Community • What is Nigeria?	• Explorations • What is Life Like in Nigeria? • How does Oil Affect Life in Nigeria?	• 3-D Map Project • Newlandia	Post-It			
Chapter 10	Ryan and Jimmy and the Well that Brought Them Together	What is the Water Crisis?	What can Children do to Reduce Water Shortage?	How can we be of Service?				• Canned Food Drive • Intergenerational Biography Project • Serving for Ryan's Well Foundation

A light bulb asks the reader to stop and think about an important point.

 A five-point star indicates that it is the reader's turn to try strategies on his/her own.

 A ringing bell alerts readers to a special note of explanation.

time, the federal *No Child Left Behind Act* (NCLB, P.L. 107–110, 2002) has hastened its decline. Today, the teaching of reading and, to a slightly lesser extent, mathematics is prioritized in most elementary schools, drastically reducing time spent on social studies (Center on Education Policy, 2008). Why is reading first? In most states, reading abilities are tested as part of NCLB, whereas social studies is not. One way to put it is this: mandated annual assessments in reading (and math) are "driving the elementary school curriculum" (VanFossen, 2005, p. 377).

Confusion over what counts as social studies, scanty knowledge of social events and affairs, and limited teacher preparation, set against clear purposes for reading and enhanced opportunities to learn to teach it, make it easy to discount social studies. Recent findings indicate that teachers devalue social studies, misunderstand its purpose, and fail to utilize powerful instructional methods (Burroughs, Groce, & Webeck, 2005; Rock et al., 2006; VanFossen, 2005; von Zastrow & Janc, 2004). We think you will find the following investigations of what is happening in schools today quite interesting.

In a survey of over 500 elementary teachers in Indiana, VanFossen (2005) found that teachers ranked social studies last among core subjects and that only one third identified its purpose as citizenship education. A range of other rationales for social studies were offered: social studies was seen as a vehicle for developing skills in language arts/reading, or for gaining life skills in good character, or for teaching specific social science content (this latter aim was predominant among upper elementary teachers). Regardless of aim, teachers taught very little social studies on average in a school day.

In a survey of 18 elementary teachers in North Carolina, Burroughs, Groce, and Webeck (2005) found that teachers focus on reading and math, marginalizing social studies instruction to less than 30 minutes per week. The majority of teachers incorporate social studies into reading instruction, using children's literature to teach about social concerns. Most try to "cover" state social studies standards with brief, superficial instruction. Teachers particularly tried to teach good character, respect for cultural diversity, and map skills.

In a survey of 320 cooperating teachers, linked to the North Carolina University System, Rock and her colleagues (2006) found a slightly higher ranking of social studies than did VanFossen, as a third core subject—after reading and math. Most teachers taught social studies two or three days a week, with students in kindergarten and fifth grade receiving the most instruction. For kindergarten, instruction focused on life skills, whereas for fifth grade, content outlined in state standards was emphasized. The majority of teachers described their teaching as standards-driven, and they embraced integration (social studies into language arts) as a satisfactory means to teach social studies.

We participated in this line of research, interviewing and observing teachers who supervised our social studies field experience (Boyle-Baise et al., 2008). We discovered an interesting twist to the trend to put reading first. Teachers were told by school administrators to prioritize reading, and they did. Yet, to them, the integration of social studies into reading represented a means of keeping social studies alive. Primary teachers discussed social studies content as it related to stories in the basal reader. Intermediate teachers focused on reading social studies textbooks well, as a means to teach skills for reading non-fiction. At the primary level, social studies teaching tended to be happenstance, or unplanned moments of explanation in relation to stories in basal readers. At the intermediate level, engaging activities, such as inquiries, role plays, or simulations, took a back seat to reading texts, mostly to stress reading comprehension. Regardless of teachers' efforts to keep social studies alive, these approaches are not ideal; they focus solely on textual learning and treat social studies as a second-class subject.

Our task is to help you see the value of social studies—as fundamental to the elementary curriculum. We will assist you in understanding purposes for social studies, in choosing powerful strategies for instruction, and in exploring substantive projects for curricular integration. We will address aims, topics, and approaches that are currently missing in much of what counts for social studies instruction: civic engagement, social justice, cultural diversity, decision-making, concept formation, inquiry learning, and service activities. In this book, we address these notions as significant aspects of democracy education.

Purposes for Social Studies: Historic Roots

Very few elementary teachers know about the origins of the social studies (Saxe, 1992; VanFossen, 2005). Over time, the central goals for social studies have been lost. Teachers often recreate social studies, according to their own aims. There is no need to reinvent the wheel. Clear purposes, sound principles, and innovative practices for teaching social studies can be found in its past. In this rest of this chapter, we reconnect you to this history.

Three competing theories are posed about the origins of social studies: (1) the continuous spontaneous existence (CSE) theory, (2) the big bang theory, and (3) the history foundations theory (Saxe, 1992). You probably think in terms of the CSE theory now: social studies is a subject, it has always been a subject, and its past is irrelevant. The big bang theory holds that social studies was invented in 1916 by the Report of the Committee on Social Studies, *The Social Studies in Secondary Education* (Dunn, 1916). The history foundation theory suggests that history was the seedbed of social studies. David Saxe (1992) suggests a fourth theory: social studies was coined by social welfare advocates, prior to 1916, as part of their humanitarian goal to improve the lives of the urban poor.

Then, as now, national committee reports on education carried great weight in setting trends for public education. The National Education Association and the American Historical Association sponsored several national reports of note for our purposes. We will take a look at the *1916 Report on the Social Studies in Secondary Education*, which was part of a larger Commission on the Reorganization of Secondary Education of the National Education Association. We also will examine a series of committees focused on the reorganization of history courses.

The 1916 Report

Why should you care about a report on social studies that is almost a century old? In 1994, Dr. Shirley Engle, an acclaimed social studies leader, provided a compelling answer to this question. In the introduction to a reprint of the Report, he wrote:

> The 1916 Report of the Committee on Social Studies is widely believed to be the most important document in the long history of citizenship education in this country. It legitimated the term "social studies" to designate formal citizenship education and placed squarely in the field all those subjects that were believed to contribute to that end. While recognizing the importance of history and the social sciences as contributing to that end, the Committee's Report recognized that citizenship is something more than mere mastery of separate disciplines. It recognized the study of social problems as a necessary part of the education of citizens. It outlined a content for the social studies which was widely adopted and has remained remarkably unchanged to this day. (Engle, 1994, p. vii)

According to the Report, "the social studies of the American high school should have for their conscious and constant purpose the cultivation of good citizenship" (Dunn, 1916, p. 9). Social studies was developed as the premier model for citizenship education. During the early 1900s, social studies emerged as a means to cultivate reflective citizens amid times marked by world war, massive immigration, rapid urbanization, overcrowded slums, inadequate sanitation, and strains on families, as well as by advances in technology, industry, and science (Nelson, 1994; Saxe, 1992). The times were thoroughly modern and a traditional, academic curriculum was perceived as outdated and ill-suited.

The *1916 Report* calls for all subjects to be "socialized" or brought into line with modern social needs and student interests. The Commission on the Reorganization of Secondary Education proposed seven "Cardinal Principles" for contemporary education. Schooling was to promote the study and practice of: health, command of fundamental processes (reading, writing, oral expression, and math), worthy home membership (literature, music, social studies, and art), vocation (career education), civic education, worthy use of leisure (enrichment for body, mind, and spirit), and ethical character (NEA, 1918). If these principles seem pragmatic, or life-oriented, they were. If they seem familiar, like the organization of education today, they are.

Social efficiency was the watchword of the day. Social efficiency stood for people's power to engineer their environments to run more efficiently—in a more orderly, productive, and safe way (Kliebard, 1986). As a model for citizenship, social efficiency meant preparation of youth to fit into society and to contribute as per one's individual capabilities. The good citizen was a "thoroughly efficient member" of his/her city, state, and nation—loyal, responsible, and respectful, industrious (Dunn, 1916, p. 9).

Fitting in, or adaptation, had a sinister side, however. To understand it, we need to examine the ideas of Thomas Jesse Jones, chair of the 1916 Committee. Jones directed social education at the Hampton Institute, a vocational training school for African Americans and American Indians. He believed in the theory of racial evolution. According to this theory, people of color formed the underclass in society because of personal deficits, rather than structural barriers (Dilworth, 2003–4). Education could be used to ameliorate these deficits and to hasten social advancement. Thus, the curriculum should focus on the development of desirable habits and ideals (e.g., obedience, thriftiness, punctuality, and industriousness) as defined by white, middle-class society (Correia, 1994; Kliebard, 1994; Nelson, 1994). As a result of civic virtue and hard work, social improvement (it was thought) would, slowly, accrue. In the meantime, Blacks and American Indians should adapt to (and accept) their present stations in life (Dilworth, 2003–4). This theory has been wholly discredited, but its tenets seeped into the *1916 Report* as appropriate for children of workers, immigrants, and people of color. Social efficiency was reformist—its goal was to focus curriculum on social needs and student interests—but it also was accommodationist—its aim was to promote adaptation and to maintain social order.

Community civics was proposed as a novel, integral aspect of citizenship education. What did it mean? To answer this question, we need to examine the ideas of Arthur William Dunn, author of the Report. Dunn incorporated his program for civic education in Indianapolis, Indiana, almost wholly into the Report. In a 1915 curriculum plan, Dunn described community civics as "training in habits of good citizenship, rather than merely a study of government forms and machinery" (1915, p. 8). The teaching of compliant habits, such as responsibility, helpfulness, cooperation, and orderliness, were outlined, along the lines of social efficiency. But Dunn also broke with this mold, arguing for a more engaged, thoughtful citizen. Community civics, proposed Dunn, should "develop political intelligence and prepare young citizens for its exercise" (p. 8). In the sixth grade curriculum, teachers were to cultivate "initiative, judgment, cooperation, power to organize knowledge around current events—all of which are civic qualities of first importance" (p. 17). Further, emphasis was "laid on what the child can *do* for the community" (italics his) (p. 17). Students were to be given opportunities to "live their civics" (Dunn, 1916, p. 22), in the school and in the community.

So, what did it mean to *live one's civics*? In Indianapolis, opening exercises (something like classroom meetings today) were utilized to foster discussion about civic behavior—including the remission of pranks! A democratic spirit was cultivated in class; the class worked together on topics of common interest. A problem method was used to teach content; for example, in sixth grade, continents and countries were investigated with a problem, such as declining international influence, in mind. School gardening cultivated civic habits, like a spirit of mutual endeavor. Additionally, community service was emphasized. As examples, children served the school as playground monitors and worked in neighborhood beautification efforts.

Where did history fit into the *1916 Report*? The Committee decided that the "best time to introduce history in the education of the child is when it is of immediate use" (1916, p. 31). An example was given: teach the history of education, commerce, or democracy

two
Citizenship as a Verb
Teaching Democracy-in-Action

Citizenship (sit´ e zen ship) v.
- learning big ideas about democracy, nationality, equality, and diversity;
- constructing a civic identity;
- practicing democratic skills; and
- participating in public affairs.

In Chapter 1, we presented a conundrum: is citizenship a noun or a verb, is it mastery of knowledge or capacity to participate, is it something one studies or something one does? In this text, we see citizenship as a verb; as learning about our nation and the world, as thinking about dilemmas of equality and equity, and as acting democratically on issues of collective concern. Envisioning citizenship as a verb does not mean relinquishing citizenship as democratic studies. Instead, it means using such studies as a springboard for deliberation, problem-solving, and community action. Walter Parker (2003, p. 19) refers to this orientation as a "knowledge-plus" position—as democratic knowledge plus civic consideration and public action, or, in short, as informed civic engagement. Presently, this orientation is hard to find in elementary schools.

Let's figure out what counts as a "good" citizen in our elementary schools today. Teachers often tell us that they "do social studies all day," or that "social studies is part of life." They interpret citizenship education as learning to get along in the classroom. This aim is significant. When children enter classrooms, they enter a civic arena, a place where collective actions and common goals matter. As Vivian Paley says of her kindergartners, school "is the first real exposure to the public arena. Children are required to share materials and teachers in a space that belongs to everyone" (1992, p. 21). Paley finds this first civic experience a perfect time to teach deliberation, or to weigh alternatives about what "we," as a class, should do. She and her students spend a lot of time considering a new rule: *you can't say you can't play*. They wonder whether the rule is "right" or "fair." Paley's deliberative response to the challenge of "getting along" is, however, rare.

Citizenship education programs tend to focus on one of the following forms: personally responsible, participatory, or justice-oriented citizenship (Westheimer & Kahne, 2004). A personally responsible citizen exhibits "good" character traits, such as honesty, integrity, respect, and compassion. This kind of citizen acts responsibly in the community: works hard, obeys rules, volunteers, and votes. In schools, this means playing by the rules, using self-control, making good choices, and doing one's personal best. A participatory citizen is involved in civic affairs, at local, state, and national levels. He/she knows how government works and has skills to participate collectively. In schools, this means investigating classroom and school concerns, making decisions that affect all students, taking part in student councils, and working on service projects. The justice-oriented citizen looks critically at systemic causes for problems such as drug addiction, obesity, homelessness, or neglect of senior citizens. The justice-oriented citizen turns social inquiry into social action in order to redress injustice. In schools this means identifying cases of inequality, unfairness, meanness, or ill treatment that are relevant to children and acting to improve them.

In most schools today, character education or life skills programs predominate. A strong point of this kind of education is that it can develop ethical, respectful individuals. However, a weakness is that it can emphasize compliant, obedient behavior, rather than deliberative, inquisitive mindsets. Also, it can emphasize the achievement of one's personal best at the expense of collective goodwill.

The participatory orientation is strongly reflected in definitions, skills, and standards promoted by the National Council for the Social Studies (NCSS 1989; 1994; Task Force on Standards for Teaching and Learning in the Social Studies, 1992). A strong point for this kind of education is that it can teach dispositions and capacities for civic engagement. However, a weak point is that it can downplay the knowledge aspect of decision-making, leading to opinionated, rather than informed, discussions. Further, it can sidestep questions about the worth of participation. Students need to consider what they are doing, for whom, with whom, at what cost, and for what benefit.

A powerful aspect of the justice orientation is that it can affirm diversity, teach equality, and foster humanitarianism. However, a challenging aspect of this stance is that it can involve teachers and students in discussions of racism or other forms of bias and hatred. These topics are controversial with no easy answers.

 Stop for a moment and consider what kind of citizenship education you have experienced. What is your experience of democratic participation or justice-oriented action? Are you likely to teach these forms? Why? Why not?

Each form of citizenship has its time and place. However, to us, personally responsible citizenship alone is a weak form of civic engagement. It is important to develop laudable individual behavior, but students need to put responsibility to work on behalf of the groups of which they are a part. The teaching exemplars, in this text, focus on participatory and justice-oriented citizenship. As noted earlier, we propose a three-part model of citizenship. Young citizens of the world (and their teachers) are: informed, reflective, and active. This model reaches back to early aims for social studies and forward to current demands for civic engagement.

Teaching Democracy-in-Action

Probably, you are quite familiar with a knowledge-focused stance from your own schooling. We will outline it as a means of review. Then, we will devote several pages to an examination of the reflection, participation, or decision-making stance, as it is likely less recognizable to you.

James Banks (1997) delineates four periods in the history of social studies: the traditional period, the social studies revolution of the 1960s and 1970s, the public issues period of the 1970s and 1980s and the resurgence of history and the rise of multiculturalism since the 1980s. As Banks notes, some of these trends were more research than practice, or the other way around; for example, when concept-based teaching was emphasized by social studies scholars, most teachers continued to teach in traditional ways. Also, these trends did not begin or end abruptly; instead, elements from one era seeped into another.

- Traditional Period, 1920–1960 (continuing today): History and geography emphasized. National patriotism developed. Glorious accomplishments of Western civilization and U.S. history underscored. Memorization of dates, places, and people stressed. Teacher talk and student response to questions emphasized.
- Social Studies Revolution, 1960–1970: Also known as the new social studies; key ideas, questions, and practices of disciplines such as history or geography stressed. Students learn to think like historians or geographers, asking questions about time, space, truth, and life—as scholars do.
- Public Issues Period, 1970–1980: Decision-making emphasized. In response to social unrest and reform, effective citizens are reflective citizens who can question democracy, see it as an unfinished ideal, and learn to act for more equality and justice.
- Resurgence of History and Rise of Multiculturalism, 1980 to today: Two conflicting trends emerge: (1) a return to the dominance of history and geography, called back-to-basics, and (2) a call to infuse multicultural content and perspectives into social studies curriculum. Standards for content mastery that attend to both trends are developed and underscored.

Stop and ask yourself, which period represents my own social studies education? Why? Give examples of ordinary and extraordinary social studies lessons from your elementary school days.

Did you recall any moments of reflective decision-making in your elementary social studies education? Although this orientation most likely received slight emphasis in your schooling, it is a perspective with a long history in the social studies field. Let's take a brief look at that history.

The authors of the *1916 Report* (Dunn, 1916) considered subject matter knowledge as a means to an end, rather than as an end in itself. Their goal was the understanding of current issues, based on the study of history, geography, economics, or other social sciences. Recall from Chapter 1 that the Committee recommended the study of history as it related to (and helped explain) present-day events or conditions. The Committee also suggested topical and problem-based studies, rather than chronological studies alone. For example, students might study current problems of genocide, slavery, or civil war by examining their historical antecedents, as well as by considering their geographic, economic, and political dimensions.

Harold O. Rugg brought ideas from the *1916 Report* to life. No one represents the reflective decision-making position more than he. As we mentioned earlier, Rugg thought of citizenship education as a three-part process: information-getting, decision-making, and community action. He called this approach the "democratic method in action" (1936, p. vii). Who was Harold Rugg? How did he shape social studies? As you read the following descriptions, consider what you can draw from his work. We will return to this point later.

From the 1920s to the 1950s, Harold Rugg was a professor of education at Teachers College, Columbia University. He also worked in the college's lab school as an educational psychologist. He spent nine years writing a textbook series that became the first unified social studies curriculum (Nelson, 1977). As Makler (2004) notes, in the 1920s and 1930s, Rugg was considered "the pre-eminent social studies educator of the time" (p. 21). As Nelson (1977, p. 64) states, "before Rugg created his *Social Science Pamphlets*, there were no social studies texts nor were there any social studies courses." His textbook series for the junior high school, *Man and His Changing Society*, influenced a decade of children in the United States. From 1929 to 1939, the series sold almost 1,400,000 copies (Winters, 1967), a huge number for the times.

Information-Getting

After World War I, Rugg sensed a new American tempo: it was "prestissimo—and its intensity fortissimo" (1926a, p. 4). Much like today, social change, economic expansion, motors, movement, building, and bigness were orders of the day. Rugg criticized the public school as lagging behind the times: "Only rarely has it succeeded in dealing with contemporary issues and conditions; never has it anticipated social needs" (1926a, p. 4).

Rugg wanted to help youth understand (and potentially improve) the society of which they were a part. He proposed the creation of an entirely new curriculum, one that dealt "directly and vigorously with the crucial forces, institutions, and problems of American civilization" (1926b, p. 148). (It is important to note that in order to develop this curriculum, Rugg read widely from social critics or "Frontier Thinkers" of his day. He studied modern society, and he urged students to do the same.)

Rugg wanted to omit subject names from courses of study. He preferred a term that signified integration, like social studies (1936). He questioned whether any student could understand the complexities of society through compartmentalized studies of history, geography, and the like. He wanted to create a new synthesis of knowledge that "ramified ruthlessly across conventional subjects" (1936, p. 336), bringing a wealth of information from history, geography, economics, and political science to bear on social events, conditions, and issues.

Rugg called his curriculum an "adventure" in understanding the drama of modern civilization. His writing was appealing, readable, and conversational. To grab students' attention, he introduced chapters with dramatic episodes, or vignettes that related to their lives. To provoke students' thinking, he raised critical questions about society, such as: Are we the richest nation on earth? To help students grasp their world, he posed big ideas, such as "standard of living" or "interdependence," and he offered many examples of each. For his time, he made liberal use of multimedia, providing a wealth of photos, drawings, graphs, political cartoons, and maps to make the study of contemporary life (and its persistent social problems) relevant, interesting, and meaningful to students.

Decision-Making

Like his colleague John Dewey (Dewey & Dennett, 1935), Rugg sought to educate youth to be thoughtful and deliberative members of their communities. Contrary to imposing one vision of society or another, Rugg claimed that "a prime necessity is the building of intelligent understanding of trends and factors and alternative courses of action in the minds of a vast minority of our people" (Rugg, 1936, p. vi). Rugg wanted youth to become social scientists. In his texts, he provided a mass of factual information for their analysis. He never answered questions as an expert from afar; instead, he invited students to engage in authentic investigations based on each chapter's guiding questions.

It is not surprising to discover that Rugg emphasized class discussions. In the introduction to the companion workbooks for the series, Rugg and his co-author, James Mendenhall, often spoke directly "to the pupils." They asked: How can you get the most from your social studies work (Rugg & Mendenhall, 1940)? They encouraged students to become informed about current events, reading a newspaper daily and a magazine monthly. They urged students to keep a scrapbook of news items, categorizing stories according to problems of the day. Rugg and Mendenhall suggested that students report on their reading to the class, exchanging ideas with their classmates. They recommended that class discussions, open forums, and debates become an important aspect of students' work.

Particularly noteworthy is the authors' advice to students about *open forums*. Students were encouraged to present their perspectives on social questions and to expect that well-informed people can disagree. Open forums "should be based upon all the facts and clear arguments that can be brought together" (e.g., Rugg & Mendenhall, 1940, p. vii). "Light, but not heat" (p. vii) was to be a class slogan, signifying calm, clear, factually based interchange.

Community Action

Rugg found citizens exploited and confused by a modern society they did not understand. He set out to cultivate a new kind of "public mind," one that was informed, deliberative, and tolerant (Carbone, 1977). He believed that ordinary people made decisions in a democracy and, therefore, needed to grasp all sides of an issue (Makler, 2004, p. 20).

Rugg considered the classroom as a prime learning community. Rugg encouraged students to learn with their classmates, through collective inquiry. Students were expected to participate in debates and open forums, write and act in short plays, go on class excursions, and serve on class committees. Rugg considered debates more limited than open forums, and he envisioned more of the latter. Plays were to be short, impromptu expressions of thoughts and feelings about important problems or historical happenings. Excursions were meant as an opportunity to learn about society first hand through visiting industries, stores, city offices, and the like. Committee service was perceived as a means of class governance.

Rugg proposed the "school-centered community" (1931, p. 288): local agencies and businesses should assist with educational activities, under direction of the school. Essentially, he proposed early forms of internship and service learning. For example, businesses should serve as "willing collaborators" (p. 291) with schools; technical skills could be developed through "short courses" in manufacturing plants, stores, and offices. Further, Rugg proposed that, as students served in the community, tolerance and civic participation could be fostered. Rugg embraced both the school and the community as educational places.

Learning from Rugg

What did you learn from the work of Harold Rugg? Let's do what we call a "Boggle" activity. Make a list of what you consider to be important contributions from Rugg. Here is our list. Let's compare the two. What is on your list that is not on ours? Why?

"Top Ten" List of Harold Rugg's Contributions to Social Studies Today

1 As future social studies teachers, we should become students of American society: reading biographies, novels, and essays and watching historical dramas, documentaries, and news shows.

2 We should think about curriculum integration as a synthesis of information from various sources in order to help students understand social topics and issues.
3 We should imagine creating a curricular adventure for social studies, writing dramatic episodes, teaching big ideas, and using multimedia to introduce and illustrate content.
4 We should consider our class as a collective inquiry group and imagine ways to help students learn with and from each other.
5 We should assist youth in doing inquiries about historical times and current events, providing text sets, news items, and other data for their discoveries.
6 We should plan class discussions, including debates and open forums.
7 We should think carefully about what the motto "light, but not heat" means for class discussions—and invite students to do the same.
8 We should plan (and let students help plan) creative writing and acting experiences, and we should go on field trips (even virtual trips).
9 We should create opportunities for students to participate in classroom and school governance.
10 We should imagine ways for students to learn with and from community people, including the provision of opportunities for service learning.

Decision-Making Today

In the 1950s, reflective social studies teaching was kept alive in Hunt and Metcalf's social studies methods textbook, *Teaching High School Social Studies* (1955). They urged prospective teachers to expose closed areas of society, such as social class, prejudice, morality, and religion, to rational inquiry in secondary classrooms. The focus on reflective citizens flowered once again in the 1970s and 1980s as the "public issues" approach (e.g., Oliver & Shaver, 1966/1996; Banks, 1990). At that time, the Civil Rights Movement and other social reforms influenced the social studies curriculum. Some educators argued that social studies should prepare citizens to think through social problems, imagine humane and just alternatives, and act to make a difference.

In 1988, Shirley Engle and Anna Ochoa published what became a popular, widely read book among social studies educators: *Education for Democratic Citizenship: Decision-making in the Social Studies*. The central thesis of the book was that effective citizens are deliberative citizens, thus, decision-making is at the heart of social studies. According to the authors:

> It is our position that the best hope for democracy lies not in indoctrination of shaky truths or in painting over the problems that plague us, but rather the cultivation of citizens who, with open eyes and awareness of democratic values, have the facility to make intelligent political judgments related to controversial issues in our society. (Engle & Ochoa, 1988, p. 5)

The authors urged educators to "stop exhorting students to be 'good citizens' according to an unquestioned view of good and help them, instead, to ask 'good questions' about their own values and those of others" (p. 7). The authors proposed what might be considered a controversial couplet for citizenship education: *socialization* and *counter-socialization*. Students should be guided to understand (and commit to) the basic values, ideas, and principles of democracy, but they should also learn to question its shortcomings and work to improve it.

Recently, Anna Ochoa-Becker updated this important work (Ochoa-Becker, 2007). Again, Ochoa-Becker argues for "movement away from presenting young people with unqualified exposition of facts" (p. 189) and toward consideration of historic and present issues. Democracy, she submits, is "learned as it is questioned" (p. 189). Ochoa-Becker urges teachers to abandon superficial studies of many topics or expansive eras, and, instead, to study small numbers of issues, in depth, with reference to large quantities of data from varied sources. This author also challenges a "sacred cow" for social studies—that information needs to be taught in chronological order. Instead, like the *1916 Report*, she suggests a topical approach: teachers and students should study topics of immediate interest, such as terrorism or genocide, looking for their historical roots, examining their geographic contexts, and searching for their cultural genesis.

The Knowledge-Plus Position

The decision-making curriculum actually is a modest change from the traditional one. History, geography, economics, politics, and cultural studies are still taught, but in a different way. You, as teacher, organize challenging studies of a few issues or topics, drawing upon social science sources (such as historical, geographic, or political information), highlighting multiple perspectives, and including deliberation on issues of concern.

Teaching decision-making does not exclude teaching history. Students can study and learn from decisions made in the past. James Leming, who is skeptical of youth's ability to think critically about complex social issues, recommends that students study historic dilemmas and learn from decisions made by leaders in the past (Leming, 2003). This proposal seems quite reasonable. Students can evaluate pro and con positions and take their own stand related to historic events. However, studies of historical issues offer just one forum for decision-making.

Students can conduct all kinds of inquiries, relevant to their lives or times, such as studies of injustice, investigations of pollution, or examinations of local issues. They can practice deliberation as the culmination of a unit of study, or as the central aspect of it. Additionally, students can participate in class meetings to appreciate and apply decision-making. Even the youngest children can decide on "ways we want our classroom to be" (Developmental Studies Center, 1996), determining, for example, fair classroom norms and policies. This varied use of fact-finding, decision-making, and action-taking is the crux of the *knowledge-plus position*. As the teacher, you help students learn about a topic, deliberate a thorny question therein, and, envision action related to the issue at hand.

From this position, citizenship is a verb; students learn democracy through studying it, questioning it, and considering actions that support aims such as tolerance, open-mindedness, and fairness.

Teaching Social Studies as Reading

Teaching social studies as democracy-in-action is rare in schools today. As we noted in Chapter 1, social studies often is placed on the "back burner" (Houser, 1995) in elementary schools. Life skills or character education still are taught, particularly in early grades. In upper elementary grades, pressure to teach to state standards has saved some time for social studies, especially for teaching history. However, with reading, writing, and mathematics driving the curriculum, time for social studies as a separate subject, with a special pedagogy, such as inquiry and decision-making, has decreased. Instead, integration is the watchword of the day.

Commonly, curriculum integration means the correlation of two subjects so that each *enhances* the other. For example, quality children's literature can bring an historical period to life. However, in today's reading-dominated milieu, social studies is not integrated with reading, but taught through it. Teachers explain social studies ideas that are embedded in stories, not for their significance alone, but in order to boost reading comprehension. Also, teachers utilize literature about memorable people and events, not to teach about the topics alone, but in order to teach skills for reading non-fiction works (Boyle-Baise et al., 2008).

We respect the resourcefulness of teachers who try to fit social studies into reading, but we stand by a different view. We think that as children work through knowledge-rich, inquiry-based, action-oriented civic engagements they can practice good reading, develop strong writing, and rehearse sound thinking. Reading can, indeed, be integrated across the curriculum through its use in a range of subjects, including social studies. We challenge you to find creative ways to teach social studies as a stand-alone subject. We urge you to become knowledgeable and excited about social studies topics and to invite your students to do the same. Times will, of course, change, but, right now, we are asking you to teach against the grain. We are asking you to be a little bit of a rebel in the classroom.

Teaching for Civic Engagement

Each chapter is written as a *civic engagement*. Civic engagements are vehicles for teaching that can help you prepare young citizens of the world. Civic engagements illustrate ways for you to help students construct knowledge, consider big ideas, practice inquiry, grapple with values, make decisions, and take civic action. Civic engagements demonstrate ways to affirm cultural diversity, include technology, and emphasize authentic assessment. The development of such projects is a tall order! We drew upon engagements that we have honed for years in our college classrooms and that we have utilized to help teacher candidates, like you, teach in the field. These civic engagements can be modeled in your college classroom and, then, adapted for your teaching in schools.

In the following sections, we provide some grounding for what you will find in each civic engagement. First, we describe and consider academic standards and principles of powerful teaching and learning as aspects of excellent social studies teaching. Next, we introduce six dimensions for citizenship education that correlate with our knowledge-plus position. Then, we outline six outstanding teaching strategies and two forms of civic engagement that bring our model of citizenship education to life.

Academic Standards

Academic standards proposed by the National Council for the Social Studies (NCSS) frame the curriculum for social studies, suggesting its scope, themes, and benchmarks. State academic standards commonly provide a more detailed description of strands, topics, and lessons for each grade level. In *Expectations for Excellence* (1994), the NCSS defines the field around ten thematic strands. Examine the ten themes below. As you can see, social studies is a broad field, including studies of culture, history, geography, psychology, sociology, political science, economics, technology and society, global education, and civics.

Ten Thematic Strands in Social Studies

1 **Culture**: studies of different cultures; beliefs, ideals, norms, language, etc.
2 **Time, Continuity, and Change**: studies of our historical roots; investigating the past, connecting it to the present, and imagining the future.
3 **People, Places, and Environments**: studies of ways that people, places, and environments interact and shape each other.
4 **Individual Development and Identity**: studies of one's personal identity and how it is shaped by one's culture, social groups, and institutional influences.
5 **Individuals, Groups, and Institutions**: studies of how institutions, such as families, schools, religious groups, government, and courts, play roles in people's lives.
6 **Power, Authority, and Government**: studies of power in U.S. society; what power is, what form it takes, who holds it; what legitimate authority is; and how minority rights are protected within majority rule.
7 **Production, Distribution, and Consumption**: studies of wants, needs, and resources, production, consumption, and distribution.
8 **Science, Technology and Society**: studies of people and technology; how does technology benefit us, how does it change our values, how can we cope with it ethically?
9 **Global Connections**: studies of health care, the environment, human rights, interdependence, ethnic conflicts, and political alliances that impact our world as a community.

10 **Civic Ideals and Practices**: studies of democratic ideals and practices of citizenship. This theme represents the central purpose of social studies.

Thinking of standards-based education as excellent education is ubiquitous today; however, the push for standards, along with the notion that "alignment" to them is essential, is a recent phenomenon—dating back only about 20 years. In 1983, a national blue-ribbon commission issued a report, *A Nation at Risk: The Imperative for Educational Reform,* that was highly critical of public education (National Commission on Excellence in Education, 1983). The commission maintained that a "rising tide of mediocrity" (p. 167) in public schools placed our nation at risk of losing its international economic pre-eminence. The report called for renewed emphasis on excellence in education, defined as a "school or college that sets high expectations and goals for all learners, then tries in every way possible to help students reach them" (p. 173).

A Nation at Risk had a great deal of influence, shaping educational reform for your generation. The report's recommendations spawned discussions of teacher quality, academic standards, graduation requirements, and standardized tests (for students and prospective teachers) that have become commonplace. Accountability is now the watchword of our times. The passage of the *No Child Left Behind Act* (P.L. 107–110) in 2002 fortified the accountability movement. Standards-driven definitions of educational excellence are the order of the day.

Standards-driven education is, however, only one view of excellence. Can you imagine other options? Many teachers think that acting upon teachable moments—serendipitous, unanticipated classroom events—is a mark of excellent education. The development of curriculum at the local level, close to students' interests and needs, is another characteristic of excellent education. Accountability as familiarity with students' backgrounds and as responsiveness to their cultural perspectives is yet another dimension of excellent education.

It is important for you to know that the NCSS standards have been criticized as well as supported. Criticisms include the following: the ten themes are little more than a rehash of traditional disciplines, such as history, geography, and political science; the standards minimize the importance of controversial issues for democratic education; the standards give insufficient attention to intellectual processes, such as evaluation of evidence, consideration of values, and participation in decision-making; and the standards give insufficient attention to citizen engagement, such as service learning and social action (Evans, 2004; Ochoa-Becker, 2001).

Arguments on behalf of the NCSS standards include the following. Social science bases for seven of the ten themes give teachers in history, geography, and economics something to aim for. Performance expectations in the standards demonstrate that the themes are interrelated and encourage teachers to highlight this interrelatedness. Intellectual processes are embedded in each theme. Finally, theme 10, Civic Ideals and Practices, showcases citizenship education as central to social studies (Adler, 2001).

Examine the NCSS standards for yourself. Do you think the themes are a restatement of social science disciplines? Do you see a focus on content mastery or decision-making? Do you see support for learning big ideas, practicing inquiry, or taking civic action?

Our position is that the NCSS standards indicate the breadth of what counts as social studies. You, as a teacher, can refer to them to select topics or themes for teaching and to find some examples of powerful teaching. The standards tilt toward becoming informed. They fall short in their support for inquiry and civic action. You will need to attend to these aspects of citizenship yourself. In each chapter, we suggest ways you can draw from, but not be confined by, existing standards for social studies.

Principles for Powerful Teaching and Learning

In addition to content standards, the NCSS developed five principles for powerful teaching and learning in social studies (NCSS, 1992). These principles can steer you toward engaging methods of instruction. Powerful social studies teaching is: (1) meaningful, (2) integrative, (3) value-based, (4) challenging, and (5) active.

- Social studies is *meaningful* when it teaches important ideas about our society and democratic citizenship and connects them to students' lives.
- Social studies is *integrative* when it crosses disciplinary boundaries, uses varied instructional activities and materials, links past struggles to present issues, and connects knowledge and skills to civic action.
- Social studies is *value-based* when it addresses controversial issues, considers ethical responses, and offers chances to reflect on the common good.
- Social studies is *challenging* when students are motivated to learn new ideas, and when the class works hard to function as a learning community.
- Social studies is *active* when students construct and think critically about their learning and when the teacher participates in learning with students.

We find these principles quite helpful as guides for teaching big ideas, practicing inquiry, and supporting civic action. Social studies should teach significant ideas, not trivial facts, and it should relate these ideas to contexts that students understand. Social studies should help students construct understandings, rather than solely learn definitions determined by others. Social studies should integrate across the social studies curriculum, demonstrating interrelationships among history, geography, and civics. Social studies should address issues that are contentious, from the classroom to the community level, using discussion and deliberation to help students consider several sides to a concern. Also, social studies should provide students with opportunities to act on behalf of the common good in their classrooms, schools, and communities.

- First, present at least two fully developed examples of an idea to students.
- Next, ask them to compare and contrast the examples.
- Then, list similarities and differences as opposites: e.g., the idea is . . . the idea is not . . .
- Finally, present a new example or non-example. Ask students to decide whether the example is/is not a demonstration of the concept.

3 **Teach for Inquiry**: Inquiry is central to the social studies. In order to make informed decisions, future citizens need to be able to locate and evaluate information. Engaging in the inquiry process helps students explore real questions and find their own answers.

- First, explain that inquiry is like a detective process. Raise an *Essential Question* (EQ) that goes to the heart of the matter and that motivates a sense of investigation.
- Next, elicit hypotheses or good guesses from students.
- Then, give students evidence, one clue (or piece of information) at a time.
- After each clue, ask students to revise their hypotheses.
- After several clues, ask students to come to conclusions.
- Compare the conclusions to the original hypotheses.
- Finally, ask students how, if at all, the investigation process changed their minds.

4 **Teach through Drama**: Role play gives children a sense of "being there," as a certain person, in a particular place or time. It can help children grasp history, develop tolerance, and practice empathy. Simulation allows children to recreate reality. It can help children enact dilemmas and "try on" different points of view.

- First, set the scene.
- Next, develop role cards for students, including things they might say.
- Then, discuss what each character might say or feel in his/her role.
- Next, enact the role play or conduct the simulation.
- If possible, allow students to act out different roles.
- Debrief what students learned from "being there" or "acting in" a certain place and time.

5 **Write to Learn:** We often ask students to write a report, articulating their new understandings by recalling factual material. Think how much more fun it could be to take on a role of a real or fictional character and write about the times from his or her point of view! RAFT is a strategy that utilizes creative writing to assess learning. It can be utilized at several points in a unit of study, as long as students have developed a reservoir of information to draw upon. RAFT stands for:

R: Role of the writer.
A: Audience.
F: Format.
T: Topic.

- First, identify the topic. The topic should be one that students have been studying.
- Review big ideas and investigations related to the topic.
- Then, ask children to imagine their role. (We like to use photographs from the time or place and ask students to write from the perspective of a person in the photo.)
- Next, share examples of writing for different audiences, in different formats. Provide important words that students might need to write, as a word wall or glossary.
- Then, give students time to write. (For the youngest students, the writing can be done together as a class.)
- Finally, ask students to share their writing through use of an "author's chair."

Discussion Web

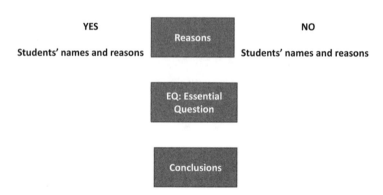

Illustration 2.1 Discussion Web.

6 **Teach for Deliberation**: A *Discussion Web* assists children's development of decision-making skills. Students learn to discuss two sides of an issue and come to consensus about it.

- Raise an EQ about a topic that is controversial and interesting to children.
- Write the EQ on the board. On either side write *Yes* or *No*. Above the question write *Reasons*; below it, write *Conclusions*.
- Next, ask students to individually answer the EQ and to provide their initial reasons. Record students' names, positions, and reasons on the board.

Stevenson, J. (1992). *Don't you know there's a war on?* New York: Greenwillow. The author reminisces about his childhood during WWII. He recalls his father's enlistment as well as his own contribution to the war effort at home.

Photgraphs and Illustrations

The Baltimore Fire (see Appendix B)
WWI and the 92nd Division (see Appendix B)

TEACH!

Become Informed

Focus In: Aunt Flossie's Hats (and Crab Cakes Later) by Elizabeth Fitzgerald Howard

Hook: Pack a small trunk with items like those mentioned in the book: old books, pictures, dried flowers, and hats (lots of hats). Include old photos of the Baltimore fire, the 92nd Division and Black soldiers in WWI, and a facsimile of a family photo album. Ask students: What can you learn about history from looking in Grandma's attic trunk? What kind of mysteries might be inside? What stories can old photos, clothes, or scrapbooks tell?

Focus Activity: Write four to five key facts from the story on sentence strips or a chart. Before reading, ask students: Do you agree or disagree with these statements? Why?

1   Aunt Flossie's hats are clues to important times in her life.
2   History is a story of fires, wars, and everyday events.
3   Older relatives, like Aunt Flossie, can teach us about history.
4   History can be told to us by people who lived through important events.

Reading: Read *Aunt Flossie's Hats* by Elizabeth Howard.

After Reading: Return to the Focus Activity. Reconsider: Do you still agree or disagree with these statements? Why? Why not?

Teach for Ideas: What is Oral History?

- **Hook:** Oral means telling or saying. How did Aunt Flossie tell us about history? Raise essential question (EQ): What is oral history?
- **Example #1:** Colonel Charles Young was the highest ranking African-American soldier at the beginning of WWI (see photo in Appendix B). He

wanted to fight in WWI and to command troops in France. However, his request was denied by the War Department. The Department said he was too ill (he had high blood pressure) and he was too old (he was 53 years old). In order to prove that he was fit for battle, Colonel Young rode on horseback from his home in Ohio to the War Department in Washington, DC. Here is his memory:

As soon as the school year was over, I rode on horseback from Wilberforce to Washington, DC, walking on foot for fifteen minutes each hour, a distance of 497 miles, to show, if possible, my physical fitness for command of troops. I there offered my services gladly at the risk of my life, which has no value for me if I cannot give it for the great ends for which the United States is striving. (http://net.lib.byu.edu/~rdh7/wwi/comment/huachuca/HI1-19.htm)

Ask students what makes this memory an oral history.

- **Example #2:** Read selections from *Through My Eyes* by Ruby Bridges. Ask students what makes this story an oral history.
- **Create a new example:** Ask students to recall the first day of school. Share multiple memories. Ask students what makes these memories oral history.
- **Assessment:** Ask students to explain, in their own words, what oral history is.

Teach for Inquiry: EQ: What was the 92nd Division?

- **Hook:** What did Aunt Flossie remember about the 92nd Division? Show illustrations in Appendix B (A.3 to A.5). Ask essential question (EQ): What was the 92nd Division?
- **Record hypotheses** (or good guesses).
- **Give students evidence**, one clue at a time. Revise hypotheses after each clue.
- **Clue #1:** Study photo of Colonel Charles Young. Tell students he was the most senior African-American officer at the time of WWI. (See Appendix B.)
- **Clue #2:** Study two photos: African Americans enlisting, and troops leaving for war (see Appendix B). Ask students if African Americans wanted to serve in WWI.
- **Clue #3:** Study the recruiting poster entitled "True Sons of Freedom." Ask students if African-American soldiers were really free. Read W. E. B. DuBois' quote about why African Americans should fight, even if they did not have equal rights at home. (See Teacher's Scholarly Knowledge.)
- **Revise hypotheses.** Come to conclusions. Answer the EQ: What was the 92nd Division?

- **Going further:** Consider: What can we learn from a person's memories? Do memories tell us all we need to know?

Think It Through

Teach through Drama: Ruby Bridges

- **Hook:** Read more selections from *Through My Eyes* by Ruby Bridges. This time, focus on the memories of Lucille Bridges, Ruby's mother, and Barbara Henry, Ruby's first-grade teacher. Ask students to consider what these memories tell us about racial inequality.
- **Role play:** Give students roles as Ruby, her teacher, her parents, parents who took their white children out of school, and people in the angry crowd. Narrate the story as children pantomime their roles.
- Ask students how Ruby's fight for equality compares with that of soldiers in the 92nd Division almost 50 years earlier.
- Help students write two or three questions to ask their grandparents (or other older relatives) about fights for equality (e.g., what do you remember about times when people fought for equality? Who fought for equality? What happened?)
- Guide students as needed to complete an oral history interview. Even the youngest students can ask relatives one or two questions and remember their responses.

Write to Learn: Oral Histories

- Share findings from interviews. Tell the oral histories.
- Help students write up the oral histories. It is easiest to write a narrative without quotations, as a story. Write from the perspective of the informant. Try the following heading: _____ (relative's name) history as told to _____ (student's name). Story boards with drawings of the oral history can serve as a reporting format for younger learners.
- Read or tell stories in an Author's Chair.
- Display all oral histories or publish them in a class text.

Take Action

Teach for Deliberation: Greensboro Sit-Ins

In our college classes, we utilize the Discussion Web to highlight (and follow up) a moment of inequality discovered through our students' oral histories. Students told stories of times when a mother fought for equal pay with a male co-worker, or when a single parent was ostracized by her community, or when an

African-American grandmother and great aunt were asked to leave a restaurant for using a "whites-only" bathroom. Particularly outstanding was a memory of a great aunt whose boss told her to dump salt and pepper on the food of patrons of color in order to force them to leave a restaurant. She was fired for her refusal. In response, we built our Discussion Web around the Greensboro Sit-ins, a moment in 1960 when four young African-American men sat down at a lunch counter reserved for whites and asked to be served. The children's book *Freedom on the Menu: The Greensboro Sit-ins* by Carole Weatherford served as the stimulus and "hook" for this lesson. We used oral histories from participants in this event as our primary data. (See Greensboro Sit-ins: www.sitins.com; and Greensboro Voices: http://library.uncg.edu/depts/archives/civrights/index.asp).

- EQ: Should Blacks and whites be served at the same lunch counter?
- Write the EQ on the board. On either side write *Yes* or *No*. Above the question write *Reasons*; below it, write *Conclusions*. Ask students to individually answer the EQ and to provide their initial reasons. Record the students' names, positions, and reasons on the board. Then, ask students to study pro and con readings, corresponding to their *Yes* or *No* position.

Yes: Interview with Ralph Johns by Eugene E. Pfaff, Jr.

EP: Why was a test of segregation made in February 1960? Why was it made in Greensboro? And why was Woolworth's chosen as the target?

RJ: Back in the late forties, I would go to Woolworth and Kress' to eat lunch, and I couldn't understand why I could sit down and eat, and yet the blacks had to stand up or take their food and leave. I would go to the S&W or Mayfair Cafeterias and watch many of my black friends walk by the window where I sat eating, and yet they could not enjoy the same privilege as an American, many who had fought for democracy in the war.

My conscience bothered me, and it broke my heart to see this disrespect given to a human being of another color than white. So from 1949 until 1960, I asked black salespersons who worked in my store and students from A&T [North Carolina A&T State] University to go to those businesses and break the law and try to get served . . . . For eleven years, I tried to get students and members of the NAACP to break their segregated barriers.

Woolworth happened to be the target because I chose it, and after eleven years—1949 to 1960—I finally asked a student who was a freshman at A&T University in my store buying shoes. I told him what I told others. "Joe McNeil, you got any guts?"

"What do you mean?" he asked. This was in December 1959.

Then I told him to get me about four students to go to Woolworth's. I would give them money to buy at different counters and get a receipt for everything they bought, and then go to the lunch counter and sit down to get something to eat. I told him that he would be told by the waitress that they don't serve Negroes—of course, the word "Negro" [was] used, not blacks then. Then I told him to call her a liar, that Woolworth's does serve Negroes, that he was served on four counters and he had the receipts to prove it. Then I told him that, naturally, she would call the manager, and he would try to evict them or call the police. But I said, if he does, then call me on the phone and I would call Jo Spivey of the Greensboro Record to send a reporter and photographer on the scene at once.

Well, Joe McNeil did not come back to my store. Dorothy Graves, who worked as a clerk in my store, said, "He's like all the rest you talked to. He ain't coming back."

But Joe did come back, February 1, 1960, with three more freshmen: Ezell Blair, Franklin McCain, and David Richmond. And they said, "We are here, Cuzzin," a nickname used by me in my many articles. Dorothy, standing there, yelled, "Praise the Lord!"

For one hour, in the back of my store, I planned strategy, telling them what to do, and gave them money to use. And I—and [told them] if trouble started, to call me on the phone. That day was the beginning of the sit-ins that swept America and flowed over into Africa.

EP: What was the status of the law regarding serving blacks at eating places?

RJ: The North Carolina law was no blacks could be seated with whites in any eating establishment or place of entertainment, or use the same toilet or drinking facilities.

No: Oral history interview with Boyd Morris by Eugene Pfaff

EP: I'm speaking today to Mr. Boyd Morris, who was the former mayor of Greensboro, former manager and owner of the Mayfair Cafeteria.

I'd like to turn now to an area of controversy and—which directly affected you as the owner of the Mayfair—and that involves the CORE [Congress of Racial Equality] picketing of the Mayfair. When did that begin?

BM: What was it, '63? In that time, they tried really forcefully to, to integrate. The law of the land was that businesses operate segregated. We were the guinea pigs of America here in Greensboro. We had no knowledge of good or bad, evil or good, whatever. And by law, we had to have restrooms for black, white, male, female. So that was the law, so that's what we knew.

EP: Were you contacted by the Human Relations Commission about your position on desegregating?

BM: Yes. I told the business leaders in the city of Greensboro when they wanted me to integrate the Mayfair Cafeteria, I was the sole owner of the Mayfair Cafeteria. And I told them, and I stand by it, I said, "Gentlemen, if each of you will integrate your places of business, if you will put ten percent black personnel into your operation, the Mayfair Cafeteria will be integrated tomorrow morning. All you've got to do is tell me at this point that you'll do it. I'll take your word for it, and I'll integrate tomorrow morning."

EP: What was their response?

BM: They said, "We're not talking about that. We're talking about integrating the Mayfair."

EP: Did you have an integrated working staff?

BM: Oh, yes, yes. And I was—more, more black than white. But—and I expect food businesses generally are more that way. But I, honestly, I had no feeling about black or white. The, the commission turned my offer around. They wouldn't go into it. So I, in my heart—and I've got to live with my God—I did what I thought was the right thing. I offered, and was rejected.

EP: Did you hire an attorney, like Mr. Benz at the S & W store?

BM: No. I was my own attorney. I was not going to do anything illegal. I told the commission, when the law of the land was changed, that you could bet your money that I would be a law-abiding citizen and operator.

- Next, switch readings, so that all students read both sides.
- Then, mix student groups, including pro and con views in the same group. Add a new reading. Hold a discussion.

New Reading: Oral history interview with Joseph McNeil by Eugene Pfaff

EP: Our interview today is with Joseph McNeil, who, along with David Richmond, Ezell Blair [Jr.] [known now as Jibreel Khazan], and Franklin McCain, conducted the first sit-in of the F. W. Woolworth Company in Greensboro, North Carolina, on February 1, 1960.

EP: Why did you and the other three men test segregation in Greensboro at Woolworth's?

JM: We were all raised in the South, and we all came up under the time when public accommodations were generally refused blacks. I think, perhaps, we all had been refused service in one form or fashion—either at restaurants, hotels—the use of restroom facilities. It was just a number of things that would call to mind that we needed to do something about.

EP: How did the four of you come to know one another?

JM: We were freshmen at A&T College at the time, well, we lived on the same floor of the dormitory, too. And we found some things in common—talked, discussed many things, I guess.

EP: Did you have any sense of the nature of race relations in Greensboro at that time?

JM: I didn't perceive race relations in Greensboro as any different from any other location in the South. Certainly, the things that hit you right out in front were no different: separate water fountains, separate sections on the bus . . . .

EP: Was there anyone who suggested, "All right, this is what we should do, let's do it."

JM: The idea was probably—you know, it's not a seed that was born in some-body's mind in the sixties. What led us, I guess, in acting that particular night was that we met, we talked, and we discussed the need to do something like this. I had previously met a fellow named Ralph Johns, who said he would be helpful to us if we would do something like this.

EP: Was there any plan that you had as to the course of your actions once you entered the store?

JM: We talked about it the night before—and we tried to figure out a response for every possible statement that could be made, or every action that could be taken or directed against us.

EP: What happened?

JM: We went in and we asked for coffee, and we were told that they couldn't serve us and that we'd have to leave. They asked one of the black help to come over and talk to us. A waitress told us we might be getting ourselves involved in something that's trouble and we'd better leave.

EP: What were your feelings as you sat there in the store?

JM: An intense sense of pride, and a bit of fear.

- Ask students to find a mutually agreeable solution to the problem.
- Share possible resolutions to the problem. Add conclusions to the web on the board.

Service Learning

The collection, posting, and publishing of oral histories are community services. Students helped to tell the memories of their relatives, and, in so doing, to share recollections of struggles for equality.

Teacher Review

How can these strategies help students *become informed, think it through*, and *take action*? Did you notice the ebb and flow of the strategies? Did you see how *Focus In* introduces students to the topic? Did you detect the ways in which *Teach for Ideas* helps students grasp fundamental concepts for the lesson? Did you discern how *Teach for Inquiry* assists students' investigation of the topic? Did you get a sense of "being there" in a place and time via *Teach through Drama*? What did you think of the *Write to Learn* activity? Did it allow students to express their learning in creative ways? Did you get a feel for the pro and con debate offered through *Teach for Deliberation*? Finally, did you begin to imagine how *Service Learning* can provide a means for students to act on the knowledge they've gained? We utilize these teaching strategies and lesson formats throughout this book. Review them, now, and familiarize yourself with this framework. Then, use this framework as a guide for the activities you create.

Making Connections

In the following chapters, we introduce you to eight civic engagements. They are: Democracy Project I and II, Worldview, History Mystery, Biography Workshop, Store, Explore, and Engage. We encourage you to practice these engagements in your college classroom, then try them out in the field. In each chapter, we push your thinking about a central question for this book: What are you going to do? Let's get started!

three
Democracy Project I
Learning about the Constitution

Walter Parker called public schools a singularly important space for "civic apprentice-ship" (1996, p. 3). Public schools, he argues, are perfect places to practice citizenship because they already possess the bedrocks of democratic living—diversity and mutu-ality. A diverse group of children live and learn together, on equal status. Schools are "laboratories of democracy" (Parker, 1996, p. 10): through teaching civic knowledge and practicing civic behavior we help youth "live" the kind of citizen they can become.

In Chapter 2, we provided three lenses for "living" one's civics: youth could learn to be personally responsible, participatory, or socially just citizens. We identified the perspec-tive of this book as correlated with the latter two forms of citizenship. Now, we round out this discussion by posing two alternative perspectives on democracy: democracy as path or democracy as accomplishment.

The perceptions of democracy as accomplishment go something like this: democracy is understandings about political institutions, skills for political behavior, and processes for political action. It is the teacher's job to familiarize youth with historic democratic documents, to help them understand how government works (e.g., how a bill becomes law, how the three branches of government function), to encourage them to maintain interest in current events, and to suggest that they vote regularly. In so doing, students can function in a representative democracy, mostly as spectators who let others do the daily work of democracy for them. This point of view is common within textbooks and academic standards for elementary social studies.

An alternative view of democracy is that it is a path that citizens walk together. Long ago, John Dewey famously said, "democracy is more than a form of government; it is primarily a mode of associated living, of conjoint communicated experience" (Dewey, 1916/1944, p. 87). Democracy, then, is something that citizens hammer out together. Rather than mostly celebrate and protect democracy, citizens must continually remake it—improving it as they go along. From this standpoint, the American tradition is more than a set of founding documents or a selection of historic events; it is a way of thinking and behaving together—democratically. When we hear calls by minority groups to heed the American dream, as in Martin Luther King's famous speech, *I have a dream . . .* , we are reminded of the path we have taken, but not realized.

In schools, the notion of walking a path toward American ideals is reflected in ongoing support for values like human dignity, freedom, equality, and liberty—particularly as these play out in the elementary classroom. It is the teacher's job to create inclusive, supportive, stimulating places to learn, where children take responsibility for themselves, care about others, and practice norms of cooperation, kindness, and fairness (Developmental Studies Center, 1996). Teachers use classroom meetings and discussions to involve students in deciding the ways they want their classrooms to be.

For us, it is reasonable (and exciting) to imagine democracy as a path that citizens walk together. Democracy is not something made in the past that youth simply carry on. It is something to work hard on, every day, as a citizen. It is a set of living ideals to cherish and challenging aims to realize. Yet, in order to walk this path, students need to understand where we (the people) have come from and where we (as citizens) might go to. Thus, this orientation demands a strong knowledge base from history, geography, civics, and the like. The *knowledge-plus* position is relevant here.

In this chapter and the next, we develop three democratic projects: *Constitution, Class Meeting,* and *Class Discussion. Constitution* offers a creative means to teach foundations of democracy—its basic ideas, principles, and structures—and to put these ideas to work in the making of a class constitution. *Class Discussion* and *Class Meeting* are formats for democratic talk. *Class Discussion* centers on the collective consideration of topics. *Class Meeting* focuses on the teaching of deliberation—as a prelude to civic action.

Constitution: What and Why?

In 2005, it became federal law to observe Constitution Day. Section 111 of Public Law 108-447 states that "each educational institution that receives Federal funds for a fiscal year shall hold an educational program on the United States Constitution on September 17 of such year for the students served by the educational institution" (Federal Register, May 2005, as located at: www.ed.gov/legislation/FedRegister/other/2005-2-054205b.htm). This act commemorates the signing of the Constitution on September 17, 1787. When you think about it, this act gives teachers a reason to annually celebrate our nation's birthday!

The timing of the event is advantageous, coming at the beginning of the school year. It allows you, as teacher, to jump start your social studies curriculum with studies of the Constitution. These studies can, then, flow in multiple directions, from learning about the Presidency, to understanding how Congress works, to considering the role of the Supreme Court. You can easily build upon this unit to develop a month or more of civic studies and actions.

Learning from Research

What do we know about children's understandings of democracy and citizenship? Over the past 30 years, a small number of studies have provided interesting information about how elementary children understand democratic government and how they can learn to act democratically. These inquiries are divided into two areas: the extent to which children grasp political ideas and processes (civic knowledge) and the degree to which children take social responsibility (social or life skills). In this chapter, we preview research on civic knowledge and in the next, we focus on social responsibility.

Grasping the Political World

Most research on children's awareness of their political and social world is somewhat dated—completed during the 1970s and 1980s. It indicates that, under the age of seven, children's civic understandings are vague, fragmented, and intuitive (making sense only to them) (e.g., Connell, 1971; Hess & Torney, 1967; Stevens, 1982). Moore, Lare, and Wagner (1985) interviewed over 200 children from kindergarten through fourth grade. They found this group to be more knowledgeable than indicated in earlier studies. Even kindergartners could explain the function of laws, courts, and police. Many could identify the President, though few had any idea what he does. Some were aware of social issues, like hunger, homelessness, and war. These studies suggested that children's conceptions of politics are emotional and personal: the President was regarded as a benevolent person who helps people, and laws were considered to be helpful and protective. Children's knowledge of laws came from personal experience, like hearing about traffic rules or watching police dramas on television. Greenstein (1969, cited in Brophy & Alleman, 2005) found a gap in fourth graders' knowledge about local, state, and national government. Children could identify figures at the national and local level, especially the President and their mayor, but they knew very little about their state.

More recently, Brophy and Alleman (2005) interviewed 96 children in grades K–3, asking them such questions as: What is government? Who is the head of our government? What is the difference between a president and a king? Who can vote? and What are taxes? Most of their findings echo the earlier studies. Most K–3 students perceive society as a benevolent place where competent people work for the government to provide individuals with what they need. There was little or no awareness of the division of lab between the President, legislators, and judges. The children focused on the President as the key law-maker and decision-maker. They had little awareness of political parties or taxes. Several findings differed from previous studies: some students saw laws as oppressive, not just beneficial, and a large group thought laws could be changed, rather than always remaining the same.

These studies also provide information about *when* children learn political knowledge. Between the ages of seven and ten, a rapid growth of political understanding seems to occur (Hess & Torney, 1967; Moore et al., 1985). Moore and her colleagues found that 20% of the children they interviewed made leaps in political knowledge in grade 2, 30% in grade 3, and 30% in grade 4. Children tend to move in leaps of conception: they learn a big idea and then fill in the details later (Connell, 1971; Moore et al., 1985). By age nine, children begin to see politics as problematic, to grasp political roles, and to understand elections (Connell, 1971; Moore et al., 1985). Between ages ten and twelve, children develop a systematic sense of the political order: they begin to understand power and conflict (Connell, 1971).

Learning Civic Ideas

Berti and her colleagues added to this knowledge base through a number of studies of Italian children in kindergarten through sixth grade. In a very important study, Berti and Andriolo (2001) found that teaching political knowledge to third graders deepened their understandings and that they retained this information the following year. This study deserves a fairly lengthy review.

From a pre-test, Berti and Andriolo learned that children did not understand big ideas, such as state, kingdom, empire, and political offices, that were presented without explicit xplanation in their textbook. They developed a curriculum to address children's misun-
-rstandings. Their curriculum was organized into 11 two-hour units, and it included
ct instruction, class discussions, role-playing (how Parliament works), and a video of
'. Andriolo (the children's teacher) taught the units in a sustained way, one unit per
from November to February.

tudents showed great progress on all items on the post-test. Almost all of the
understood political offices, could name the head of state, and could explain
was chosen. A majority understood that the state was both a territory and a
hority. Two thirds knew that laws came from civil codes, penal codes, and the
Significantly, there were very few regressions when children were tested
ter.

n a comparison classroom, where no political knowledge was taught,
od few political concepts in either the pre- or the post-test. These find-
irect, systematic teaching of political knowledge works—children can
'erstandings of political ideas and processes, whereas few changes
owledge without such teaching.

the World

In a related study, Barton (1997a) found that students lacked the background knowledge needed to grasp topics in their textbooks. Fourth- and fifth-grade American students did not understand the American Revolution because they did not understand taxes—what they are, how they are collected, and what they are used for. Since taxation without representation is a key issue for the Revolution, students need to comprehend taxation in order to comprehend the war. This finding emphasizes the need to teach children the big ideas that underpin democratic studies.

What do these inquiries mean for you, as teacher? By the time children leave elementary school, they can develop a well-informed political orientation. They learn in bits and starts, helped along by big ideas. It is never too early to begin to teach political knowledge; children are more aware of their political world than you might imagine. Children need to learn what government is and how it works: why it is needed, what it does for people, and how it is funded. They need to grapple with who does what for whom at what level of government. This content is weighty, challenging, and interesting stuff. Curriculum that is restricted to the identification of leaders or symbols is simply insufficient for this task.

Teacher's Scholarly Knowledge

Constitution

- **Constitution Day:** Constitution Day (or Citizenship Day) is an American federal holiday that recognizes the ratification of the U.S. Constitution. It is observed on September 17, the day the Constitution was signed by the Constitutional Convention in Philadelphia, Pennsylvania. The law establishing the holiday was created in 2004 with the passage of an amendment by Senator Robert Byrd to the Omnibus Spending Bill of 2004. The act mandates that all publicly funded educational institutions provide educational programming on the American Constitution on that day. In May 2005, the United States Department of Education announced the enactment of this law and noted that it applied to any school receiving federal funds of any kind.

- **The United States Constitution:** The United States Constitution is the supreme law of the United States of America. The Constitution consists of a preamble, seven articles, 27 amendments, and a paragraph certifying its enactment by the Constitutional Convention. The Preamble is a statement of purpose. The Preamble, especially the first three words ("We the people"), is one of the most quoted sections of the Constitution. These three words denote that the Constitution did not come from a king or an emperor, but from *the people* themselves. **Article I** establishes the legislative branch of government: the U.S. Congress, including the House of Representatives and the Senate. The Article establishes the manner of election and qualifications of members of each House. In addition, it outlines legislative procedure and indicates the powers of the legislative branch. **Article II** describes the presidency (the executive branch):

procedures for his/her selection, qualifications for office, the oath of office, and the powers and duties of the office. It also provides for the office of Vice President of the United States, and specifies that the Vice President succeeds to the presidency if the President is incapacitated, dies, or resigns. **Article III** describes the court system (the judicial branch), including the Supreme Court. The article requires that there be one court called the Supreme Court; Congress can create lower courts whose judgments are reviewable by the Supreme Court. Article Three also requires trial by jury in all criminal cases, defines the crime of treason, and charges Congress with providing for a punishment for it. **Article IV** describes the relationship between the states and the federal government and among the states. For instance, it requires states to give "full faith and credit" to the public acts and court proceedings of the other states. It also establishes extradition between the states, as well as laying down a legal basis for freedom of movement and travel among the states. Article Four also provides for the creation and admission of new states. **Article V** describes the process necessary to amend the Constitution. It establishes two methods of proposing amendments: by Congress or by a national convention requested by the states. As of 2008, only the first method (proposal by Congress) had been used. **VI** establishes the Constitution, and the laws and treaties of the United States made in accordance with it, to be the supreme law of the land, and that "the judges in every state shall be bound thereby, anything in the laws or constitutions of any state notwithstanding." **Article VII** sets forth the requirements for ratification of the Constitution. The Constitution would not take effect until at least nine states had ratified it in state conventions specially convened for that purpose.

- **History of the Constitution:**[1] The Articles of Confederation was the first form of government for the United States. It established a firm league for friendship. But there were problems: states could be asked to contribute to the country's needs, debts, or wars, but they did not have to comply. The President had no definite powers, nor was there any overall legal system. In 1786, George Washington, Alexander Hamilton, and others suggested a Grand Convention to improve the Articles. The meeting took place from May 14 to September 17, 1787. In all, 55 delegates attended, though they came and went over the summer. The delegates elected George Washington President of the Convention. Then they decided to keep the proceedings secret. Although the summer was blistering hot, the delegates met behind closed windows and locked doors, guarded by sentries. Delegates were sensitive to the notion of a *national* government, so they called it the *federal* government, which gave power to the states *and* to the central government. Edmund Randolph, Governor of Virginia, proposed the Virginia Plan, which eventually was selected as our government's organization. The plan identified three branches of government, the Executive, the Legislative, and

---

1 We encourage you to read *A History of Us: From Colonies to Country* (1999) by Joy Hakim for a lively, intriguing history of the Constitution that brings the delegates and their debates to life in ways that students will enjoy.

the Judicial, which checked and balanced each other. A major debate took place over state representation in Congress. Large and small states sought equal representation for their interests. In the Great Compromise, delegates decided that all states, large or small, would have two representatives in the Senate, while the House of Representatives would reflect the number of inhabitants in a state. The practice of slavery also was a very troubling issue. Delegates argued over how slaves would be counted in a state's population. Slaves could swell a state's population, or not be counted at all. In the Three-Fifths Compromise, delegates decided to count five slaves the same as three free white men. Further, the Northern states wanted to end slavery, but in order to achieve a federal government, they compromised yet again. They allowed the slave trade to continue for 20 years, until 1808. Of the 55 delegates, 39 delegates, from 12 states, signed the Constitution. The Constitution was sent to the states, which held conventions to consider it. By June of 1788, nine states had ratified the Constitution, officially making the United States a nation. Many of the original framers were troubled that the Constitution did not include a description of individual rights. In 1791, Americans added a list of rights to the Constitution. The first ten amendments, known as the Bill of Rights, were ratified in 1791.

Teaching Resources

Children's Literature

Allen, K. (2006). *The U.S. Constitution*. Mankato, MN: Pebble Plus, Capstone Press. This simply written, large-format book introduces the U.S. Constitution: what it is, when and why it was written, what it does, and why it is important. It is very brief (150 words), but it is well illustrated and suitable for use with primary age children.

Fritz, J. (1987). *Shh! We're writing the Constitution*. New York: G. P. Putnam's Sons. This readable, engaging book provides a detailed explanation of the Constitutional Convention, including the major debates among delegates. It is 44 pages in length, and more suitable to upper than lower elementary. It probably should be read in several sittings.

Kennedy, E. M. (2006). *My Senator and me: A dog's eye view of Washington, DC*. New York: Scholastic Press. This whimsical book provides a glimpse of the work day of a Senator, from the point of view of his trusty dog! The story is very accessible to children who can learn a great deal about Washington, DC, and Congress by following Splash, Senator Kennedy's dog—and, oh, following the Senator too.

Maestro, B. (1990). *A more perfect union: The story of our Constitution*. New York: Collins. This simple, attractive, informative book covers the birth of the Constitution from the initial decision to hold the convention, through the summer meetings in Philadelphia, the ratification struggle, the first election, and the adoption of the Bill of Rights. The book is marketed to a 9–12 audience, but should be accessible to primary children as well.

Pearl, N. (2004). *The U.S. Constitution (American Symbols)*. Mankato MN: Picture Window Books. This book begins with James Madison introducing himself and asking the question: "What is the U.S. Constitution?" The book oversimplifies the answer, condensing the Constitution's history into 24 pages. But children should be drawn in by the attractive illustrations, and the book should be suitable to primary grades.

Travis, C. (2001). *Constitution translated for kids*. Dayton, OH: Oakwood Publishing. This book translates each section of the Constitution into everyday language for kids.

Internet Sites

Since mandated observance of Constitution Day went into effect, an abundance of internet websites have been developed that offer teachers a wealth of primary sources, lesson plans, and interactive games for students. Several major sites, which provide links to many others, include:

> National Constitution Center: www.constitutioncenter.org
> EdSITEment, National Endowment for the Humanities: www.edsitement.neh/gov/
> The National Archives: www.archives.gov/national-archives-experience
> Democracy Kids, Center on Congress: www.democracykids.org
> Ben's Guide to Government for Kids: http://bensguide.gpo.gov/

Illustrations

First page of the Constitution: We the people: www.archives.gov/education/lessons/constitution-day/

Interactive Game

Save the Bill of Rights: The idea behind this game is that the National Computer has crashed. Students must help find the lost amendments to the Constitution. Students click on illustrations of a church, school, prison, home, and the like to find the amendments. There is a self-answer key. It's a fun way to introduce the Bill of Rights.

TEACH!

In our college classes, we model the following lessons, then we invite pre-service teachers to follow our example. During our demonstration, most of the class takes notes, using the lesson plan guides in Appendix A. One small group serves as reviewers: they observe carefully and, then, share their perspectives on the strengths and weaknesses of the lesson. Next, we work individually with a couple of volunteers to help them prepare to teach

Candidate #3

- College: none
- Career: postmaster, lawyer, U.S. Representative, store owner, state congressman, captain in U.S. Army, public speaker
- Religion: no specific denomination
- Married with four children
- Age: 56

Candidate #4

- College: City College of New York
- Career: soldier for 35 years, infantry officer, four-star general, Presidential Assistant for National Security
- Religion: Protestant
- Married with three children
- Age: 63

Candidate #5

- College: Wellesley College, Yale Law School
- Career: lawyer, U.S. Senator
- Religion: Protestant
- Married with one child
- Age: 59

Candidate #6

- College: Yale University, Harvard Business School
- Career: Business man, state governor
- Religion: Protestant
- Married with two children
- Age: 60

Clue #4: Provide data about the candidates' ethnicity and gender. Ask students if this additional information changed their minds. Why? Why not?

> Candidate #1: African American, male
>
> Candidate #2: European American, female
>
> Candidate #3: European American, male
>
> Candidate #4: African American, male
>
> Candidate #5: European American, female
>
> Candidate #6: European American, male

Conclusions: Decide who among this group is most qualified to be President.

Assessment: Make a new list of qualifications for President.

 It's your turn! Practice teaching the next Inquiry activity. Remember, the process of detection motivates student interest. Turn facts into clues! Provide one clue at a time, revising hypotheses as you go along, just like a detective. Now, you give it a try!

Teach for Inquiry 3.2: What do members of Congress do?

Hook: Exhibit the graphic of Three Branches of Government (from Ben's Guide to Government: www.bensguide.gov). Ask the EQ: What do members of Congress do?

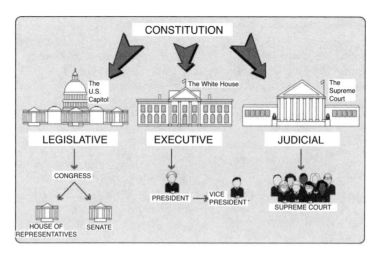

Illustration 3.3 Three Branches of Government.

Hypotheses: List students' initial hypotheses (good guesses) on the board.

Clue #1: Refer to the website for Democracy Kids (www.democracykids.org). Click on: Facts of Congress. Then, click on: What does Congress do? Three tasks for Congress are presented, along with relevant examples: (1) Congress passes laws, (2) Congress decides how to spend money, and (3) Congress shapes foreign policy (although this last task can be challenging for children to grasp, plenty of examples are provided). *Revise hypotheses.*

Clue #2: Refer to the website for Democracy Kids (www.democracykids.org). Click on: What do legislators do? This selection provides information about what a Congressperson does on an hourly basis in: "A Day in Congress," or "Back Home." *Revise hypotheses.*

Clue #3: Read aloud *My Senator and Me: A Dog's-eye View of Washington, DC* by Senator Edward Kennedy. Ask students to listen for three things the Senator does each day. Make a list of students' recollections after the reading. *Revise hypotheses.*

Conclusions: Answer the EQ: What do members of Congress do?

Think It Through

Teach through Drama: Constitutional Convention

Hook: Examine a mural which depicts delegates to the Constitutional Convention: www.archives.gov/exhibits/charters/charters_murals.html. Over several days read aloud *Shh! We're Writing the Constitution* by Jean Fritz. Note the Convention's setting, central characters, and major debates.

- For biographical sketches of the delegates see: www.archives.gov/exhibits/charters/constitution_founding_fathers.html
- For primary-age students, keep roles simple: George Washington, Convention President, James Madison, scribe, Benjamin Franklin, oldest delegate, and other delegates identified only by state.
- For intermediate students, re-examine the mural above. Select a representative from each state by name. Those highlighted in the book by Jean Fritz include:

    - Edmund Randolph: Virginia
    - John Dickinson: Delaware
    - Luther Martin: Maryland
    - George Washington: Virginia
    - Benjamin Franklin: Pennsylvania
    - James Madison: Virginia
    - Alexander Hamilton: New York
    - Elbridge Gerry: Massachusetts
    - William Patterson: New Jersey
    - Oliver Ellsworth: Connecticut

Create a role card for each delegate. Note things he probably said at the Convention. Review the role cards with students. (We like to secure cards with string to hang around students' necks as part of their "costume.")

ROLE PLAY

- Set the scene. Create a raised platform for George Washington. Cover tables with green cloth. Close window blinds, shut the door. Make a thermometer that shows 90 degrees.
- Discuss possible actions, feelings, and dialogue. Consider what delegates might say and do. Review the major debates. Practice George Washington's stern look. Practice jumping up to speak in excitement, and the like.
- Invite students to play out their roles.
- Stop and "freeze frame" in the midst of the play. Ask students to share how their character is feeling right now.
- Switch roles and do the play again. Freeze frame several times.

ASSESSMENT

- Recall the actions and feelings of the characters. Consider why they acted as they did.
- Ask students to share what they learned from participation in the role play.

It's your turn! Rehearse a role play! Create a role play to dramatize the EQ above: What do members of Congress do? Here are some ideas to help you get started. Review website for Democracy Kids (www.democracykids.org). Make a list of what happens: "In Congress," and "Back Home." Select an issue that is pertinent to your students, such as: What should be done about lead-poisoned toys that have come from China? Make role cards, including possible dialogue for: Senators, Aides, Citizens, and Lobbyists.

Take Action

Teach for Deliberation: Count Me In![3]

Hook: Review the *Three Branches of Government* chart (p. 52). Ask students: What does it mean to represent a state in Congress? Help students think through the idea of "representation." The student council is a good example. If necessary, conduct a mini-role play on representation in which a couple of students "represent" the wishes of your classroom at a school meeting.

SEMINAR (PREPARE TO TALK)

Example #1: Study the website: www.congress.org. Identify the Congressional representation for your state and district. Information is listed by district (accessible by zip code), so you will have to enter multiple districts to identify all the Representatives for your state. If you click on the names of Senators or members of the House of Representatives, photographs, political, and biographic information will appear. Place the photos on a map of your state to illustrate your Congressional representation.

Example #2: Examine the U.S. Census website: www.census.gov. Look for the Population Finder. Identify your state and click on "go." The population of your state will appear. Ask students: What does population have to do with the representation of our state in Congress?

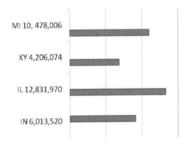

MI 10, 478,006

KY 4,206,074

IL 12,831,970

IN 6,013,520

Illustration 3.4 Population of States, 2006.

3 This lesson was adapted from "Geographically Speaking," a plan on the PBS Kids website: www.pbskids.org.

Example #3: Use this same website to find the population of neighboring states. Make a bar graph of this information. Illustration 3.4 is an example for Indiana, the home of one of the authors.

DISCUSSION WEB (TIME TO TALK)

Ask an EQ: Should large states and small states be represented equally in Congress? Write the EQ on the board. On either side write *Yes* and *No*. Above the question write *Reasons*; below it, write *Conclusions* (see Illustration 2.1 on p. 26). Ask students to silently answer the question and to think of a reason for their answer. Ask students to share their thinking. Write students' names and reasons on the board under *Yes* or *No* columns.

Readings/Discussions: Read *Yes* or *No* readings (see below), according to students' initial responses.

TABLE 3.3 Should Large States and Small States be Represented Equally in Congress?

Yes	No
<ul><li>In the past, the votes of all the states, no matter what their population, counted the same.</li><li>All people might not be educated enough to make good decisions about their government. The same number of educated people should be selected from each state to make decisions.</li><li>The Congress should be small, just one house or group. It should have several executives or leaders at its head.</li><li>If small states do not have equal representation, large states will gang up on them.</li></ul>	<ul><li>The larger states have more people, so they should get more votes in the Congress.</li><li>The national government should be more concerned with all the people instead of each state. A certain number of people should have a representative in Congress.</li><li>There should be one person in Congress for every 30,000 people.</li><li>The larger states do not have any reasons to gang up on the smaller states. We will be one nation. We must decide for the good of all.</li></ul>

- Switch readings, so that all students read both sides.
- Mix student groups; include *Yes* and *No* views in the same group. Ask students to share their views and reasons for holding them.
- Add a new reading for the mixed group. Provide the opposing plans considered by the Constitutional Convention: the Virginia Plan (favored by large states) and the New Jersey Plan (favored by small states). Ask students to consider why each plan made sense to delegates from larger and smaller states, respectively (see Table 3.4).

Conclusions: Ask students to rethink the EQ. Determine if anyone changed his/her mind, and, if so, why? If not, why not? Outline the Great Compromise that ensured the passage of the Constitution: the Senate has two members with two votes for every state; the House of Representatives has representatives according to the state's population.

TABLE 3.4 Opposing Plans at the Constitutional Convention

The New Jersey Plan	The Virginia Plan
<ul><li>The government should be a federation of states, as it is now.</li><li>Each state should have an equal vote.</li><li>The government should be one legislative body with several leaders.</li><li>The government should be small.</li></ul>	<ul><li>There will be three branches of government.</li><li>The executive branch is the head and is responsible for running the government.</li><li>The legislative branch will be made up of two houses which will make laws.</li><li>The House of Representatives will be elected directly by the people.</li><li>The Senate will be smaller. It will be elected by the House of Representatives.</li><li>The third branch will be the judicial branch. It will make sure that laws are constitutional and obeyed.</li></ul>

It's your turn! Practice teaching a Discussion Web! Try this EQ: Should we (the students) have a Bill of Rights? Here are some ideas to get started. Hook attention by displaying the Bill of Rights (see www.archives.gov/exhibits/charters/bill_of_rights.html). Prepare for discussion by playing the interactive Constitutional game: **Save the Bill of Rights!** (www.constitutioncenter.org). Create *Yes* and *No* readings relevant to your school and class. For a new reading, compare Classroom Rules to a Classroom Constitution. Give it a try!

Civic Action: Make a Classroom Constitution[4]

A Caveat: In our experience, youth (and teachers too) commonly equate democracy with voting. Though majority rule is an essential aspect of democracy, another viable option is to decide by consensus, coming to a mutually agreeable conclusion. In making a Classroom Constitution, some things can be jointly decided. Possibly, you will want to teach and practice *class meetings* and *discussions* in concert with making the class constitution. In the next chapter, we focus on these pedagogies.

Hook: Invite students to participate in making a plan for a democratic classroom. Explain democracy as a plan to take part in operating the classroom for the benefit of all. In small groups, ask students to describe their ideal for an equal, fair, and respectful classroom. Create a T-chart from students' responses.

Step #1: Recall the Preamble to the U.S. Constitution. Assist students in writing a preamble for their Classroom Constitution that addresses their visions for a democratic classroom.

---

4 The Making of a Class Constitution draws upon ideas in a lesson plan created by Mary Ellen Daneels of Community High School in West Chicago, Illinois, for Congress Link: www.congresslink.org.

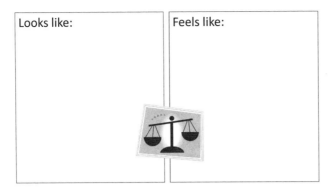

Looks like:	Feels like:

Illustration 3.5 Our Democratic Classroom.

Step #2: Review the parts of the U.S. Constitution. Recall that the Constitution establishes responsibilities, qualifications, and selection processes for three groups: the President, Congress, and Supreme Court. The Classroom Constitution should, similarly, set rules and roles for the teacher, students, aides, parents, and other parties to the classroom.

Step #3: The development of the class constitution is dependent on your age group. For younger children, it can simply focus on policies for teachers and students; for older children, it can replicate the Articles of the U.S. Constitution. Given this developmental variance, we provide activities suitable for primary and intermediate levels.

Primary Level: Provide three spaces to write and revise rules and roles for teachers, students, and parents. We like to use large pieces of butcher block paper because it seems more like we are creating a document than just writing on the white or black board. We have found it useful to organize the discussion around the consideration of "Responsibilities" and "Rights." The youngest students can understand notions of "Jobs" and "Promises" for each group. This activity can be done in the group as a whole or, for students with a bit more intellectual maturity, in cooperative groups.

Intermediate Level: Translate the purpose of each Article in the U.S. Constitution for the students. Then, work slowly through each one, establishing rules, rights, and responsibilities for each area as appropriate to your class. Here are a few ideas to help you begin.

- Article I: establishes Congress, which makes laws. Describes qualifications of, election to, and terms for office. For your classroom, help students think through the creation of a student council that will work with you to make classroom policy. Or, as is our preference, help students grasp ways to participate directly in democracy through class meetings. A class, which is much smaller than a nation, can include everyone in decision-making, determining class policies, and settling common problems. The class constitution should set guidelines for organizing a student council or for holding class meetings, as well as specify the types of decisions in which students can participate.

- Article II: establishes the executive power as vested in the office of the President. Describes qualifications of, election to, and terms for office. Of course, you and your students can create the office of Class President and Class Vice President. You can elect children to these offices, or provide a means for all to take turns serving in these roles. If teaching the voting process is relevant to your situation, the making of this constitution offers a meaningful way to discuss majority rule. Or, you can identify yourself as the permanent class leader, inviting students to help you consider wise, democratic leadership. Additionally, your group can select a temporary, rotating class leader to assist with class meetings and other, limited, democratic activities.

- Article III: establishes the Supreme Court as the supreme law of the land and requires trial by jury in criminal cases. Judicial review, as evaluation of the actions of one's peers, is likely to be fraught with difficulty. However, consideration of problematic situations via class meetings can be instructive. If your school utilizes Conflict Resolution as part of a Peaceable School plan, you can establish peer mediation as an aspect of your classroom constitution.

- Article IV: requires each state to honor the others' public acts, records, and legal reports. According to the intentions of this article, your classroom policies should relate to and reinforce your school policies. A powerful possibility is to invite your school administrator to "ratify" your Classroom Constitution, working with him/her to amend the constitution as needed to align with school goals and guidelines. At the very least, your Classroom Constitution should not conflict with school policies. However, given the predominance of Character Education, along with its aims for personally responsible citizenship, constitutional classroom governance is likely to prompt a more participatory stance.

- Article V: describes the process utilized to amend the Constitution. A Classroom Constitution should be a living, breathing, flexible plan—not one set in stone. Therefore, regardless of students' level of intellectual maturity, a process for amendment should be included. The U.S. Constitution can be amended by a two-thirds vote of the Representatives and Senators, which is a feasible classroom option. A strong sense of consensus among students is practical too.

- Article VI: establishes the U.S. Constitution as the absolute law of the land. It binds Congress people and judges, by their word, to support it. For a classroom constitution, all students, regardless of age group, should sign the final document, indicating their support for it.

- Article VII: outlines the procedure for ratification of the Constitution. For a classroom constitution, regardless of age group, parents should "ratify" or approve the document.

Step #4: Give students the opportunity to sign the constitution. Work hard to obtain all the signatures, modifying the document if necessary to resolve students' concerns.

Step #5: Send copies of the document home for "ratification" by parents. This is an opportunity to inform parents of your plan for classroom governance.

Teacher Review

Students won't learn about democracy by osmosis. Research indicates that "if you teach it, they will learn"; even young students can grasp and retain political notions. You, as teacher, need to carefully present and practice core democratic ideas, skills, and processes. It is not easy to teach something as abstract, complicated, and just plain distant from students as the U.S. Constitution. This topic is often reduced to formulas, such as the three branches of government, or given over to boring memorization. It's a challenge to make the Constitution come alive as a set of daring decisions about the ways our country should be. Yet, we challenge you to do just that.

Let's take a few moments to consider your readiness for this task. What, if anything, do you need to learn about the historic process of creating the U.S. Constitution? Do you know who attended the Constitutional Convention, from what state, with what views? Do you understand the major dilemmas that writers faced? Can you translate the words and ideas of the Constitution in ways youth can understand? What scholarly knowledge will you need to develop in order to teach this democracy project?

Envision your classroom as a place that cultivates democratic knowledge. Write a note to yourself about what you foresee. Ask yourself: what will you, as teacher, do?

Making Connections

Educating youth about the U.S. Constitution might be one of the first, and most demanding, tasks you undertake during the school year. The recognition of Constitution Day in mid-September can be seen as both an obligation and an opportunity to help children begin to understand who they are as citizens. The Constitution is not just a document; it represents America in the making. Founding fathers debated its tenets fiercely, marking the process with several major compromises, such as maintaining slavery, which reverberated far into the future. The examination of the Constitution affords many chances to practice citizenship-as-a-verb: rehashing the central debates of the Founders, deciding who is qualified to be President, and making a classroom constitution. Going far beyond a single day's celebration, prolonged study of the Constitution offers you an initial impetus to help youth become informed, think it through, and take action.

four
Democracy
Project II
Talking
Democratically

If democracy is a path that we walk together (and we think it is), then we must learn to talk together, listening respectfully to others' views, offering our own, finding common ground, and hammering out solutions. Unfortunately, we have observed the predominance of "social studies as reading" and "teaching as telling" in many elementary classrooms (Boyle-Baise et al., 2008). These phrases stand for teaching that is centered on textual modalities, supplemented by teacher explanations. Students "read" their social studies, focusing on fiction and non-fiction stories in basal readers in primary grades or on textbooks in intermediate grades. Regardless of level, teachers tend to ask, and students tend to answer, short, recall-type questions based on their reading.

This kind of teaching is not the "stuff" of democratic talk. Instead, imagine classrooms where students make collective decisions—about their learning, their classroom policies, and their relationships with one another—through class meetings oriented toward the common good. Or, imagine classrooms where students investigate and consider important questions via discussions. These classrooms are the kind Harold O. Rugg envisioned as part of democracy-in-action. We, too, argue for the worth of democratic talk. It is a key aspect of "doing" citizenship as a verb; it is thinking and acting together, making and taking mutual decisions that develop a collective "we."

In this chapter, we focus exclusively on Teaching for Deliberation, demonstrating several ways to promote democratic talk. We utilize the Focus In format to build interest in the topic at hand, but we set the other outstanding teaching strategies aside, at least for now. Instead, we present and ponder strategies for holding *Class Meetings* and cultivating *Class Discussions*.

Class Meetings and Discussions: What and Why?

Class meetings and class discussions are moments of democracy-in-action. They can promote social understanding, practice democratic skills, and nurture collective spirit. Class discussions can help students try out ideas and forge common understandings. Class meetings can foster deliberation, a weighing of alternatives that is, arguably, at the heart of democracy.

Most educators (us included) hold a monolithic view of discussion, seeing it as a singular form of lively interchange. But what constitutes good discussion, and how do teachers encourage it? Parker (2003) outlines two types of discussion: seminar and deliberation. A seminar has an inquisitive feel; the class wonders: what does this mean? A deliberation has an action tone; the class decides: what should we do? We think that, as a couplet, seminar and deliberation can be quite powerful for elementary students. For young students, deliberations can flounder in mere opinion. Seminars can supply a solid base of information for deliberation.

Discussion Web, a structured consideration of pro and con views, is a powerful means to *Teach for Deliberation*. It is intentionally located at the end of our sample units, as a culmination of learning. *Teach for Ideas* and *Teach for Inquiry* can serve as "seminars," or opportunities, for students to gain the understandings needed for participation in a Discussion Web. However, a seminar of informational activities also can be developed as part of (and as an introduction to) a Discussion Web (as we illustrated with *Constitution* in Chapter 3).

Class meetings also foster deliberation. They can function as a time to plan studies, to check in on student activities, and/or to consider (and possibly resolve) classroom problems. In this chapter, we showcase a meeting of each type, as suitable for primary or intermediate children. We have successfully utilized class meetings as a means of governance, not only with youth, but in our college classes, with prospective teachers like you!

High (Town) Council is a role play that "puts it all together"; students discuss classroom or school policies, first, in small groups and, second, with their selected representatives, making decisions, mostly through the vote, based on majority rule. High (Town) Council illustrates and implements representative democracy, with deliberation at its very core. It can be utilized as a one-time simulation, or, for much more fun, as an ongoing means of classroom governance.

We won't mince words: it is incredibly difficult to foster discussion/deliberation in elementary classrooms. Classrooms tend to be expository (telling) places, rather than discursive (talking) places. Yet, as Benjamin Barber (1984, p. 173) contends: "at the heart of a strong democracy is talk." As noted in the research section below, teachers can support discussion and deliberation through the provision of scaffolds, or tools for dialogue, and through their communication of the value of student thought and talk.

Learning from Research

In this chapter, we review inquiries that help us understand how children learn to act democratically. In the last 20 years, educators have questioned whether civic education, alone, can develop caring, cooperative, and civil citizens (Berman, 1997). The development of civic competence—learning the principles, structures, and processes of democratic government and gaining skills to make informed decisions—is seen as too limiting. Instead, educators propose an expansion of civic education to include social responsibility. Social responsibility focuses on a person's relationship to others and with the larger social and political world. Primary attention is given to the way children *work with* and *care for* others.

Whereas citizenship education is allocated mainly to social studies, social responsibility cuts across the curriculum—as the promotion of good character and ethical actions. In schools, this impetus commonly is called the teaching of life or social skills. Unfortunately, and this is a significant point, many teachers, particularly in primary grades, tell us that they don't teach social studies, instead they teach life skills. Or, they think that teaching life skills IS social studies. We encourage you to see civic competence and social responsibility as two complementary (and indispensable) aspects of democracy education.

Four processes support the development of social responsibility: (1) pro-social modeling by parents, teachers, and other significant individuals, (2) cooperative relationships with others, (3) perspective-taking, and (4) learning to manage conflicts effectively. Let us examine research related to each one.

Berman (1997) provides an overview of research on children's development of social responsibility. A range of studies indicate that children develop caring relationships when parents reason with them about moral conflicts, involve them in family decision-making, behave in socially responsible ways, and set high moral expectations. Further, in contexts where cooperation and friendship is present, peers can also have an impact on moral development, especially on building mutual respect. Additionally, empathy can be nurtured by helping children take the perspective of another. The resolution of conflict, if dealt with directly and honestly in a safe atmosphere, can promote moral growth.

A significant, bold, and expansive study of the development of social responsibility was conducted by the Developmental Studies Center (Battistich, Watson, Solomon, Schaps & Solomon, 1991; Berman, 1997). The Center created the Child Development Project (CDP) to develop pro-social character, moral behavior, and social responsibility in children. The CDP was a school-wide project, integrated throughout three elementary schools in California. The CDP had five major components: cooperative learning, class meetings, and three helping activities—responsibility for classroom chores, participation in peer tutoring, and engagement in school and community service. Class meetings were particularly important, serving as opportunities for students to set rules, solve problems, and take actions to improve the classroom environment. Teachers focused on empathy and perspective-taking through extensive use of children's literature that addressed issues of equality, equity, and concern for others.

Researchers followed two student cohorts, for a five-year period, in three CDP schools. They compared these students with those in three similar elementary schools. Their findings show significant development of social responsibility in CDP schools. Students in CDP schools were observed engaging in more pro-social behaviors—giving affection, support, and encouragement to their peers—than students in comparison schools. In classrooms where students participated in class meetings, discussed pro-social literature, and worked cooperatively, they scored highest on a "sense of community" questionnaire. Further, students in CDP schools demonstrated greater perspective-taking skills and more effective ways of resolving conflicts than in comparison schools.

Additionally, case studies by Ann Angell (1998; 2004) in upper elementary Montessori classrooms indicate that classroom meetings help students learn skills for deliberation and conflict resolution that contribute to peace in the classroom. Notably, the purpose and outcomes of classroom meetings differed across the schools where Angell taught. Her class in a private, upper-income school effectively used parliamentary procedure to resolve conflict, build consensus, and make decisions. Her class in a public, culturally diverse, inner-city school used meetings successfully to build a sense of community across cultural and social differences.

Inquiries by Terence Beck (2003; 2005) suggest that scaffolding (or direct support) helps elementary students consider complex social questions. Beck helped two fourth-grade teachers plan 12 lessons that focused on deliberation. Students read and discussed chapters from the We the People (Center for Civic Education, 1988), a basic text on the U.S. government. Students were taught a Steps-Plus-Roles process (Herrenkohl & Guerra, 1998). Small groups used three steps to guide deliberation: find the problem, generate solutions, and make decisions. Then, small groups reported their results and their classmates took on Audience Roles, questioning the report—like a teacher might. Beck found that the introduction of problem-solving steps and audience roles led to dramatic increases in students' talk. Notably, teachers' response to student talk impacted discussions greatly. When teachers engaged in "authority talk," students talked less and tried to find "right" answers more; when teachers engaged in "inquiry talk," students talked more and offered a range of solutions.

What does this research suggest for your teaching? Students can learn to discuss and deliberate, but you will need to provide direct support for them to do so. Classroom meetings offer a fruitful venue for deliberation. The practice of steps for problem-solving, along with student review of discussions, can help students learn to talk, think, and make decisions together. Your role in discussion and deliberation matters. In order to foster democratic talk, you should be willing to adopt an inquiry stance, encouraging students to express their thoughts, rather than using the occasion to assert your own.

Teacher's Scholarly Knowledge

Part I: Classroom Meetings

There are three types of meetings: planning, check-in, and problem-solving.[1] Planning meetings particularly are suited to the beginning of the school year when decisions are made about the democratic ethos of classroom life. Check-in meetings focus on how the class is learning. They especially are applicable to the evaluation of a plan or an activity. Problem-solving (or consciousness-raising) meetings offer a means to raise awareness about general problems or respond to specific situations. When consciousness-raising is a goal, children's literature can provide a stimulus for discussion. Notably, class meetings should not only focus on problem-solving or students' (and your own) enthusiasm for them can wane quickly.

A Caveat: You, as teacher, need to develop an environment that is conducive to classroom meetings. Students need to become acquainted with one another, building a sense of classroom community. Additionally, the establishment of ground rules is a prerequisite for class meetings. Ground rules should support free and fair participation and respectful treatment for all students. You can create ground rules with students: something like the following:

Classroom Meeting: Ground Rules

•One person speaks at a time.

•Listen to each other.

•Allow each other to disagree.

•No putdowns.

•No blaming.

Illustration 4.1 Ground Rules for Classroom Meeting.

The physical set-up for meetings is critical too. All participants, including the teacher, need to be seated at the same level—able to see and hear one another easily. Obviously, a circle of participants works well. Finally, you, as teacher, will need to model respect for students' ideas: inclusion of even the most quiet students and thoughtful treatment of their responses. Opportunities to demonstrate this commitment arise every time you engage in question and response activities with students. You can wait patiently for students to answer, recognize their contributions as good ideas, summarize their thoughts, and encourage them to add more—all of these responses indicate your thoughtful, respectful engagement with student ideas.

1 This section on classroom meetings relies heavily on ideas from Ways *We Want Our Class to Be* (1996) by the Developmental Studies Center. We encourage you to read this book for an extensive treatment of classroom meetings.

Majority Rule or Consensus: Most of us equate democracy with majority rule. We tend to teach students to vote on decisions, from a very early age. However, majority rule sets up winners and losers, possibly fueling feelings of disgruntlement, or, worse, rejection. Certainly, majority rule is significant for democracy—and must be taught. Yet coming to consensus is crucial too; it illustrates receptivity and builds community. In order to teach democracy in its fullest sense, consensus, too, must be taught. Consensus means that everyone can live with the decision, even if it is not someone's first choice. Reaching consensus is just plain tough; sometimes meetings will end without it. At times, it can be sufficient to raise awareness of an issue, then come back to it later for a decision. The Child Development Project (Developmental Studies Center, 1996, pp. 36–37) outlines five steps for coming to consensus:

1 Define the problem or issue in concrete terms.
2 Brainstorm solutions.
3 Discuss solutions: combine, develop, or compromise on ideas.
4 Reach consensus: ask students if everyone can live with the solution. If they can't, consensus has not been reached.
5 Evaluate the decision: at a later time, discuss how the decision is working.

After brainstorming, the class may be faced with a large number of alternatives to consider. In order to sift and winnow among possibilities, students can: (1) explain the advantages and disadvantages of each idea, then eliminate problematic ideas or combine good ones; (2) identify choices that they can't live with, explain why, then eliminate those ideas; and (3) identify choices they can live with, explain why, then consider these ideas as foremost for consensus.

Part II: Class Discussions

As noted earlier in this chapter, discussions can be differentiated into seminars, or explorations of topics, and deliberations, or deciding how to resolve a problem. A Discussion Web offers a little of both: students read pro and con passages, discuss them with their classmates, and then decide upon a "should" question related to the topic at hand. A range of informational activities can serve the purpose of seminars, *Teach for Inquiry*, for example. Most importantly, young citizens should become informed as a basis for thinking it through and as a prelude to taking action.

A seminar can be prompted by a text that is potentially mind-altering, meaning it has the power to surprise, alert, or disturb the reader (Parker, 2003). For older students, Parker utilizes famous speeches, essays, letters, and films as seminar texts. For younger students, children's literature can reveal new issues, introduce novel ideas, and/or clarify democratic values. Two of our favorite works of this kind are *Encounter* by Jane Yolen, which depicts the landing of Columbus from indigenous views, and *The True Story of Ruby Bridges* by Robert Coles, which tells a true story of school desegregation as experienced by a six-year-old African-American girl. Reading these stories aloud never fails to prompt serious discussion of social, cultural, or moral issues. The point is to find a piece of literature, a poem, or a song that dramatically presents a significant aspect of your topic.

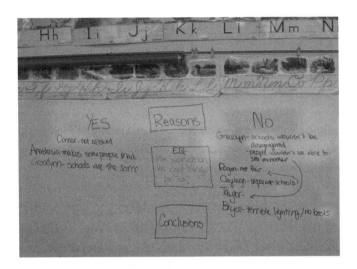

Illustration 4.2 Second Grade Discussion Web on *The True Story of Ruby Bridges*. Spencer, IN, 4/08/08.

For a seminar, an opening question is central (Parker, 2003). It should be genuine, perplexing, and go to the heart of the matter. Previously, we identified such questions as EQs: they open discussion to multiple possibilities, like (as illustrated above) "Was segregation the right thing to do?" A seminar is free-flowing: it moves along according to what participants say. Your task, as teacher, is to encourage wide participation. You might push the question a bit by asking: Who agrees, disagrees, or can say more about this topic? Or, you can exhibit your attentiveness (and, thus, your esteem for student talk) by summarizing student points. For students, a list of rules or procedures, like the following, can set expectations for the discussion:

Citizen Talk

- Listen to one another.
- Add to what other people say.
- Support your ideas with facts from the book.
- Respect the ideas of everyone.

Over the years, we've learned that seminar/discussions are rare in elementary schools. Instead, teacher-led question–answer sessions suffice for discussion. In Teach! we provide a few, quick, easy strategies to prepare youth for seminar participation.

Teaching Resources

Children's Literature

Couric, K. (2000). *Brand new kid*. New York: Doubleday Dell Books. Lazlo S. Gazky is a second-grade exchange student from Hungary. All the kids make fun of him for his pink lips, odd hair, and strange accent. Then Ellie and Carrie, two classmates who initially joined in the taunting, have a change of heart. They teach the rest of the kids that Lazlo is no different than any of them. This story can initiate discussion about compassion and differences.

Hurwitz, J. (1991). *Class president*. New York: Scholastic Press. An election for class officers will be held in fifth grade. Julio is interested, but campaigns for his friend Lucas instead. As he does so, his leadership skills become apparent, including acting as a spokesperson with the principal. Eventually, his classmates elect him class president. This chapter book can supplement the role play: High (Town) Council.

Lovell, P. (2001). *Stand tall, Molly Lou Melon*. London: Penguin New Readers. Molly Lou Melon is short, clumsy, and has buckteeth. Her grandma has always told her to walk proud, smile big, and sing loud, and she takes that to heart. But then Molly Lou has to start in a new school. The class bully calls her "SHRIMPO!" and "BUCKY-TOOTH BEAVER!" Molly Lou puts him in his place—in a very satisfying way. This book can initiate discussion of bullying or teasing.

Meddaugh, S. (1994). *Martha calling*. New York: Houghton Mifflin. Martha is a dog who suddenly begins speaking after she eats a bowl of alphabet soup. When Martha wins a vacation in a telephone contest, there is a problem: NO DOGS ALLOWED. Martha disguises herself as a human and successfully presents her position (dogs allowed) to other guests. This book is suitable for primary children, but its message can stimulate discussion about inclusion and exclusion (and fighting for fairness) among older children as well.

Seuss, Dr. (1954). *Horton hears a Who*. New York: Random House. Horton the Elephant hears a cry for help from a speck of dust, and spends much of the book trying to protect the infinitesimal creatures that live on it from the trickery of other animals. Horton wins in the end by persuading the "Who's" to make as much noise as possible to prove their existence. Horton represents kindness, trustworthiness, and perseverance, and he teaches the value of all people, no matter how small.

Teague, M. (2008). *Letters from the campaign trail: LaRue for mayor*. New York: Blue Sky Press. Ike LaRue, a hilarious, ingenious dog character, finds his civil liberties at risk when Hugo Bugwort, a mayoral candidate, proposes anti-dog policies. Bugwort collapses at a campaign rally, and Ike helps rescue him, causing Bugwort to rethink his positions.

This book is a fun introduction to political policy debate. It is a good fit for High (Town) Council.

Internet Sites

The Taft Institute for Government: www.taftinstitute.org. This foundation promotes civic education for teachers and students. It sponsors an election simulation for classrooms in which students take on roles of actual candidates running for office. See the simulation for *Maxiopolis* as a resource for developing a role play for High (Town) Council.

TEACH!

Set the stage for democracy! Read one or more of the books previewed above. Explain that an ideal, democratic classroom is a place where everyone feels safe, cared for, respected, fairly treated, able to express his/her ideas, and able to learn. Help students consider ways in which each story illustrates democratic ideals.

Take Action: Class Meetings

Focus In: Horton Hears a Who by Dr. Seuss. **Hook:** *Read the story aloud. Encourage younger students to repeat key lines in chorus, such as "no matter how small."*

Focus Activity: Before and after reading: Ask students to consider questions such as the following:

- Why does Horton believe that you are important, "no matter how small"?
- Why is Horton treated badly by other jungle residents: the monkeys, the vultures, etc.?
- Does Horton choose to help or is he forced to? What kind of elephant does that make him?
- Would you protect the small and the weak? Why or why not?

Going Further: Ask students to relate Horton's story to good citizenship. Probe their ideas: Would Horton be considered a good citizen if he were an American? Why or why not?

Teach for Deliberation: A Planning Meeting (in two parts)

MAKING A DEMOCRATIC CLASSROOM: PART I

Before the Meeting: Form groups of three or four, with seats facing inward, so each student can look directly at her or his tablemates. Invite students to role-play a planning committee for the ideal democratic classroom. Ask students to suggest classroom norms that will make their classroom democratic. Challenge them to go beyond the usual—be polite, raise hands, and take turns—to talk about real conditions that need correcting, like teasing, bullying, or unfriendliness.

Open the Meeting: Explain that the purpose of this meeting is to create classroom norms that make the class an ideal democratic place.

Step #1: Ask students: What makes an ideal democratic classroom? You can create a "good" scenario, the best possible, or a worst-case scenario, but we suggest both, just for fun, keeping in mind that most real classrooms are a mix.

Step #2: Categorize these ideas as pertinent to the teacher, students, or other parties in the classroom. Ask planning committees to discuss which ideals are most important. Put a star by ideals that are important. Suggest four or five ideals.

Step #3: Share and discuss the group's chosen ideals. Ask if others support these ideals. Garner reasons for support and identify ideals that seem objectionable to one or more members of the community. If possible, revise the ideal so it becomes acceptable to all. List, revise, and restate ideals until the class is satisfied with the outcome.

Close the Meeting: Reflect on the meeting. Ask what seemed to go well, or poorly: How did everyone get along? Did every member feel their views were considered? Was there anything that was done that one or more students disliked? Consider improvements for the next meeting.

MAKING A DEMOCRATIC CLASSROOM: PART II

Before the Meeting: Post ideas from Part I. Read aloud *Martha Calling, Brand New Kid,* and/or *Stand Tall, Molly Lou Melon.* Ask students what the stories can teach them about the ideal classroom. Consider: do the stories offer new ideas or reiterate those from Part I?

Open the Meeting: Explain that the purpose of this meeting is to continue to decide upon what makes a democratic classroom. Invite students to continue their role play of a planning committee for the ideal classroom.

Step #1: Post signs that read: *Equality, Fairness, Responsibility,* and *Respect.* Ask students to recall examples of each from the stories you have read aloud.

Step #2: Ask committees to categorize their ideals from Part I under these values. Encourage them to provide reasons for their decisions.

Step #3: Share the categorizations. Consider: do the ideals relate to everyone; for example, is fairness similar for teachers and students? Point out that the value categories are norms or standards for democratic conduct. Ask students what they will like best about a classroom that operates according to these ideals.

Step #4: Translate the categories into a Class Constitution or Plan for a Democratic Classroom. Create a written document that represents class discussions. Ask students to sign the document, indicating their support for it.

Step #5: Develop a procedure to amend the document. Emphasize that this document is a living plan. Students will be able to amend it throughout the year. *(You can fold the final steps of this meeting into the Making of a Class Constitution.)*

Close the Meeting: Reflect on the meeting. Ask what seemed to go well, or poorly. Consider improvements for the next meeting.

 It's your turn! Remember: these engagements are intended for you to try in your college classroom, as a rehearsal for their utilization in schools. Hold a meeting! Consider how to make your social studies methods class an ideal democratic place.

Teach for Deliberation: A Check-in Meeting

WHAT DID WE LEARN?

Open the Meeting: Explain that the purpose of this meeting is to check in with students to see what they are learning. Invite partners to make a list of what they learned. Ask them to star any commonalities.

Step #1: Ask partners to share their lists, particularly the starred items. Generate discussion with clarification questions, such as what was especially hard, easy, or exciting to learn, or what did the class learn together, or what did you learn about working with others?

Step #2: Record students' ideas on the board. (Transfer to class notes or a class newsletter to send home later.)

Close the Meeting: Ask students for any further observations about the day. Point out accomplishments you observed. Ask them to practice with their partners answering a question often asked upon their return home: What did you learn today?

Teach for Deliberation: A Problem-solving Meeting

WHAT'S THE PROBLEM?

Before the Meeting: Post the five steps for coming to consensus noted earlier. In child-friendly language these steps can read:

1 What's the problem?
2 Give ideas to fix it.
3 Discuss the ideas.
4 Choose one idea that is fair to all.
5 How did our idea work?

Open the Meeting: Remind students of the steps above. Encourage them to focus on "solutions," not "culprits," or on what can be done, rather than on who acted problematically. Prompt students' thought about the problem. We like to read a children's story about the problem at hand, such as *Brand New Kid* or *Stand Tall, Molly Lou Melon.* There is a wealth of such stories, and we encourage you to find your own favorites.

Step #1: Define the problem. Help students find the actual cause of the situation. Look at the problem from several angles: Why is it a problem? Why is it happening?

Step #2: Generate solutions. Brainstorm possible solutions in pairs. Share the solutions.

Step #3: Discuss the solutions. Determine advantages and disadvantages to each one. Identify solutions students cannot live with, and seek their reasons why. Identify solutions students can live with, and ask them to explain why.

Step #4: Reach consensus. Modify solutions until they are acceptable to the group. Ask students: Is this a decision everyone can live with? If the answer is yes, the solution is accepted. It might be the case that heightening awareness of the problem is sufficient. Then, consensus does not need to be reached.

Close the Meeting: Ask students to reflect on the meeting. Explain that solutions should be considered temporary. Set a trial period for practicing and, then, evaluating the solution.

Take Action: Class Discussions

Teach for Deliberation: Getting Ready for Discussion

TALKING TOGETHER

- **Activity #1:** Allow students to talk as loud as they can for 10 seconds, then as soft as they can for 10 seconds. Develop a hand motion that indicates each one (we place our hands far apart or touching).
- **Activity #2:** Ask students to talk in a middle voice. Name this voice the "inside voice," or "discussion voice." Connect this voice to an appropriate hand signal, such as hands a little apart.

- **Activity #1:** Place students in small groups. Give each student three to five small objects (we use poker chips). Ask students to talk about a question of importance at the moment. Each time a student speaks, he/she must give up a chip. When students are out of chips, they are out of turns to talk.
- **Activity #2:** Discuss what happened with the exercise above. Ask students why participation from all students is valuable for a discussion.

QUALITIES OF GOOD DISCUSSION

- **Activity #1:** Help students role play a wonderful (and terrible) discussion.
- **Activity #2:** Identify characteristics of a good discussion. Create a T-chart of what a good discussion looks like and sounds like.

TABLE 4.1 T-Chart: Good Discussion

Looks Like	Sounds Like
▪ Students taking turns.	▪ That's a good idea.
▪ Students participating.	▪ Tell me more what you mean.
▪ Students nodding.	▪ I would like to add to your idea.
▪ Students smiling.	▪ The book said that too.
▪ Lots of different students talking.	▪ I would like to add a different idea.

Teach for Deliberation: Holding a Discussion

Seminar: The conditions for a seminar are well considered above. Identify and read (aloud if necessary) a vivid piece of children's literature. Pose an EQ that provokes discussion. Remind students of expectations for discussion. Prepare to ask probing, encouraging questions. You are ready to go!

Fishbowl: Imagine standing outside a fishbowl and looking in. You can see the gyration of fish and swirl of fauna. Fishbowl stands for observation from the outside in. It is a simplified version of the Steps-Plus-Roles process described in the research above. You, as teacher, select a small group of students to observe a discussion, looking carefully for its good qualities.

 Note: Allow students to switch roles so that they are not only participants or observers.

"Putting It All Together": Simulate a Government

Civic Action: High (Town) Council

As noted at the outset of this chapter, High (Town) Council can serve as a single simulation or as a means for ongoing classroom governance. Town Council is at its most fun when a policy that matters is hotly debated. For younger students, assign roles pertinent to the issue, such as parents, children, custodian, or school principal, to prompt their thinking from multiple perspectives. As teacher, you can simply select (and rotate) children to play roles as council members. For older students, a representative democracy can be simulated. As teacher, you can form small, deliberative communities, like districts, with selected (or elected) leaders, and hold an election (from among district leaders) for council members.

Before the Simulation: Read aloud a book like *Letters from the Campaign Trail: LaRue for Mayor* or *Martha Calling*. Ask students to consider what it means to propose and defend a public policy: Why are policies put forward? What, if anything, can change citizens' minds? Where, if at all, does deliberation fit in?

Open the Simulation: Explain that in this simulation students will enact a town council, a local form of democratic government. Each student-citizen is a member of a district (committees or groups), which selects representatives who advise the High (Town) Council about their needs, wants, and values. Each district selects a local (district) leader and a person to serve on the High Council. Thus, each group has two leaders. The High Council meets after each district meets.

The role of classroom citizens is to suggest and consider policies or rules that respond to daily issues and that strengthen their democratic classroom, You, as teacher, can stimulate debate by proposing rules for equal play, fair share, or responsible resource use, as in the following illustration.

Bill for Equal Play
The rule is proposed that boys and girls have an equal chance to take part in all sports teams and games.

Bill for Fairness
The rule is proposed that resources are shared among groups so that no one is without supplies like crayons, pencils, and paper.

Bill for Responsible Use
The rule is proposed that paper, water bottles, and cans be reused or recycled by our classroom.

Illustration 4.3 Proposing a Policy.

Step #1: Citizens in each district draw up a proposal related to the problem at hand, or discuss a rule recommended by the teacher. Each district can use consensus or majority rule to come to a decision on their position.

Step #2: Report and review the proposals generated by districts. Look to see if similar ideas hold across districts; for example, is equality or fairness universally valued? Do potential rules for classroom equality hold anything in common?

Step #3: The High Council should sit in front of the room and each district should face them. Remember, one council member represents each district. The district leader presents a proposal, and its rationale, to the High Council. Each district should do the same until there are a set of proposals (written on the board) for council consideration. High Council members then ask for discussion for or against each proposed rule. Time should be allowed for objections, questions, and new ideas. After listening to both positive and negative views, the High Council meets and decides on the rules (probably by majority rule).

Step #4: Post the results of the High Council meeting. A class newspaper or podcast or other form of announcement will do. Remind all students that decisions of the council apply to all who reside inside the classroom borders, including the teacher!

Close the Simulation: Reflect on the game, district communities, laws and rules, and the idea of representative democracy in general. Ask what seemed to go well, or poorly. Consider improvements for the next High (Town) Council.

Going Further: Legislation can now proceed, with districts introducing bills or laws for the consideration of their fellow districts and, subsequently, for their proposal to the High Council. Like classroom meetings, High (Town) Council can be convened regularly, as a central aspect of classroom governance.

Teacher Review

Democracy projects are at the heart of civic education. Democracy education can easily tilt toward civic knowledge, particularly in our test-dominated, standard-oriented, accountability-driven milieu. However, civic knowledge is just one facet of democracy education, and here we have demonstrated ways to balance knowing with discussing and deciding. Young citizens of the world need to engage in democratic talk, considering, deciding, and taking action together.

Let's take a moment to consider your readiness to foster classroom deliberations. Can you see yourself sharing power in the classroom with your students? Can you see yourself limiting teacher talk in order to encourage student talk? Can you see yourself guiding a class meeting or prompting a class discussion? Why or why not?

Management systems that set strict "if–then" policies for behavior and punishment, or that reward children for good conduct with trinkets or playtime, do not foster deliberation or allow collective decision-making. Arguably, these approaches devalue democracy and diminish its practice. Yet they are routinely applied in schools. Now that you have studied alternatives, what will you, as teacher, do?

Making Connections

Class meetings and class discussions exemplify democratic talk. They are at the heart of democracy-in-action. They represent the engagement in "civic engagement." Look back at the definition of social studies, delineated in Chapter 1. As noted, the primary purpose of social studies is to *help young people develop the ability to make informed and reasoned decisions for the public good* as citizens—locally, nationally, and globally. After reading this chapter, this definition should take on new meaning. You should now be able to think about and teach informed decision-making. Additionally, you now have at hand more powerful means to teach social studies; class meetings and discussions are meaningful, value-based, challenging, and active in the best sense of these terms. They derive from student concerns, help them contemplate issues, foster their critical thinking, and spur their civic participation. These formats can genuinely prepare young citizens for their roles in the world.

five
Worldview
Developing World-mindedness

All the People like us are WE,
And everyone else is THEY.
And THEY live over the sea,
While WE live over the way,
But—would you believe it?
THEY look upon WE,
As only a sort of THEY!

Rudyard Kipling, *Selected Verse* (Harmondsworth: Penguin, 1977), pp. 289–90
(emphasis ours)

Your students are young citizens of the world, who, like us, inhabit an increasingly shrinking globe, one in which there is a rapid evolution of trade, communications, environmental changes, and all manner of issues. Knowledge itself is increasingly available to nearly everyone through the internet and world-wide news coverage, and governments have to work very hard to keep secrets from their own populations. In short, the whole world is in touch with each other and there are all types of exchanges—ecological, social, political, and economic—down to the very basics of existence such as food, clothing, and shelter.

Human global interaction is not something entirely new; rather it is a process that is more rapid and obvious than ever before. Indeed, humankind has been sharing, invading, and borrowing each other's materials, goods, lands, and ideas since time immemorial, even back to cave days and before. Waves of exploration and discovery brought new exchanges, especially of food, clothing, shelter, and modes of living. These ways of being are "cultural universals" (Brophy & Alleman, 2005, p. vii): aspects of life that have existed in all cultures, past and present. Food and clothing can be studied from many viewpoints, including cultural, geographic, and economic, and they are easily applied to the daily lives of children. For the purposes of this chapter, we focus on foods and agricultural products as an aspect of worldwide exchange, a subject that we hope stirs students "in the gut," sparking interest in global connections.

A real problem with global relationships is the human tendency toward ethnocentrism: a feeling and attitude that "we" are better than anyone else and that our culture, country, team, family, or school is better than any other place or group. Ethnocentrism can build team spirit or instill a sense of pride, but it also can allow arrogance or a sense of exception that renders other folks and their lifestyles exotic, weird, or, at worst, subhuman. Seeing the human family as ONE is a good start toward social understanding, whereas seeing oneself or one's own country as better than the rest is a troublesome step toward international error, prejudice, and animosity.

You have to decide where to strike a balance, which is not easy as we all have our prejudices and preferences. However, as teachers (and socialization agents) of young children, we have a deep and abiding responsibility to broaden horizons and build a sense of tolerance or, at least, open-mindedness about our views and treatment of others. We take the position that you, as teacher, should work toward building a sense of world-mindedness in youth—a sense of global existence, interchange, and connectedness.

In this chapter, we provide ideas and lessons to teach "world-mindedness," or to help children see their world as interconnected and interactive and place themselves within it as buyers, sellers, customers, and citizens. After all, what we eat or wear can be subjects of great debate. Food and trade can often raise health, safety, welfare, and economic issues that affect lives, lands, and livelihoods all over the world.

Worldview: What and Why?

Worldview is a way of thinking about the globe, its people, places, and history. A worldview typically expresses one's values, beliefs, and assumptions (Spradley & McCurdy, 2003). People do not necessarily share worldviews; rather, their views articulate their cultural expectations. It can be quite challenging to question one's worldview; it is a "taken-for-granted" perception of the "way things are." In this chapter, we define worldview broadly, as a way of looking at the world as a whole, as one place that we, as humans, share. Worldview places us, our country, and our concerns in a global context. This point of reference might be novel for you and, possibly, for your students. As memebrs of the most the most powerful country in the world, U.S. citizens have the luxury to centralize and elevate our perspectives. We tend to wear "blinders of ethnocentrism" that stymie the need to develop world-mindedness (Merryfield et al., 2008, p. 7).

For youth, however, attention to world culture and events can come quite naturally through films, media, literature, music, art, foods, and clothing. The old Expanding Horizons curriculum, the idea that children and young adults must begin where they live, so to speak, by comprehending first their family, then their neighborhood, city, state, country, and finally, the world, can be sharply questioned (Moore, Lare, & Wagner, 1985). In an age of internet and instant communication, children learn about global trends and events easily and quickly, perhaps understanding less than adults, but still aware of people, places, and problems in the "news." Some social studies educators argue that world-mindedness is built and reinforced by attention to issues of the day that affect each of us, and our youth, in terms of both information and feelings (Case, 1993).

There are many ways to teach worldview. In this chapter, we focus on the Columbian Exchange as an example of global interchange with ripple effects lasting hundreds of years. Why begin Worldview with Christopher Columbus? Children commonly are introduced to our country's history through the story of Christopher Columbus. His "discovery" of America serves as a foundation for their thinking about us, our country, and our place in the world. As the editors of *Rethinking Columbus*, an alternative examination of the Columbus story, maintain: "The 'Columbus-as-Discoverer' myth teaches children whose voices to listen for as they go out into the world—and whose to ignore" (Bigelow & Peterson, 1998, p. 10).

Stop for a moment and ask yourself: What is the difference between notions of "discovery" or "encounter?" Did you envision a new finding in relation to the first term and an exchange in regard to the second? Arguably, the discovery of America ignores indigenous peoples, but an encounter recognizes their existence. Our goal is to help you "rethink" Columbus, as a cultural, economic, and agricultural encounter, or as a global interchange, with far-reaching consequences, particularly in regard to the foods we eat. Rather than simply celebrate Columbus Day as an American beginning, we invite you to approach the day as an opportunity to teach world-mindedness.

Our big project for this chapter focuses on the history of foods: their origins, diffusion, and exchange. The Columbian Exchange is a starting point for the consideration of worldwide distribution, and consequences thereof, for food and food products. We invite you to teach big ideas of "encounter" and "exchange," using mapping, primary resources, and multiple perspectives, to investigate the origins and diffusion of foods, and to discuss and debate current economic and ecological issues related to food production.

Learning from Research

World-mindedness is: acceptance of other cultures, concern with the world's problems, realization of interconnectedness, and recognition of one's world citizenship (Lathong, cited in Merryfield et al., 2008). Teaching world-mindedness commonly includes foci on cultural differences, as well as on cultural universals (things humans share in common), on perspective consciousness (understanding and appreciating others' points of view), and on human choices, as they impact our world (e.g., Anderson, 1979; Hanvey, 1976; Kniep, 1986; Merryfield, 1998; 2001). A special case is made to emphasize values of respect for others' perspectives, particularly awareness of other nations' views and attitudes, as well as sensitivity to the moral dimensions of human activity, such as human rights and gender equity (Boulding, 1988; Pike & Selby, 1995).

Based on five years of research in P–12 classrooms in Hong Kong, Japan, and the United States, Merryfield, Lo, Po, and Kasai (2008) identify five elements of global education that build world-mindedness: (1) knowledge of global interconnectedness, (2) inquiry into global issues, (3) skills in perspective consciousness, (4) open-mindedness (as recognition of bias, stereotypes, and exotica), and (5) intercultural experience and competence. Notably, Merryfield (2001) argues that, in today's world, the inclusion of diverse perspectives in the curriculum is no longer sufficient. We also need to help children critically examine the Eurocentric framework that divides the world into "us" and "them," consider alternative ways of seeing the world, and grasp the complexity of global human interaction and exchange.

So, what do these proposals mean for elementary education? Case (1993) offers a simplified approach to teaching worldview that is relevant for the elementary level. He defines two key dimensions for global perspectives: substantive and perceptual. The substantive dimension refers to "knowledge of people and places beyond students' own community and country" (p. 318). The perceptual dimension refers to orientations, values, and sensitivities through which students view the world. Case submits that perceptions grow from substantive knowledge; however, it is quite possible that the two dimensions develop hand in hand. Case outlines five global perceptions to develop in children: open-mindedness, anticipation of complexity, resistance to stereotyping, inclination to empathize, and non-ethnocentrism (thinking one's group is superior to others).

So, what do teachers usually teach in regard to worldview? Merryfield (1998) and Kirkwood (2002) conducted in-depth, qualitative studies that included elementary, middle, and secondary teachers, ranging in expertise from exemplary global education teachers to novices. Their findings suggest that, regardless of school level or degree of expertise, teachers tended to focus on the study of culture (or ways of life). They aimed to teach tolerance and foster cross-cultural appreciation. In Merryfield's studies, teachers also taught the "nightly news" as a means of connecting global studies to students' lives. Exemplary global education teachers, however, went further. They also taught pressing global issues such as human rights, the slave trade, child labor, and war. As one example, a fourth-grade teacher in Merryfield's studies included themes of inequality and privilege in a unit on immigration.

There is very little research that focuses explicitly on teaching world-mindedness to elementary students. In teaching about Japan, the elementary teachers in Kirkwood's study (2002) tended to emphasize cultural universals, as things we all want and need, such as loving families, safe homes, self-esteem, and personal appreciation. Additionally, they tended to "posthole" or interject information about Japan into the curriculum at opportune moments. For example, they read a story about Japan during language instruction or created a story problem oriented to Japan during math.

In another study (Meyer, Sherman, & MaKinster, 2006), researchers sought to learn how third graders responded to the Japan BRIDGE (Bringing Relevant Internet Dialogue to Global Education) Project, an introduction to Japanese culture. The investigators analyzed lessons, interviewed students, and collected their work. They found that lessons tilted toward the substantive, or knowledge-based, dimension of global perspectives, focusing, yet again, on cultural universals, such as food, clothing, and shelter. The perceptual dimension was mostly neglected; students' ideas and perspectives were rarely sought out, discussed, or challenged. These researchers call for more explicit attention to perceptions, such as open-mindedness, empathy and non-ethnocentrism in globally oriented curricula, possibly through cultural comparison, rather than through a singular focus on one country's values and views.

What does this research mean for you, as teacher? In the development of worldview, knowledge of people and places is not enough. Rather, it can serve as a starting point for students' consideration of others' perspectives and situations, as impacted by powerful countries, economic pressures, environmental conditions, and the like. Helping students develop sensibilities, such as open-mindedness, tolerance, and empathy as well as consciousness of their own national orientations, also is as crucial to worldview. Global interconnectivity, however, should be seen not only as a matter of news and views, but also as a matter of citizens' moral and ethical decisions. The decisions we make daily, about food, clothing, transportation, and communication, can have profound short and long-term effects on people we may never meet, but may learn to care about.

Teacher's Scholarly Knowledge

Big Ideas for Worldview

Worldview may, itself, be seen as a big idea, one that is recognized by NCSS as Standard 10: Global Connections. We are using the expression "worldview" because we feel that is clearer and more pointed than "global education" or "world history"—terms often applied to teaching about the world. Worldview is based on the development of world-mindedness, a sense of inclusion, or a perception of the world as interrelated and interconnected, where all people are seen as human beings with feelings, rights, and values. Worldview also encompasses some of the values that we think lie at the heart of good social studies teaching: empathy, sharing, open-mindedness, and tolerance. Worldview works against what are, arguably, three of the deepest and most abiding problems of human beings:

- **Ethnocentrism:** The attitude that our culture and society, nation or people are superior to all others, or the best of all, and that others who are unlike us are strange, exotic, and perhaps not quite human.
- **Egotism:** The attitude that we are at the center of the universe, and that our feelings are most important, or those of our family and friends, and the rest don't count very much, or perhaps we can ignore them if at all possible.

- **Econocentrism:** The attitude that what really matters is how to make money, "making a buck," and being successful and having lots of material goods, without considering the costs to others, or to the environment, or to political relationships.

In addition to these attitudes, there are several key ideas that can be developed whenever discussing human global development. These six related ideas are largely borrowed from anthropology and sociology and concern the ways that people and cultures interact: contact, cooperation, and conflict; and diffusion, adaptation, and assimilation.

- **Contact, cooperation, and conflict:** These terms describe how people meet, get along, and eventually react to each other, working together or fighting and arguing with each other.
- **Diffusion, adaptation, and assimilation:** Diffusion is a term that describes the way things, ideas, and people travel from one place and time to another, while adaptation and assimilation describe how cultures receive and alter each other's inventions and ideas, and populations. Immigration, for example is the actual movement of people, who carry their culture and attitudes, as well as goods, from one place to another, changing themselves and their hosts in the process, either purposely or unwittingly.

The Columbian Food Exchange

We encourage your study of *America's History in the Making*, a teacher's workshop developed by the Annenberg Foundation at www.learner.org/channel/courses/amerhistory/.

Although intended for teachers at the ninth- to twelfth-grade level, this site contains a wealth of information that can be adapted for the elementary school. Study, in particular, Unit Two: *Mapping Initial Encounters.* The information below is drawn from the overview of this unit.

- When Columbus arrived in North America, indigenous peoples inhabited every part of the continent. Consequently, as Europeans and Africans explored this new land, they had a wide variety of encounters.
- Shortly after Columbus landed in the Caribbean, the Spanish began spreading across Florida and then into the interior of North America. The French, Dutch, Swedish, English, and other Western Europeans soon joined the Spanish. Russians, and even representatives from the young United States, later joined them.
- The linking of the eastern and western hemispheres marked the beginning of a truly global and interconnected human history, a process known as the Columbian Exchange.
- Native Americans adopted European animals, such as horses and cattle, and tools, such as metal knives or guns. Foods from the Americas such as corn, tomatoes, chilies, and potatoes were adopted, not only in Europe, but globally.
- In the Americas, needs for labor, particularly to grow and harvest foods for export,

resulted in the introduction of slavery. First, native people were enslaved; then, when they began to die from disease, slaves were brought from Africa.

- Although many elements of the Columbian Exchange can be considered positive—new food supplies, livestock, and better diets—negative aspects include diseases that wiped out American populations, the African slave trade, and eventual conquest of the Americas by Western European nations.

You also can study the history and diffusion of individual foods that were part of the Columbian Food Exchange. Each of the books in the "Biography of Foods" series describe ways in which the Age of Exploration (including Columbus' voyages) spread foods around the world, often enslaving people to produce crops in the process. The primary question for each book is: How did that get here? Younger children can gain global awareness and consider worldwide interdependence simply by answering this question. Older students can explore social, cultural, and environmental effects of production and consumption, building world-mindedness. In *Teaching Resources*, we review and annotate several of these books at some length.

Eagen, R. (2006). *The biography of sugar.* New York: Crabtree Publishing Co.
Gleason, C. (2006). *The biography of cotton.* New York: Crabtree Publishing Co.
Gleason, C. (2006). *The biography of rubber.* New York: Crabtree Publishing Co.
Morganelli, A. (2006). *The biography of chocolate.* New York: Crabtree Publishing Co.
Rodger, E. (2006). *The biography of chocolate.* New York: Crabtree Publishing Co.
Zronik, J. (2006). *The biography of rice.* New York: Crabtree Publishing Co.

We also suggest that you read Book One, *The First Americans* (1993), from Joy Hakim's ten-volume American history series, *A History of US* (New York: Oxford University Press). These well-written textbooks present a mix of social, political, and military history. Each volume richly illustrates the daily life, cultural attitudes, contemporary concerns and dilemmas, and political climate and events that bring our nation's history "to life." In Book One, chapters 15–18 relate to the Columbian Exchange. Upper elementary students probably can read the book independently. You can draw materials from the text for younger learners.

Teaching Resources

Children's Literature

Christopher Columbus

These books offer a range of views on Columbus, from celebrated explorer to cruel fortune-seeker. Most are of the former variety. The books can be used to stimulate student critique of the ways Columbus is portrayed. Questioning the notion of "discovery" can lead the way for viewing Columbus' venture as cultural, social, economic, and agricultural exchange.[1]

DISCOVERY-ORIENTED BOOKS

De Kay, J. (2001). *Meet Christopher Columbus.* New York: Random House. In this book, Columbus' hope for wealth is downplayed in favor of his quest for adventure. The excitement of exploration and the appeal of spreading Christianity are touted as primary reasons for Columbus' travels.

D'Aulaire, I., and D'Aulaire, E., (1996). *Columbus.* San Luis Obispo, CA: Beautiful Feet Books. This edition is a reprint of a classic. The D'Aulaire book is an artifact of racist treatment, calling native people "savage" and "heathen," but it remains a top-seller today.

Gleiter, J., and Thompson, K. (1995). *Christopher Columbus.* Orlando, FL: Steck-Vaughn. This easy-to-read biography stops after the first voyage, when Columbus returned to Spain as a hero. During the second voyage, Columbus enslaved the Tainos to produce riches. By stopping after the first voyage, the book avoids the tawdry aspects of the Columbus story.

Young, R. (1996). *Christopher Columbus and his voyage to the new world.* Englewood Cliffs, NJ: Silver Burdett Press. This book cheers Columbus on to discovery. The title of the series of which this book is a part sums it up: "Let's Celebrate."

ENCOUNTER-ORIENTED BOOKS

Fritz, J. (1997). *Where do you think you are going, Christopher Columbus?* New York: Putnam Juvenile. This book questions Columbus' motives and presents native people's views. But it pokes fun at Columbus in a way that can trivialize indigenous concerns.

Yolen, J. (1992) *Encounter.* San Diego: Harcourt, Brace, Jovanovich Publishers. Columbus' landfall in San Salvador is told through the eyes of a Taino boy. This meeting is treated as a cross-cultural encounter, not as a colonial discovery. The book portrays a sense of loss from the Taino perspective and unsettles Eurocentric, egotistic views of the Columbus story.

Histories of Food

Eagen, R. (2006). *The biography of bananas.* New York: Crabtree Publishing Co. Bananas originated in the Malay Archipelago, then traveled to Hawaii and Africa through trade. During the Age of Exploration, a Portuguese missionary brought bananas from the Old World to the New. With the advent of refrigeration, bananas could be kept fresh long enough to be shipped to North America. The United Fruit Company, a U.S. business,

---

1 The review of books about Columbus draws from Bill Bigelow's article, "Once upon a Genocide," in Bigelow & Peterson (1998), pp. 47–55.

monopolized the banana trade, paying workers low wages. Banana plantations leave giant holes in rain forests, plus pesticides endanger workers. The banana trade has worldwide implications!

Eagen, R. (2006). *The biography of sugar*. New York: Crabtree Publishing Co. On Columbus' second voyage, he brought cows, pigs, and sugar cane along. Sugar already had a long history, moving via trade, conquest, and missionary work, from New Guinea to Asia, India, and Africa. Sugar cane cultivation spread through the Caribbean islands to South America through Spanish and Portuguese colonists. Sugar cane harvesting required a large number of laborers. Europeans enslaved native peoples, then, when they died, brought slaves from Africa to meet the demand. The story of sugar certainly teaches worldview.

Internet Sites

America's History in the Making: www.learner.org/channel/courses/amerhistory/. This website offers an online teachers' workshop on America's early history. Unit Two: *Mapping Initial Encounters* focuses on the Columbian Exchange.

Food Timeline: www.foodtimeline.org/food2a.html. This website is devoted to the histories of food! There is a good list of foods that were part of the Columbian Exchange, as well as links to lesson plans about foods.

Curriculum Programs

Bigelow, B., and Peterson, B. (1998). *Rethinking Columbus: The Next 500 Years* (2nd ed.). Milwaukee, WI: Rethinking Schools. This compilation of resources challenges the Columbus myth and reinstates the views of native peoples. A greatly expanded second edition has over 100 pages of new material, including an exciting role play, "The Trial of Columbus."

TEACH!

THE COLUMBIAN EXCHANGE

PART I: WHAT IS THE COLUMBIAN EXCHANGE?

What people ate or drank, what they wore, or how they lived at any given time reflects their personal values and the values of their society, but also many hundreds or even thousands of years of cultural diffusion, the slow borrowing and adaptation of ideas and things from one place to another. The Columbian Exchange is, arguably, a superb starting point for the development of world-mindedness; it is the story of how food, clothing, religion—our very values and views—got here from there and back again.

Become Informed

Focus In 5.1: Encounter by Jane Yolen

Hook: The caravel, shown below, was a lightweight, maneuverable ship favored by sailors in the fifteenth century. Columbus sailed a caravel to the "New World." Compare illustrations of Columbus' ships in *Encounter*. First, show the ships from the sailor's point of view.

Illustration 5.1 Spanish Caravel. Source: Ricardo Manuel Silva de Sousa from Shutterstock.

Next, ask students to imagine what it might look like from the standpoint of a boy in the Americas who had never seen such a ship. Compare this picture with the first illustration in *Encounter*, which depicts Columbus' ships as winged, bird-like monsters. Explain that *Encounter* is seen through the eyes of a native boy. Ask students to look for more comparisons between the boy's views and the explorer's views.

Focus Activity: Write four or five key facts from the story on sentence strips or a chart. Before reading, ask students: Do you agree or disagree with these statements? Why?

 Note: The following statements are appropriate for younger learners. You will need to increase their levels of difficulty and sophistication for older students.

1 People were already living in America when Columbus landed.
2 Island people thought Columbus and his men were strange creatures.

3 The island chief and Columbus exchanged treasures.

4 Columbus was hunting for riches, not looking for friendship.

Reading: Read *Encounter* by Jane Yolen.

After Reading: Return to the Focus Activity. Reconsider: Do you still agree or disagree with these statements. Why? Why not?

Going further: Ask the children to wonder: Why is this book called *Encounter*, not discovery? Write down their responses and save as a link to the next lesson.

Teach for Ideas 5.1: What is the Columbian Exchange?

Hook: Ask students to recall the gifts between explorers and native people in *Encounter*. Start to develop a Connecting Web, like the following.

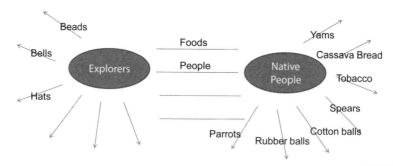

Illustration 5.2 Connecting Web: Columbian Exchange.

Example #1: Watch a video overview of the Columbian Exchange at *America's History in the Making*: www.learner.org/channel/courses/amerhistory/.

Example #2: Display and discuss *The Alphabet of Things that the Americas Gave to the World* (Illustration 5.3).

Example #3: Read chapter 17 from *The First Americans*, in the *History of US* series by Joy Hakim. This chapter provides details, illustrations, and charts of foods and animals involved in the Columbian Exchange.

Create a new example: List food exchanges that continue today. As examples, what foods do Latino-American and Asian-American immigrants bring with them? To spur children's thinking, set up a facsimile of an international grocery aisle in your classroom.

A: avocado, amaranth, asphalt	O: Oklahoma
B: buffalo, beaver pelts, Brazilian dye	P: potatoes, parrots, pumpkins, popcorn, pineapple, pecan, papaya
C: canoe, corn, chocolate, cassava, cotton, cashews, catfish, chilis	Q: quinine, quinoa
D: democracy, dyes, dogsleds	R: rubber
E: ecology	S: squash, silver, sunflowers, sweet potatoes, succotash
F: fertilizer, food preservation	T: turkey, tapioca pudding, tomatoes
G: gum, guano deposits, grits	U: USA Constitution (influenced by Iroquois)
H: hammock, hominy, hickory nut	V: vanilla
I: impeachment, ipecac	W: wild rice, witch hazel, words
J: jerky, Jerusalem artichoke	X: xylophone
K: kidney beans, kayaks	Y: yams
L: libraries, long pants, llamas	Z: zero, zucchini
M: moccasins, manioc, medicines	
N: nuts, names of states	

Illustration 5.3 The Alphabet of Things that the Americas Gave to the World. Source: Jack Weatherford, *Indian Givers: How the Indians of the Americas Transformed the World*, New York: Fawcett Columbine, 1988. Adapted from a list in *Rethinking Columbus* (Bigelow & Peterson, 1998).

Assessment: Ask students to explain the Columbian Exchange in their own words.

Teach for Inquiry 5.1: Who was Christopher Columbus?

Hook: Show a variety of illustrations of Columbus from the books outlined above. Compare illustrations from discovery-oriented books and encounter-oriented books. Ask students to share what they know about Columbus. Recall their ideas about Encounter vs. Discovery. Raise the EQ (Essential Question): Who was Christopher Columbus?

Record hypotheses (or good guesses).

Give students evidence, one clue at a time. *Revise hypotheses after each clue.*

Clue #1: Break students into groups. Ask them to examine children's trade books about Christopher Columbus. Explain that they will be "bias detectors," searching for words, phrases, and illustrations that portray Columbus as: explorer or gold-seeker, courageous or cruel, or hero or villain. Illustration 5.4 can be used to direct this activity.

Clue #2: Compare the stories of Columbus' first and second voyages. Assist youth in reading a letter from Christopher Columbus in 1493 to Luís de Santangel, Treasurer of Aragon, Spain. You will find a copy in Book One of *A History of US* by Joy Hakim, Chapter 16, page 79. Then, read the first part of Chapter 17 in this text. Ask students to "detect" what changed in Columbus' worldview from his first to his second voyage.

Who was Christopher Columbus?
Acting as Bias Detectors

Bias words for: Hero

- Brave, smart, determined
- Curious, wise, explorer
- Religious, or godly, took Christian faith to heathens
- Discovered America
- Took things back to Spain to help describe America
- Wise, fair leader

Bias words for: Villain

- Thief, kidnapper, enslaver
- Gold-seeker
- Ignored natives' religion
- Encountered people who were already there
- Stole things to take to Spain to show-off as treasure
- Slave master, murderer

What did you find?

Illustration 5.4 Who was Christopher Columbus?

Clue #3: Ask students to compare the world maps in Illustrations 5.5 and 5.6, before and after the voyages of Columbus. Certainly, Columbus changed people's worldview, literally—a larger world became known. Note the "American" land mass, incorrectly depicted as a long, narrow, island, rather than a continent, but, nevertheless, present as a new part of the world.

Illustration 5.5 Map Prior to Columbus. Martellus, World Map, 1489. Courtesy Library of Congress, Geography & Map Division, G1005 1482 Vault.

Revise hypotheses. Come to conclusions. Answer the EQ: Who was Christopher Columbus?

Illustration 5.6 Map Following Columbus. Waldseemüller, World Map, 1507. Library of Congress, Geography & Map Division, www.loc.gov/rr/geogmap/waldexh.html.

 Note: It is vital to present a fair, balanced view of Christopher Columbus. We suggest that you caution students to think of Columbus as neither entirely courageous nor wholly cruel. He bravely set out to find a new trade route where none had gone before, yet his own ethnocentric worldview allowed him to treat native peoples with unacceptable savagery.

Think It Through

Write to Learn 5.1: Encounter with Christopher Columbus

Hook: Once again, show students illustrations from the book *Encounter* by Jane Yolen. The illustration of Columbus and his men going ashore is particularly powerful. Ask students to imagine they are members of Columbus' crew or of the Taino tribe. Consider the possible views and feelings of both.

Review: Create a set of illustrations that capture these two perspectives. Allow students to select a role from which to write. Rehearse a imaginary dialogue between crew members or tribal people, or between the Taino boy and other native people. Make a word bank of terms that might be needed for writing.

RAFT:

R: Role of the writer
A member of Columbus' crew or a Taino youth.

A: Audience
People in the future, who will live after you.

F: Format of the writing
An oral history, a letter home, or a journal entry.

T: Topic
A moment of encounter between people from "Old" and "New" Worlds.

Assessment: Read the writings from an author's chair.

Take Action

Teach for Deliberation 5.1: Was the Columbian Exchange a Good or Bad Thing?

Hook: Remind students of their critical examination of Christopher Columbus. Ask them to think deeply about the Columbian Exchange: was it a good or bad thing?

Discussion Web: Write EQ on board. Write *Yes* or *No* on either side. Above the question write *Reasons*, and below it, write *Conclusions*. (See Illustration 2.1 on p. 26.) Ask

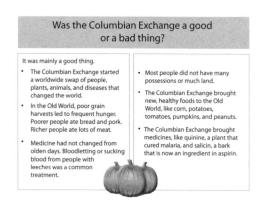

Illustration 5.7 Was the Columbian Exchange a Good Thing?

Illustration 5.8 Was the Columbian Exchange a Bad Thing?

students to silently answer the question and to think of a reason for their answer. Ask students to share their thinking. Write students' names and their reasons on the board under the appropriate *Yes* or *No* columns.

Yes or No Readings: Read in small groups, according to initial responses. Yes: It was mainly a good thing. No: It was mainly a bad thing.

Switch readings, so that all students read both sides.

Mix student groups, including *Yes* and *No* views in the same group. Ask students to share their views and reasons. Ask students to try to find a mutually agreeable solution to the problem.

Share as a class.

Conclusions: Ask students if anyone changed his/her mind, and, if so, why? If not, why not?

PART II: HOW DID THAT GET HERE?

As mentioned earlier, studies of the biographies (history, exchange, growth, and production) of foods that evolved as part of the Columbian Exchange can deepen and extend students' grasp of this topic. Pre-service teachers with whom we've worked have successfully developed and taught lessons on the history of chocolate, bananas, and popcorn to primary children. Their main goal was to introduce younger children to the world through locating, mapping, and learning about sources of their favorite foods. In the following lessons, we draw from their curricular ideas, adding some of our own to focus on labor issues related to the growth and harvest of chocolate.[2]

Become Informed

Focus In 5.2: The Biography of Chocolate by Adrianna Morganelli

Hook: Make up an informal geography and food test. Ask students: How did that get there? We know food moved from the new world to the old (and vice versa) because of the Columbian Exchange. Where does your favorite chocolate bar come from? Where did the banana you ate for lunch come from? What does the sugar on your cereal have to do with Christopher Columbus? Let's find out! Tell students they will study where chocolate comes from, how it is grown and produced, and how it is made into bars of candy.

Focus Activity: Write four to five key facts from the story on sentence strips or a chart. Before reading, ask students: Do you agree or disagree with these statements? Why?

2 Some aspects of the following lessons on chocolate draw from a unit of study originally developed in 2007 for second grade by two pre-service teachers at Indiana University, Julia Merrin Holcombe and Stephanie Chomanczuk.

1 Chocolate is made from the beans of the cacao tree.
2 Cacao trees first grew in the rain forests of South and Central America.
3 People first used cacao beans to make a frothy, sweet drink.
4 Cacao beans can only be grown in the tropics or warm weather lands.
5 The number of cacao beans is getting smaller from shrinking rain forests and diseases that harm the plant.

Reading: Read pages 4–7 from *The Biography of Chocolate*.

 Note: This book is a non-fiction book that packs facts on each page. It must be examined carefully, not simply read aloud. We suggest that you copy select pages for students.

After Reading: Return to the Focus Activity. Reconsider: Do you still agree or disagree with these statements. Why? Why not?

Going further: *Locate lands where chocolate is grown on a large, display-size, world map.* Pinpoint where most cacao is grown—Africa—and where most chocolate is consumed—Europe. Explain that many African farmers and plantation workers cannot afford to buy chocolate as a finished product because their wages are too low. Ask children what can be done to address this problem. Record and save their responses for later in the unit of study.

Teach for Ideas 5.2: What is the History of Chocolate?

Getting Ready to Teach: Create a *timeline* for the history of chocolate, as appropriate for your grade level. For primary grades, you can try these designations of time: Before Columbus, After Columbus, During Control by Spain, Chocolate Moves to Africa, The Birth of the Chocolate Bar, and Chocolate Goes to Hershey, Pennsylvania.

Create *picture/fact cards* from the illustrations and information on pages 10–21 of *The Biography of Chocolate* by Adrianna Morganelli. We created such *picture/fact cards* by

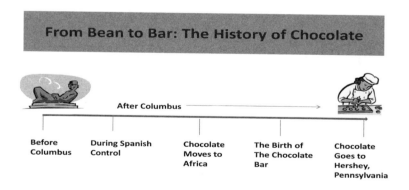

Illustration 5.9 From Bean to Bar.

making color copies of photographs in the biography books, cutting out their outlines, gluing them onto construction paper, adding factual information to the back of the cards and then using magnets to display them on our white board as examples for students.

Hook: Ask students: What is the history of chocolate? Did you know people in Mexico and Central America drank chocolate before Columbus? Can you imagine how chocolate got from Mexico to Europe?

Example #1: Study picture/fact cards (illustrations and information) from pages 10–11 of *The Biography of Chocolate.*

> Example: On the front: Illustration of Aztec tribute. On the back: The Aztec people lived in the dry highlands of Mexico. Cacao trees did not grow well there. The Aztecs traded with the Mayan people for cacao beans. They learned to make a chocolate drink from the beans, like the Mayans did. The beans were so valuable, they were used as money. Rulers required their people to pay them a tax in cacao beans.

Select students to read the cards. Discuss their meanings. Use magnets to place them on a timeline, like the one in Illustration 5.9.

Example #2: Study picture/fact cards from pages 12–13 of *The Biography of Chocolate.* Select students to read the cards. Discuss their meanings. Place them on a timeline.

Example #3: Study picture/fact cards from pages 14–15 of *The Biography of Chocolate.* Follow the same procedure above.

Example #4: Study picture/fact cards from pages 18–19 of *The Biography of Chocolate.* Follow the same procedure above.

Example #5: Study picture/fact cards from pages 20–21 of *The Biography of Chocolate.* Follow the same procedure above.

Create a new example: Ask students to develop another description on the timeline: what chocolate means to them today.

Assessment: Ask students to explain the history of chocolate in their own words, orally or through a written or illustrated task.

Teach for Inquiry 5.2: Did Slaves Make Chocolate?

Hook: Ask students what they remember about slavery and the Columbian Exchange. What happened when Spain and Portugal took control of lands in the new world? When they wanted gold, what happened? When they wanted to plant, grow, and harvest big crops, like sugar cane, what happened to the local people? Raise the EQ for this lesson: Did slaves make chocolate?

Hypotheses: Record students' initial hypotheses.

Give students evidence, one clue at a time. Revise hypotheses after each clue.

Clue #1: Make copies of the illustration of Aztec cacao workers on page 16 of *The Biography of Chocolate*. Describe what is shown: After Columbus' voyages, the Spanish defeated the Aztecs, took control of their lands, and developed cacao plantations. The Spanish forced Aztecs to harvest and process cacao beans on their plantations.

Clue #2: Make copies of the illustration of African workers on page 17 of *The Biography of Chocolate*. Describe what is shown: When many Central and South American workers died from disease, a labor shortage occurred. The Spanish, Portuguese, and Dutch plantation owners brought in Africans to work as slave labor in their fields.

Clue #3: Make copies of the photographs on pages 22 and 23 of *The Biography of Chocolate*. Describe the photographs: Farmers receive little money for cacao beans, although buyers of chocolate, like us, pay a lot for it. Most of the money earned on chocolate goes to companies who make and sell it. Farm workers often earn only food and lodging for their work. Fair Trade is an effort to convince chocolate manufacturers to refuse to buy cacao beans from plantations or farms where workers are not paid well.

Revise hypotheses. Come to conclusions. Answer the EQ: Did slaves make chocolate?

Going further: Learn more about the Fair Trade Movement. Our local health food stores offer products, such as coffee, that are produced and manufactured through Fair Trade. Invite store owners to share their knowledge of Fair Trade and of their stores' involvement in it.

Think It Through

Teach through Drama: From Bean to Bar: How Chocolate Gets Here

GETTING READY TO TEACH

Make a *life-size process graph* of the growth, production, and distribution of chocolate. Our pre-service teachers created a table display for second graders that went from an artificial cacao tree, to a basket of cacao beans, to a burlap bag marked "25lbs. of Cacao Beans," to a chocolate candy bar. Create or add illustrations to the world map of *Chocolate Lands*. Use arrows to depict movement of chocolate from growing to consuming nations—from there to here.

Hook: Discuss each aspect of the process depicted in the display. Ask students what kind of jobs might be involved with each step in the chocolate-making process. Show a movie clip of chocolate-making. A short, kid-friendly film of the chocolate-making process can be found on the Hershey's Chocolate website: www.hersheys.com. Click on *Making Chocolate*. You can skip the last section on Hershey Products to reduce the commercialization of the film.

Roles: Roles for the role play can include: Farmer, Harvester, Shipper, Factory Worker, and Grocery Store Clerk. Use photographs from *The Biography of Chocolate* (pages 23, 24, 26, 28, and 31) as *role cards* (you will need to create your own for grocery clerk). Describe the role on the back of the card. (Save the role cards to use in the *Writing to Learn* lesson.)

> Example: Cacao Tree Farmer: My job is to grow cacao trees on small farms. I work in places that have warm climates such as Mexico, South America, or Africa because the trees need warm weather, sunshine and rain to grow. I prune trees so they don't get too tall to harvest the cacao pods easily, and I constantly check trees for diseases.

ROLE PLAY

- Set the scene. Create simple props, as necessary.
- Keep the role play simple, extemporaneous, and unrehearsed.
- "Freeze frame" in the midst of the play. Ask students to share what they are doing right now.
- Switch roles and do the play again. Freeze frame several times.

ASSESSMENT

- Discuss the actions of the characters. Recall each step in the process of Bean to Bar.
- Ask students to share what they learned from participation in the role play. How will the students choose the format for their writing?

Write to Learn 5.2: Chocolate-Making: What's your Role?

Hook: Review the lessons in this unit of study. Focus particularly on the world map of Chocolate Lands and on the display of the chocolate process from Bean to Bar. Recall the roles and role play acted previously. Invite students to select a chocolate-making role as a perspective from which to write.

Review: Review the roles. Post words that will assist students with their writing, such as cacao, tropics, plantation, disease, Mexico, South America, Africa, shipping, manufacturing, factory, process, and, of course, chocolate.

RAFT:

R: Role of the writer
Invite students to select from among the following roles: Cacao Farmer, Cacao Harvester, Shipper, Factory Worker, or Grocery Store Clerk. Give each student a copy of the role card, with description, as appropriate to his/her choice.

A: Audience
We suggest having children write to another class of students who want to learn about where chocolate comes from, how it is produced, and how it gets to their grocery stores.

F: Format of the writing
Write a letter to the new class explaining your role in getting chocolate from there to here.

T: Topic
Making chocolate.

Assessment: Students read their writing from an author's chair.

Take Action

Organize opportunities for your students to share their knowledge, questions, and criticisms of the Columbian Exchange with others. Here are some suggestions for taking action.

Civic Actions

- Make a world map of the food exchange. Post it, with explanations, in a central place in your school. Arrange for your students to give talks about the display as an alternative to usual Columbus Day activities.
- Hold a public debate about the value of the Columbian Exchange. Invite other classes, teachers, parents, and the like.
- Write accurate versions of the Columbus story. You might call them "Bias Alerts." Attach them to library books as another side to the Columbus story.
- Make a list of healthy foods that we inherited from native peoples. Post the list in your cafeteria. Start an Eat Healthy campaign based on what you learn.
- Find out more about where your favorite foods come from. Do another "biography" of food. Gather information from your own class about the origins of favorite family foods. Make a world map that shows the origins of foods. Post it in your cafeteria too.

Teacher Review

As you look back over this chapter, what have you learned about teaching worldview? What does it mean to teach world-mindedness? What makes the story of Christopher Columbus a good place to begin teaching global awareness? What aspects of world-mindedness does this exercise emphasize? Can you identify substantive (knowledge) and perceptive (views and values) aspects of world-mindedness in this example? Is it a good idea to introduce world interchange through biographies of food? Why or why not? How can you move beyond teaching about one country or culture to emphasize interrelationships and interconnectedness?

Do you agree or disagree with the following statement: teaching *about* culture, especially focusing on cultural universals, or things humans share, is not enough to prompt global understanding. If you agree, what are your reasons? If you disagree, what else is needed? Stop and consider: What does it mean to develop world-mindedness for young citizens of the world in this day and age? What will you, as teacher, do?

Making Connections

At the end of Chapter 1, we presented the definition for social studies currently endorsed by NCSS (1994): "the primary purpose of social studies is to help young people develop the ability to make informed and reasoned decisions for the public good as citizens of a culturally diverse, democratic society in an interdependent world." This chapter should deepen your grasp of this aim. Your job, as an outstanding social studies teacher, is to help youth realize that they are local, national, and global citizens—all at once. This task requires challenging ethnocentrism, fostering multiple perspectives, and targeting global interconnections. Plus, it means considering people, places, and events in the world as topics for discussion and issues for action. You can envision the following chapters from a global, as well as a national, perspective. What kind of History Mysteries might you foster about a place or condition in the world? Who might you select for a Biography of a world leader? What does Store and economic decision-making gain from taking a worldview of the problem?

six
History Mystery
Rediscovering our Past

History is not just a march through time. It is not just learning the main date. As history educators Linda Levstik and Keith Barton (2001) note, history is an enormous family drama, full of plots, twists, and turns. History is our story; it shows us our past, and it suggests our future. The end is not predictable, and we are still in the middle of the story. History is mysterious; it already happened, and its memory can only be pieced together from remnants of the past. History is the pursuit of our story; it can kindle our curiosity and engage our passion—if only we will let it.

In elementary schools, however, students often find history boring. Commonly, history is taught as content to cover, rather than as an adventure to discover (e.g., Barton, 1997b; VanSledright & Frankes, 2000). It is presented as a story already told, by someone else, about someone else. It becomes a frozen image that must be learned for reasons children may not understand. In this chapter, we focus on good history teaching, particularly on the benefits of approaching history as mystery. Let's stop for a moment and consider several proposals for good history teaching.

Good history teaching moves beyond lists of people, places, and dates to develop in-depth understanding. The NCSS (1994) considers in-depth treatment, rather than superficial coverage, as a principle of powerful teaching and learning—it makes topics more meaningful to students. As Levstik and Barton (2001, p. 10) argue, "Knowing more facts does not necessarily mean greater understanding; students may learn more facts without having any idea what they mean or why they're important." Good history teaching focuses on big ideas, such as revolution, civil war, or suffrage, provides a sense of "being there" in times past, and offers reasons for studies of historic events.

Good history teaching helps students "read" history. Reading history is different from reading for general comprehension. Sounding out words or figuring out their meanings in context can assist students in reading content, but not necessarily in grasping historical information. Myra Zarnowski (2006, p.10) outlines five "rules of the game" that can help students make sense of history:

1 historical context: help students identify similarities and differences between the past and present;
2 historical truth: help students use historic fiction to develop a sense of life in the past;
3 historical accounts: help students realize that historical accounts are created from bits of incomplete evidence;
4 multiple perspectives: help students recognize that people in the past did not see things in the same way; and
5 historical significance: help students consider reasons why historical events are important to study.

In order to help students make sense of history, Zarnowski (2006) proposes a type of "teaching shorthand." Teachers should: (1) emphasize historical thinking, (2) read historical literature, and (3) provide hands-on experience. Teachers should ask thought-provoking questions, such as: What was life like then? What evidence makes you think that? Why is it important to know about . . . ? Teachers should read quality non-fiction and fiction works about the times under study. And teachers should encourage students to "do" history, questioning, discussing, and debating about the past.

Good history teaching, then, approaches history as a mystery—as a voyage of discovery (Gerwin & Zevin, 2003). Students study raw data from history, such as photographs, newspaper articles, and political cartoons, to figure out the story, like a detective. This approach invites students to explore a topic in depth, tapping into historical times, probing evidence, and considering alternative viewpoints. Moreover, for a history mystery, students "do" history by constructing their own versions of the past. As noted in Chapter 2, we consider history mystery as an attitude, as well as a method; it is approaching history curiously, piecing stories together from remnants of the past.

History Mystery: What and Why?

In this chapter, we focus on teaching history through inquiry—on doing or constructing history. As noted above, recollection of history is stressed more than its investigation. Students will, in all likelihood, need structure and support to "do" history. Levstik and Barton (2001) suggest that teachers provide an *apprenticeship* in inquiry, modeling, and

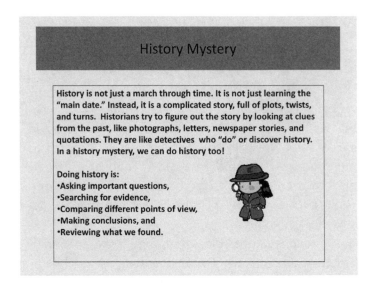

History Mystery

History is not just a march through time. It is not just learning the "main date." Instead, it is a complicated story, full of plots, twists, and turns. Historians try to figure out the story by looking at clues from the past, like photographs, letters, newspaper stories, and quotations. They are like detectives who "do" or discover history. In a history mystery, we can do history too!

Doing history is:
•Asking important questions,
•Searching for evidence,
•Comparing different points of view,
•Making conclusions, and
•Reviewing what we found.

Illustration 6.1 History Mystery.

practicing processes of historical discovery and examination. As they note: "students have to learn what it is to ask and answer historical questions—how to find information, how to evaluate sources, how to reconcile conflicting accounts, how to create an interpretive account" (p. 14).

Our civic engagement for this chapter is the creation of a museum-like exhibit around the Women's Suffrage Movement. Why focus on Women's Suffrage? In common practice, teachers (and textbooks) tend to emphasize men's history—truly his-story! Holidays spur celebrations of the feats of Columbus, Washington, Lincoln, and Martin Luther King. Textbooks concentrate studies on political eras, wars, and conquest. As Ann Bausum (2004, p. 7) notes in her award-winning book about women's suffrage: "except for a few scattered figures, women had apparently stayed home while history happened." She goes on to say, "That's a shame, because the history of how women fought for and won the vote is one of the great stories about the growth of our nation" (p. 8). This story has democracy at its heart: for 72 years, from 1848 to 1920, women fought for their right to vote, to have a say in running their country, and they did it through non-violence, without taking up guns or swords. This story deserves to be discovered by students as an example of the path toward the achievement of democratic ideals that we all trod.

Learning from Research

Contrary to popular belief, elementary children can learn to think historically, going beyond memorization of famous people and important events. During the past 15 years, a small body of research has demonstrated that children can develop a sense of chronology and learn skills of historical inquiry.

Chronological Time

Children understand chronological time, but not as adults do. Matthew Downey (1994) found that children rely on visual clues (e.g., fashion, architecture, and technology) to figure out historical time. Linda Levstik and Christine Pappas (1987) learned that second graders use broad designations for time, such as "long ago," whereas fourth to sixth graders use more highly differentiated categories for time. Based on this research, Keith Barton and Linda Levstik (1996) asked 58 children from kindergarten through sixth grade to place nine photographs, which included a variety of visual clues, in order from "longest ago" to "closest to now" (p. 426). Not surprisingly, they learned that children's temporal distinctions, or classifications for time, and their time vocabulary, specifically dates, gained in sophistication over time.

In regard to classifications of time, students from kindergarten to grade 2 distinguished time as a dichotomy—something happened either long ago or close to now. By grades 3 and 4, children made three distinctions: old and older, close to now and now, and in the middle. By grades 5 and 6, children differentiated all the photos and used historical information to compare pictures. In regard to dates, primary grade children guessed dates randomly. Third and fourth graders began to estimate dates by century and decade. Fifth and sixth graders used conventional terminology, such as the late 1900s.

Children grasped the mathematical meaning of dates before they could connect them to specific historic information. Third and fourth graders assigned odd dates to photos, but then went backward or forward in time by standard increments, say, each photo was ten years apart. By fourth grade children connected photos to background knowledge, and by fifth and sixth grade, children's accuracy with dates and information increased greatly. However, children in all grades thought of time in a unilinear fashion: first there were pioneers, then there were cities. It was difficult for them to understand that pioneers and cities existed simultaneously, but in different geographic locations.

History as Inquiry

History is not only a topic, but a process—an inquiry into the past and, then, a reconstruction of it. The *National Standards for History* (National Center for History in the Schools, 1996) call for historic inquiry, teaching students to sift evidence, analyze sources, question evidence, and construct historic accounts.

Bruce VanSledright (2002) taught 23 fifth graders in a suburban, East Coast school to do historic inquiry. VanSledright found that all students could learn processes of historical investigation. Students learned to consider the reliability and perspective of data and to construct evidence-based interpretations. However, some students' reading difficulties or propensity to rush to judgment hindered their participation in inquiry. Other evidence indicates that after fifth graders were taught about the nature of history and work of historians, their knowledge and thinking about history became more sophisticated (Brophy, VanSledright, & Bredin, 1992). Students realized that history encompasses all of the past, including the lives of ordinary people, and they recognized that historians tap into a range of sources for information. However, it was difficult for students to make historical interpretations; they expected inquiry to establish facts indisputably, and they struggled to incorporate conflicting information.

Linda Levstik and Keith Barton (1996; and Barton, 1997a) found that third, fourth, and fifth graders could learn to evaluate the reliability of historic sources, but they had great difficulty connecting this activity to the construction of historical accounts. Sometimes, students ignored evidence and made up their own conclusions.

What do these investigations suggest for your teaching? You can teach historic time. Visual clues can help children determine time. However, the use of conventional dates, such as 1492, before grade 5 will very likely be meaningless to your students. Instead, you can help your students distinguish "long ago" from "now," and you can use mathematical timelines to deepen their grasp of time. Further, you will need to carefully demonstrate the complexities of any one period; pioneers and cities can exist at the same time.

Additionally, students can do historical inquiry. However, the undertaking will require a good deal of scaffolding, or support. Students will need help in the creation of narratives based on data, particularly the inclusion of conflicting evidence within them. Teaching history as mystery must be developed as an *apprenticeship in inquiry*.

Teacher's Scholarly Knowledge

- **Suffrage:** From the Latin word *suffragium* meaning approval and the right to vote.
- **Women's Suffrage Movement**: The Women's Suffrage Movement was the struggle to gain the same right to vote as men. With a few exceptions, like Kuwait and Saudi Arabia, women today have the same voting rights as men. However, this was not always the case. During U.S. colonial times, voting was limited to adult males who owned property. Many people thought that property owners had the strongest interest in good government; therefore, they were the best qualified to make decisions. In the early nineteenth century, changing social conditions and the idea of equality led to the beginning of the suffrage movement. By then, more women were receiving an education. Women also began to participate in reform movements and take increased interest in politics. Women and men began to question why women were not also allowed to vote.
- **Suffragist:** A person who works for voting rights is called a *suffragist*. Sometimes women who fought for suffrage were called suffragettes, but that term was considered derogatory. Most women referred to themselves as suffragists, and that term is preferred today.
- **Seneca Falls Convention:** The Seneca Falls Convention, held in Seneca Falls, New York, on July 19 and July 20, 1848, was the *first women's rights convention* held in the United States, and as a result it is often called the birthplace of feminism. Early advocates for women's suffrage *Elizabeth Cady Stanton* and *Lucretia Mott* organized the convention.

At Seneca Falls, a group of American women and men met to discuss the legal limitations imposed on women. Their consciousness of those limitations had been raised by their participation in the *anti-slavery movement*. Many of the attendees were also abolitionists whose goals included universal suffrage. Attendees created the *Declaration of Sentiments*, which outlined the rights to which they felt women were entitled. They used the language and structure of the *United States Declaration of Independence* to underscore their claims as American citizens.

- **19th Amendment:** *The right of citizens of the United States to vote shall not be denied or abridged by the United States or by any State on account of sex. Congress shall have power to enforce this article by appropriate legislation. (Passed by Congress June 4, 1919. Ratified August 18, 1920.)* In 1870, the 15th Amendment to the Constitution gave all citizens, regardless of race, color, or previous condition of servitude, the right to vote. Advocates for suffrage, particularly *Elizabeth Cady Stanton* and *Susan B. Anthony*, fought hard to add the word "sex" to the 15th Amendment, but they were not successful. The 15th Amendment pitted race against gender. Imagine the frustration of women who fought for the end of slavery AND women's suffrage for 30 years, only to have their fellow (male) activists tell them to wait a little longer. Some Southern white men did not want to enlarge numbers of African American voters by enfranchising Black women. Some Northern and Southern suffragists tried to increase support for women by arguing that white women could outvote African-American citizens.

- **Civil disobedience**: Deliberate, but non-violent, disregard of custom and law, on the grounds of conscience, in this case in order to gain voting rights. Women championed their cause through speeches, rallies, petitions, and writings. During the last five years of the fight, from 1913 to 1918, some suffragists tried more militant tactics. Some advocates went to jail and suffered ill-treatment, rather than pay fines for trumped-up charges, such as disrupting traffic. Women's groups split over strategies for victory. The National American Woman Suffrage Association (NAWSA), led by Carrie Chapman Catt, favored a moderate, lobbyist, state-by-state approach to suffrage. Alice Paul and Lucy Burns advocated for the passage of a federal amendment to the Constitution. They formed the National Women's Party and used militant tactics, such as picketing the White House and criticizing the President, to champion their cause. Catt, however, came to the defense of Burns and Paul when they and their supporters received brutal treatment during their imprisonment.

- **Leaders of the movement:** The Women's Suffrage Movement spanned 72 years, from 1848 to 1920. The fight extended across several generations of women, sometimes in the same family. *Elizabeth Cady Stanton, Lucy Stone*, and their daughters worked for the cause for much of their lives. Most leaders were women and most were white. White suffrage leaders in the early years of the movement included *Elizabeth Cady Stanton, Lucretia Mott*, and *Susan B. Anthony*. In the later years, white leaders included *Carrie Chapman Catt, Alice Paul, Lucy Burns*, and *Harriot Stanton Blatch*.

African-American activists organized their own, segregated, clubs to raise support for the cause. Suffrage leaders of color included *Sojourner Truth, Frances Parker,* and *Ida B. Wells-Barnett.* In 1913, Paul and Burns organized a parade to rekindle interest in women's suffrage. A compromise was struck in order to involve Southern and Black women. The Black women walked in a segregated group at the rear of the parade. Wells-Barnett refused to participate in this compromise and, instead, walked with white leaders. In 1916, Carrie Chapman Catt developed the "Winning Plan" for gaining the vote, which included social action at the state and federal levels. Her plan eventually won the passage of the 19th Amendment on June 4, 1919.

Teaching Resources

Children's Literature

Bausum, A. (2004). *With courage and cloth: Winning the fight for a woman's right to vote.* Washington, DC: National Geographic Society. This non-fiction chapter book is suitable for upper elementary. It describes the entire fight for women's suffrage, focusing on the last ten years. It shows women struggling to win the vote, not to merely receive it. It treats the movement with nuance, allowing students to see different points of view among leaders.

Fritz, J. (1995). *You want women to vote, Lizzie Stanton?* New York: G. P. Putnam's Sons. This non-fiction chapter book is lengthy, but appealing. It should be read aloud to upper elementary students. It traces the life of Elizabeth Cady Stanton with honesty and humor. It is a great introduction to the times in which suffrage leaders lived.

Harness, C. (2003). *Rabble rousers: 20 women who made a difference.* New York: Dutton's Children's Books. This anthology includes five leaders of the suffrage movement, both white women and women of color. The portraits are short and suitable for children's research. The idea of "rabble rousers" focuses on social activism.

Karr, K. (2005). *Mama went to jail for the vote.* New York: Hyperion Books for Children. This fiction picture book is a "must read" because it chronicles the final days of the Women's Suffrage Movement, focusing on acts of civil disobedience. The main character seems to be Inez Milholland, who led a famous march on Washington, DC, on March 3, 1913. Details in illustrations should be pinpointed. For example, the jail is the Occoquan Workhouse, a place of terrible treatment for suffragists.

McCully, E. (1995). *The ballot box battle.* New York: Alfred A. Knopf. This picture book introduces the idea of women's suffrage through the eyes of a young girl who is befriended by Elizabeth Cady Stanton. Cordelia accompanies Mrs. Stanton on one of her unsuccessful efforts to vote. This story is an engaging introduction to suffrage for younger students.

Rustad, M. (2002). *Susan B. Anthony*. Mankato, MN: Capstone Press, Pebble Books. We love this first biography for children. It depicts the life of Anthony simply, through photographs. The timeline is a wonderful introduction to the march of time in a person's life. For those who think women's suffrage is too difficult for primary children, read this book.

White, L. (2005). *I could do that! Esther Morris gets women the vote*. New York: Farrar, Staus and Giroux. This fictionalized account of the life of Esther Morris takes the fight for suffrage from the federal level to the states—all the way to Wyoming! It is a good balance for books that focus on East Coast leaders and activism in Washington, DC. It is suitable for young learners, portraying activism as something an ordinary person "can do."

Films

The following films will deepen your scholarly knowledge as a teacher. However, clips of film from each can be used as a visual resource for children.

Burns, K., and Barnes, P. (1999). *Not for ourselves alone: The story of Elizabeth Cady Stanton and Susan B. Anthony*. New York: PBS Home Video. This film describes the early years of the Women's Suffrage Movement, focusing on the partnership of Elizabeth Cady Stanton and Susan B. Anthony. The first five minutes of this film show footage of a turning point in the movement, the 1913 March on Washington. A clip of this march can complement the story. *Mama Went to Jail for the Vote*.

Garner, K. (2004). *Iron jawed angels*. New York: HBO Home Box Office. This film depicts the final years of the suffrage battle, focusing on the partnership of Alice Paul and Lucy Burns. The militant tactics of the National Women's Party are highlighted. Chapter 4 (Women on a Horse) and 10 (Silent Sentinels) are most suitable for children's viewing and depict significant aspects of the struggle.

Internet Sites

National Women's Hall of Fame: www.greatwomen.org. Search by the name of the leader. Includes a photo, birth and death dates, and brief biography. You will probably have to rewrite the bios as they are written for an adult audience.

Alice Paul website: www.alicepaul.org. This website offers a number of photographs of suffrage leaders, including Alice Paul. The children's version of her biography is readable for upper elementary students. The *Researching Alice* page provides avenues for students (and you) to investigate Ms. Paul's life.

American Memory, Library of Congress: http://memory.loc.gov/ammem. Search: Women's History, then Women's Suffrage. Of particular interest are Selections from the

National American Women's Suffrage Association, 1848–1921, and By Popular Demand: Votes for Women Suffrage Pictures, 1850–1920. Also search for Women of Protest. You will find records of the National Women's Party, including photos of parades and pickets.

The National Women's History Project: www.legacy.org/index.html. This website provides an overall history of the Women's Suffrage Movement, including a timeline. It links the past to the present by including information about women's issues today.

The Oracle Education Foundation: www.library.thinkquest.org. This website hosts youth-made web-quests, or think-quests. Look for Think-quest Jr.—completed by elementary children in relation to social studies. Then, find a think-quest made by fifth graders about women's suffrage: *Women Who Turned the World*. This think-quest includes a timeline, biographies, trivia quiz, and links to more information.

TEACH!

Become Informed

Focus In: The Ballot Box Battle by Emily McCully

Hook: Ask students what a "ballot box battle" might be about. Create a ballot box and a voting simulation. Discuss a classroom issue. Ask the students to vote, but allow only the boys to place their ballots in the box. Explain that women were not always allowed to vote and that this story will begin to describe their battle for the vote.

Focus Activity: Write four to five key facts from the story on sentence strips or chart. Before reading, ask: Do you agree or disagree with these statements? Why?

1 Voting is part of being a good citizen.
2 Only men should be able to vote in the U.S.A.
3 Women can be good citizens just like men.
4 Women should battle to get the right to vote.

Reading: Read *The Ballot Box Battle* by Emily McCully.

After Reading: Return to the Focus Activity. Reconsider: Do you still agree or disagree with these statements? Why? Why not?

Teach for Ideas: What is Women's Suffrage?

Hook: Show a photo of the "silent sentinels," women picketing the White House in 1917. Explain the photograph. Ask students to think about: What were women waiting for? What is liberty? Why did getting the vote mean winning liberty? Let's find out!

Illustration 6.2 How Long Must Women Wait for Liberty? Courtesy Library of Congress, Manuscript Division, http://hdl.loc.gov/loc.mss/mnwp.160032.

Example #1: In a file folder, glue a photograph of "suffering" on one inner page and a photo of "suffrage" on the other. Place a long piece of paper (suitable for writing a list) under each. In small groups, ask students to write down words that describe each (help emergent readers as needed). Ask students to share their findings: compare and contrast. Make a listing of attributes of each: suffering is/suffrage is.

Example #2: Read aloud one of the historical nonfiction or fiction books above. We like either *I Could Do That! Esther Morris Gets Women the Vote* or *Mama Went to Jail for the*

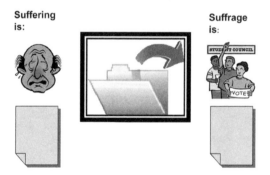

Illustration 6.3 What is Suffrage?

Vote as examples. Both books illustrate suffrage, the first at the state level, the second at the federal level. Before reading: ask students to listen for the meaning of suffrage. After reading: list their comments on the board. Extend the list from example #1.

Example #3: Show the following flyer from the National American Woman Suffrage Association (ca. 1912) listing reasons for women's suffrage (you can find it through the American Memory website under: Votes for Women! The women's reasons . . .).

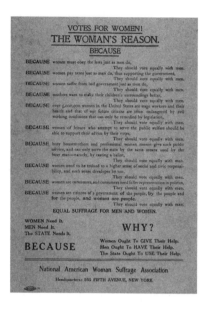

Illustration 6.4 Votes for Women! Courtesy Library of Congress.

Create a New Example: Allow students to vote on a class or school issue. Guide their discussion to the importance of "having a say" in the way their class/school is run. Ask them again: Why did women think getting the vote meant getting liberty?

Assessment: Ask students to explain in their own words what women's suffrage is.

Going Further: Start a word wall with ideas that students will encounter in their studies of this topic. See the following example.

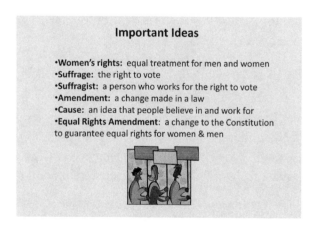

Illustration 6.5 Important Ideas for Suffrage.

Teach for Inquiry 6.1: Learning to "DO" History

In order to deepen student's grasp of historical inquiry and construction, you should teach them how to "read" history. Find ways to focus on the five rules for making sense of history: historical context, historical truth, historical accounts, multiple perspectives, and historical significance. Several of our favorite exercises follow. The aspect of "sense-making" that each supports is highlighted.

EXERCISE 6.1D: COMPARING LIFE THEN AND NOW (HISTORICAL CONTEXT)

We like to use activities from *My Backyard History Book* by David Weitzman (1975) to help students grasp historical context. The book focuses on everyday, local history that students can find in their own "backyard." Two of our favorite activities are "Pop, Mood, and Rock" and "Hand-Me-Down History." For the first, students ask their parents or caregivers about the music they listened to in their younger days. For the second, students make a family archive by placing old photos, documents, or artifacts in a box. You can imagine other options! In order to teach historic context, it is important to compare findings from then and now, sketching similarities to and differences from times past.

EXERCISE 6.1B: HISTORY IS ONLY PART OF THE STORY[1] (HISTORICAL ACCOUNTS)

At the end of the school day, ask children to write an account of their day. Number each paper, from 1 to 5 (in repeated groupings) if possible. (For emergent readers, help small groups write accounts. You will need at least four accounts.) Ask students to pass their papers in. Next, crumble up groupings of papers and toss them in the trash:

- Group one: Lost to fire.
- Group two: Lost in moving to a new building.
- Group three: Kept by an unknown person.
- Group four: Lost because of carelessness.
- Group five: SAVED

Read group five aloud. Explain that this account is now the history of the day. Students usually proclaim: my story is lost! Just so; history is only a partial account, saved from bits and pieces of information.

EXERCISE 6.1C: THERE IS MORE THAN ONE VERSION OF THE STORY (MULTIPLE PERSPECTIVES)

Read aloud *The True Story of the Three Little Pigs* by John Scieszka (Harmondsworth: Puffin Books, 1996). This children's story is rewritten from the wolf's perspective, introducing the notion of multiple viewpoints. Ask students to rewrite a common historical story, such as Christopher Columbus, as told from a different point of view, such as that

---

1 This activity is commonly used at the Truman Presidential Library to teach children about the partialness of historical accounts.

of native people's stance. The "wolf's point of view" can be used as a metaphor for the consideration of multiple perspectives in historical accounts.

EXERCISE 6.1D: FIND THE EVIDENCE! (HISTORICAL ACCOUNTS)

Organize a "retrieval file" for student inquiries. Title a file folder with the topic under study. Glue pockets that will hold 3" × 5" cards to the inside of the file. Designate pockets for different types of evidence. Organize experienced readers into inquiry groups to find evidence about several topics, and then to incorporate their findings into larger stories—like finding pieces of the puzzle. Help emergent readers find information for one collective class file.

Illustration 6.6 Retrieval File: Protests.

EXERCISE 6.1E: INQUIRY IS A DETECTIVE PROCESS

Inquiry is a process. It is finding and *considering* clues. Each Teach for Inquiry in this book demonstrates this process. First, students propose hypotheses, then they consider pieces of information or evidence, revising their hypotheses as they go along. By now, you should be familiar with the inquiry process; perhaps you have tried to teach one of our sample lessons. Before you set students on their inquiries, practice the process yet again. Remember that, according to the research above, students have trouble creating historic narratives based on evidence. Students tend to make up their own tales, regardless of the evidence. You should help students connect their evidence to their conclusions. You can model the following Teach for Inquiry as a guide for students' own investigations.

Teach for Inquiry 6.2: Why Did Suffragists Use Protests to Get the Vote?

- **Ask an Essential Question** (EQ): Why did suffragists use protests to get the vote?
- **Elicit hypotheses** from students.
- **Give students evidence**, one bit of data at a time. Ask them to consider each clue, then to revise their responses to the EQ.

- **Clue #1:** Examine the front page of the *Woman's Journal*. What can you learn from the headlines? *Revise hypotheses.*

Illustration 6.7 *Woman's Journal and Suffrage News.* Courtesy Library of Congress.

- **Clue #2:** NWP members picket International Amphitheater, Chicago, where President Woodrow Wilson delivers a speech. October 20, 1916.

Illustration 6.8 Women Picket, 1916. Courtesy Library of Congress, Manuscript Division.

- **Clue #3:** Lucy Burns, NWP leader, in jail; arrested for disrupting traffic, November 1917.

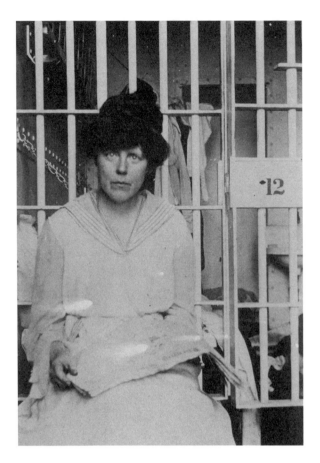

Illustration 6.9 Lucy Burns: Jailed 1917. Courtesy Library of Congress, Manuscript Division.

- **Conclusions:** *Revise hypotheses.* Come to conclusions. Answer EQ.

Think It Through

Teach through Drama: Susan B. Anthony Trial

Set the scene: Give students copies of the cover of Trial Proceedings (Illustration 6.10). Explain that Susan B. Anthony was tried and convicted in 1874 for illegally voting for President in November 1872. She claimed that she was a citizen according to the 14th Amendment, with the right to vote. The judge said the 14th Amendment did not include women.

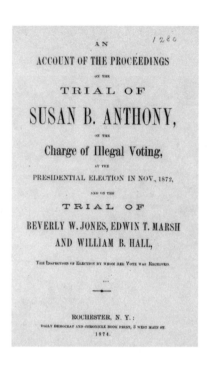

Illustration 6.10 Trial of Susan B. Anthony. Courtesy Library of Congress, Prints and Photographs, LC-USZ62-60762.

Here is the 14th Amendment (passed in 1866, ratified in 1868).

AMENDMENT XIV

All persons born or naturalized in the United States, and subject to the jurisdiction thereof, are citizens of the United States and of the State wherein they reside. No State shall make or enforce any law which shall abridge the privileges or immunities of citizens of the United States; nor shall any State deprive any person of life, liberty, or property, without due process of law; nor deny to any person within its jurisdiction the equal protection of the laws.

Translated for children this means:

Anyone born in the United States, or given citizenship by the United States, is a citizen of the United States and a citizen of the state where they live. States cannot make or enforce any laws that limit the rewards or protections of any citizen of the United States. No state can take away any citizen's life, freedom, or belongings without proper use of the law. Every person is given the same protection under the law (Travis, 2001, see p. 46).

The 14th Amendment gave former slaves full rights as citizens. It assumed the new rights went to men though, not to women. Anthony argued that she was a citizen and should have all the rights and protections due a citizen, including the right to vote.

- **Develop role cards** for students; including things they might say.

Susan B. Anthony

(In her own defense) It is not illegal for me to vote. The 14th Amendment makes every person born in the U.S. a citizen. All citizens have the same rights and protections. The amendment does not say women are not citizens. I am a U.S. citizen. I can vote.
(At the end) I will not pay a penny of this fine!

Jurors

#1: Is she a citizen? The amendment gave freedom to former slaves, not to women!
#2: She is breaking the law!
#3: Women do not have the right to vote!
#4: Maybe she is a citizen. Maybe she can vote.

Judge

(At the beginning) We now start the trial of Susan B. Anthony. She voted for President in 1872. We have to decide if she broke the law.
(At the end) We find you guilty. You are fined $100 for voting.

Audience Members

#1: Women should stay home! They shouldn't vote. It is not a pretty thing for women.
#2: I think she is very brave.
#3: Miss Anthony is standing up for all women. She is right!

Imagine roles: Discuss what each character might say or feel in his/her role.

Enact the play. Freeze the role play at certain dramatic points and ask students how their character feels at that moment. Do the play twice so students can act out different roles.

Think it through: Was Anthony guilty? Why or why not?

It's your turn! Develop a role play of the Women's Suffrage Parade in Washington, March 3, 1913. Here are some ideas to get started. Read: *Mama Went to Jail for the Vote* by Kathleen Karr. Study the photo of the Parade (below). Show chapter 4 of the film *Iron Jawed Angels* (Woman on a Horse). Ask children to imagine "being there" with their mother, in the parade. Make role cards for marchers, onlookers, and policemen. Enact the play. Think it through: Was the parade a good idea? Give it a try!

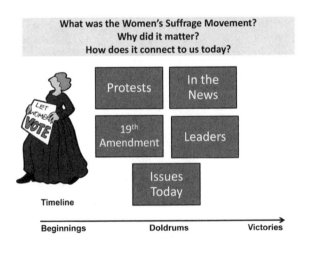

Illustration 6.11 Parade in Washington, 1913. Courtesy Library of Congress, Manuscript Division.

Take Action

Civic Action: Demonstrating the Women's Suffrage Movement

Your students can take action by teaching others! Organize the study of the Women's Suffrage Movement around the making of a museum-like exhibit. Utilize the exhibit to

Illustration 6.12 Exhibit: Women's Suffrage Movement.

showcase what students learn. The following graphic suggests multifaceted dimensions for this display.

 Note: This exhibit is intended as a culmination of students' studies. It can present what students have learned already, through the previous activities, or it can prompt further inquiry, writing, and dramatizing. You will find more tips for teaching inquiry, writing to learn, and teaching through drama (as presentation techniques) inside this action project.

INVESTIGATE!

This exhibit is a product of class study. Develop your study as a class inquiry, teaching students to "do history" as part of the process. The process and results can be as simple or sophisticated as the maturity of your students allows. In the following pages, we offer formats to help you guide this investigation.

You, as teacher, should provide all evidence needed for students' inquiries. Place primary sources, such as photographs or news articles, in students' retrieval files, mark texts they should read, and indicate websites they can search on their own. Here is a sample retrieval folder that organizes students' investigation of suffrage leaders.

Find

Biographies: Women's Suffrage Leaders

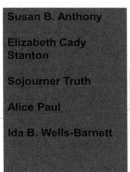

Susan B. Anthony

Elizabeth Cady Stanton

Sojourner Truth

Alice Paul

Ida B. Wells-Barnett

Directions:
Find: www.greatwomen.org.
Click on: Women of the Hall.
Search by: Last name.
Read the biography.
Decide on 4-5 important things to remember.
Write them down on your 3X5 cards.
Place them in the pocket for each person.

Illustration 6.13 Retrieval File: Biographies.

Read

Rustad, M. (2002) *Susan B. Anthony.* Mankato, MN: Capstone Books.

Davis, L. (1998). *Susan B. Anthony: A photo-illustrated biography.* Mankato, MN: Capstone Books.

Study

Susan B. Anthony after she tried to vote in the presidential election of 1872

Illustration 6.14 *The Woman Who Dared*, Daily Graphic, vol. 1, no. 81 (June 5, 1873). Courtesy Library of Congress, Prints and Photographs Division.

Complete

TABLE 6.1 Suffrage Leader: Susan B. Anthony

What we learned	• She started the Women's Suffrage Movement. • She worked with Elizabeth Cady Stanton. • She tried to vote in the 1872 election. She was fined $100. • She gave speeches and held meetings for suffrage on stagecoaches, steamboats, and railroad cars.
Views we found	• She was against the 15th Amendment because it gave Black men the vote, but not women. Other people thought this Amendment was alright because at least some more people gained the right to vote.
Questions we have	• Did Susan B. Anthony ever get to vote? • Was her fine just? Right? Lawful? • Should we fine someone for disobeying a law? What if he or she thought the law was unjust?

WRITE!

For students, determining what to write often proves to be the most challenging aspect of an investigation. Posting retrieval charts, like that above (Illustration 6.13), allows

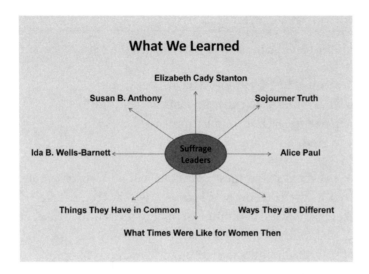

Illustration 6.15 Concept Map: What We Learned.

students to see and consider their findings. Additionally, students can create conceptual mappings of findings, again pushing them to identify and present their data.

PRESENT!

Plan your exhibit as a class. Students can create physical, museum-like, or electronic, web-based exhibits. In either format, the inclusion of a timeline is a "must." Students, and their audience, need to gain a sense of time from the exhibit. An illustrated timeline is an effective tool for understanding for all elementary students. Remember that primary students do not yet grasp dates, such as 1920, but they do understand the passage of time. For these students, large designations of time, such as Beginnings, Doldrums (the suffragists' own term for post-Civil War years), and Victories are sufficient.

Rehearse students' presentation of information. We have assisted prospective teachers in preparing their classes for exhibitions. Here are a couple of techniques that help youth display their knowledge.

- Arrange a "Teach In," where your students teach others. Help youth determine three significant ideas from their studies. Place markers on the floor: #1, #2, and #3. Guide students in moving (literally) from idea 1, to 2, to 3 and, while doing so, explaining each idea. This rehearsal is also effective for preparing introductory, explanatory, and closing remarks.
- Hold an exhibit opening! Create a program with students as masters/mistresses of ceremony and presenters of information. Prepare other students as "roving reporters" who explain the exhibit to guests, informally, as they ask questions. Rehearse with a set of questions that guests are likely to have. Invite the press! Assign a couple of roving reporters to meet the press!

Teacher Review

Let's reflect on this effort and its outcomes. Ask yourself the following questions:

- Did you gain a sense of history as mystery?
- Did you grasp what it means to teach students to "read" history?
- Do you feel prepared to teach the inquiry process?
- Are you ready to guide an inquiry-centered study?

You might have answered yes to these questions, but still worry about the extent of preparation involved in the creation of a History Mystery. Yes, it takes work, it takes research, and it takes passion and commitment to develop a constructive, inquiry-based project such as this. Ask yourself: Is it worth it?

Recently, one of us visited a fifth- to sixth-grade classroom to observe social studies instruction. The teacher organized students into small groups where they read their text-book aloud, stopping to consider questions raised by the teacher or her two aides. The reading focused on ancient Mesopotamia, highlighting inventions that changed inhabit-ants' lives. Students worked with the teacher to complete a comparison chart: inventions (on one side) and why they were important (on the other). The textbook was the sole resource. Although a timeline and small map were included in the text, they were not referenced.

 Think back on this teaching occasion. How can this lesson be revised to become a History Mystery? What is the mystery at hand? What clues can be highlighted? What resources can be utilized? Where, if at all, can the textbook fit in?

We can imagine a mysterious presentation of Mesopotamia. Where was it? What happened there? Why was it important? What is civilization? What makes it ancient? Were there any curious customs or valiant leaders? What did children do there? We invite you to kindle your curiosity (and that of your students) by treating history as mystery.

Making Connections

History Mystery is really more a perspective than a product; it is a way of looking at the past, through a stance of inquiry and a search for evidence. Many topics or themes can be approached with a sense of mystery, or a readiness to discover information, mull it over, and tell its tale. How much more fun for children and you, their teacher, than reiterating pre-digested, ready-made accounts!

In the Preface and in Chapter 2, we made the case for in-depth, integrated, interdis-ciplinary social studies. History Mystery is a tool that can help you and your students examine various topics through a historical lens. Certainly, it is easy to imagine intersec-tions between History Mystery and Biography Workshop. Rather than spotlighting an intriguing person for a day or two, think about investigating their life to find reasons for their significance. Further, histories and biographies are situated in times and places; geographic locations, political situations, and economic conditions can easily be drawn into a History Mystery.

A sense of inquiry is central to all these chapters. Civic engagement has multiple meanings: students engage in learning, while learning to engage as citizens.

seven
Biography Workshop[1]
Composing Citizens' Life Stories

Outstanding citizens are people who take action to make a difference. Imagine what students can learn from studying the life and times of an outstanding citizen! They can grasp citizenship and envision civic action through a real life story. They can see that ordinary people, as well as elected leaders, take action to champion human dignity, challenge inequality, and achieve social justice. They can imagine themselves as citizens who fight to improve democracy.

In this chapter, we examine a powerful means to teach and learn about outstanding citizens: the development of cooperative biographies. Tarry Lindquist, an elementary social studies teacher-of-the-year, called this approach a gift, passed along—teacher to teacher—as a special way of teaching history and citizenship (Lindquist, 1997). Similarly, this project was passed along to us by several colleagues, Professors Walter Parker (University of Washington–Seattle) and Myra Zarnowski (Queens College, New York) who utilized it to "do history" with teachers like you (Parker, 2005; Zarnowski, 2003). Currently, the development of cooperative biographies is a staple of the social studies methods course at Indiana University, where Lynne and her colleague Leana McClain guide their ongoing revision and mutation. Our focus on outstanding citizens is one of many possibilities for biography. We invite you to try this form of biography, to translate it for use in your own classroom, and to pass the idea on to another social studies teacher.

1 We want to acknowledge and thank Senior Clinical Lecturer Leana McClain at Indiana University for her assistance with the development of the biography project for Rosa Parks.

Cooperative Biographies: What and Why?

A cooperative biography is a book-making project in which small groups of students collaborate to investigate an outstanding citizen, and then use their information to write and illustrate a book about the citizen's life, including his/her efforts to make a difference. It is an integrative endeavor that teaches history, geography, and civics, draws upon drama, music, and art, and utilizes reading, writing, and illustrating skills. It is a form of History Mystery that focuses on the life and times of exceptionally engaged citizens. Further, as students investigate people's lives, they *do history*, collecting and evaluating evidence, and creating a credible account. When the biographies are completed collaboratively, students also learn to work alongside others.

Every effort should be made to select lives that are fascinating and that exhibit contributions of diverse citizens to democracy. Fascinating lives allow students to witness courage in the face of hardship and to engage with struggles for the common good. Attention to diversity allows students to recognize the trials and triumphs of men and women from a range of social, ethnic, economic, religious, and physical ability groups.

As we discussed in Chapter 3, democracy is unfinished; it is a path that citizens walk together as they create and recreate democracy. Over time, democracy should not only regenerate, but advance, embracing more people, realizing more equality, and resulting in more fairness. Biographies should capture this process, showing people in action, endeavoring to improve democratic life.

You can learn to teach cooperative biography by first writing your own. The following task sheet on page 125 outlines this engagement. Our pre-service teachers tell us that the outline works well, not only for their "first try," but as a structure for their students' composition of biographies too.

What should students know and be able to do as a result of their engagement in cooperative biography? Recall that, in our view, good citizens are informed, reflective, and active. Biographies can serve to demonstrate examples of extraordinary citizenship: they can help students envision engaged citizenship through the lives of people who have made a difference. As we teach biography, we focus on the following goals. As you see, some goals target civic content and others highlight skills associated with investigating, writing, and publishing historical accounts.

Content goals:

- Students should understand that biography is a person's life story.
- Students should understand that people live in particular places and times.
- Students should understand that people's stories illustrate multiple perspectives.
- Students should realize that a person can take action to improve democracy.

Process goals:

- Students should be able to utilize data to develop a credible account.
- Students should be able to construct a timeline of a person's life.

Cooperative Biography: Learning about Outstanding Citizens

What is it?

It is composing biographies of outstanding citizens. It is absorbing and doing history. It is an authentic way to integrate history, geography, civics, and language arts.

What outstanding citizens might students study?

James Madison	Abraham Lincoln	Thomas Jefferson
Susan B. Anthony	Jane Addams	Chief Joseph
Eleanor Roosevelt	Martin Luther King	Ida B. Wells

How does it work?

Decide upon learning objectives.
- Students should understand that people live in particular places and times.
- Students should understand that people's stories illustrate multiple perspectives.
- Students should realize that a person can take action to improve democracy.
- Students should be able to utilize data to develop a credible account.
- Students should be able to compose and publish a biography.

Select a subject.
- Select a person whose life illustrates powerful ideas of history, geography, and democracy.
- Select a fascinating life. Select a person about whom there are plenty of materials.

Introduce the project.
- Assess what children know.
- Explain objectives or targets for the project.

Investigate the lifestory.
- Read a book. Watch a film. Sing a song. Do a role play.
- Study a map. Make a timeline. Create a retrieval file.
- Collect data about early, middle, and later times in the citizen's life.

Prepare for writing.
- Identify events in the citizen's life that students found interesting.
- Select four or five events as topics for "chapters," or lifestories.
- Place students in cooperative groups to write each chapter.
- Emergent readers: the class writes together, as a teacher-guided activity.

Make a book.
- Write and illustrate chapters.
- Write a "Citizens Take Action" page; show the citizen making a difference.
- Make a timeline, map, and word list.
- Add an "Author's Note" to explain your decisions about writing history.
- Create a book cover and title page.

Illustration 7.1 Cooperative Biography: Learning about Outstanding Citizens

- Students should be able to compose and publish a biography.
- Students should be able to collaborate to investigate and write a biography.

Learning from Research

Why teach citizenship through biography? Children are interested in history that focuses on people (Barton, 1994). Children can grasp the past through lives of individuals (Barton, 1997a). They can connect with people's feelings and begin to understand their actions in historical times (Campbell, 2008; Levstik, 1989). They can wrestle with social issues, opposing values, and multiple perspectives when they are highlighted in children's literature (Houser, 1999; Tyson, 2002). Let's examine this research and connect it to the biography project.

History as People's Lives

Personal stories can make history come alive. However, children can fail to situate people within their times, missing the impact of the periods in which they live. In a study of fourth- and fifth-grade classrooms, Keith Barton (1997a) found that students thought of history almost entirely in terms of the actions of individuals, particularly of famous people. Even when the teacher explained political tensions or economic realities, students perceived events as enacted and changed by individuals. This point is emphasized in several other studies (e.g., Brophy, VanSledright, & Bredin, 1992; Lee & Ashby, 2000; McKeown & Beck, 1994), and it is pertinent nationally and internationally (den Heyer, 2003; Hallden, 1998).

Personal stories can make history more inclusive, highlighting the lives of a variety of men and women. Not surprisingly, children tend to omit women (and minority groups) from history. In a study of fifth graders, Wineburg (2001) found that boys tended to exclude females from their drawings of historical scenes. Girls drew women, but sparingly, mostly as male helpmates.

Historic Fiction: A Sense of Being There

Historic fiction can speak to students' need to humanize history—to see how people lived and felt in other times. Linda Levstik (1989) conducted a year-long case study of a fifth grader, and she found that the student's historic understanding developed greatly through her reading of historic fiction. The student enjoyed a sense of "being there" and hearing the story told through the characters' eyes. The complexity of novels such as *The Witch of Blackbird Pond* (Speare, 1958) or *My Brother Sam is Dead* (Collier & Collier, 1974) helped this student ponder moral dilemmas, consider causation, and identify multiple perspectives in history.

Susan Campbell (2008) studied the understandings gained by fifth graders from their reading and discussion of historical fiction. Students worked in literacy groups to read selections from the Scholastic series *Dear America*, which portrays fictional characters in historically accurate and stressful situations. Like Levstik, Campbell found that students were drawn to affective or emotional motivations of characters and utilized them to make sense of a character's actions. She submits that personal connections helped students develop historical understandings of things such as historic context, multiple perspectives, and uses (or abuses) of power.

Literature about Social Issues

Children's literature with controversial issues embedded in it can help youth grasp social dilemmas and envision means to address them (Houser, 1999; Zarnowski, 1998; Tyson, 2002). Cynthia Tyson (2002) studied an urban sixth-grade classroom in which students read *Leon's Story* (Tillage, 1997), about life during Jim Crow Laws, and *SeedFolks* (Fleischman, 1997), about the creation of a neighborhood garden from an abandoned city lot. She found that discussions of the books helped students analyze social problems, define social action, and think of themselves as citizens who could take action.

What do these inquiries suggest for you, as teacher? Biography (and autobiography) can humanize history. Biographies can provide personal, emotional, and complicated views of the times in which central characters lived. When students connect personally to characters, they can use this acquaintance to support more complicated understandings of history.

Moreover, biographies of outstanding citizens can focus students' attention on efforts to achieve democratic ideals. Biographies of outstanding women, people of color, and other under-represented groups can counterbalance the traditional focus on men in history. Yet you will need to find ways to situate individual lives within social, political, and economic trends of the day. Historic fiction and non-fiction that probes social issues can bolster biographies, helping students expand their focus from individual greatness to social influences on people's lives.

Teacher's Scholarly Knowledge

 Note: For this engagement, we ask you to wear two hats! Think of yourself as both a student and a teacher of biography. We invite you to write a biography yourself as a vital prerequisite to teaching the process to youth.

In the following pages, we provide suggestions to help you investigate, and then create, a biography of one outstanding citizen, Rosa Parks. We selected Rosa Parks because she personified the qualities of a young citizen of the world. She was informed, reflective, and active. She literally sat down in order to stand up for equal rights for African Americans. Parks' life encompassed the Civil Rights Movement, and children can learn about these days through her eyes. Stories of this movement touch our very souls as citizens. They can help us understand why democratic rights are a prize worth fighting for.

There is an old adage that "you can't teach what you don't know." As part of your preparation for any in-depth unit of study, you need to become an expert on your topic. In Tarry Lindquist's fifth-grade classroom, she and her students study their subject for three weeks before writing a biography (Lindquist, 1997)! Imagine how much you need to know to guide such an in-depth study! Lindquist invites her students to think of the project as a journey; in order to recall their journey, they should pack their "mental baggage" (p. 103) with souvenirs and take careful notes. In the next few pages, we provide suggestions for packing your mental luggage, or preparing to teach about Rosa Parks.

Reading about Rosa

Our pre-service teachers begin to construct their scholarly knowledge by reading *Rosa Parks: My Story* by Rosa Parks (1992). This autobiography is written on the middle-school level, so it can be read aloud as chapters for upper elementary students, but it is a wonderful resource for you too. Our pre-service teachers tell us that it is a book they can't lay down. Possibly like you, our pre-service teachers are surprised by how little they know of the Civil Rights Movement and of Rosa Parks' life. The story covers about 80 years of Mrs. Parks' life, countering the notion that nothing notable happened after the famous Montgomery Bus Boycott. Read and discuss the book in class, then make a timeline of events that marked Mrs. Parks' life (see pp. 177–178).

Nothing can replace an in-depth reading of biography. So, rather than list a few interesting facts about Mrs. Parks' life, we pose some questions to guide your reading of *Rosa Parks: My Story*.

- **Rosa's early years:** When Rosa was ten, she defended herself from a white boy who threatened to hit her. What does her response suggest about her character? What does it tell us about the tenor of the times? How do you think her grandparents' attitudes and actions influenced her way of seeing the world? Rosa's mother was a teacher. What influence did she have on Rosa's education? What did Rosa learn at Miss White's school that would, eventually, support her refusal to move from her seat on a segregated bus?
- **Young adult years:** Do you think Raymond Parks was a good match for a future civil rights heroine? Why or why not? What did it mean for a young Black woman to have a high school diploma in those days? In what ways did Rosa's efforts to register to vote represent larger societal problems with equality? How, if at all, did Rosa's work with the NAACP prepare her for the bus boycott?
- **Bus Boycott**: Did Rosa refuse to give up her seat because she was too tired, as the story often goes? If she was tired, what was she tired of? Do you agree with Mr. E. D. Nixon that Rosa Parks was the "perfect plaintiff" for a case that challenged segregation? What was life like for Rosa Parks during the Montgomery Bus Boycott?

- **After the boycott**: Did Mrs. Parks simply fade away after the boycott? To what extent did her activism continue? Rosa Parks received the Presidential Medal of Honor in 1992, after the publication of *Rosa Parks: My Story*. Find out more about this award.

Studying Primary Documents

Study primary resources from the times and consider ways to utilize them in your future classroom. The Alabama Archives provide a wealth of artifacts about the Montgomery Bus Boycott, including the Montgomery Bus Code, a list of demands by African-American citizens, newspaper stories about the boycott, and even a mug shot (a student favorite) of Rosa Parks' arrest (www.archives.state.al.us/teacher/rights/html). We highlight a sample of these resources in the figures below.

C. 6, § 10   MONTGOMERY CITY CODE   C. 6, § 13

Sec. 10. Separation of races—Required.

Every person operating a bus line in the city shall provide equal but separate accommodations for white people and negroes on his buses, by requiring the employees in charge thereof to assign passengers seats on the vehicles under their charge in such manner as to separate the white people from the negroes, where there are both white and negroes on the same car; provided, however, that negro nurses having in charge white children or sick or infirm white persons, may be assigned seats among white people.

Nothing in this section shall be construed as prohibiting the operators of such bus lines from separating the races by means of separate vehicles if they see fit. (Code 1938, §§ 603, 606.)

Sec. 11. Same—Powers of persons in charge of vehicle; passengers to obey directions.

Any employee in charge of a bus operated in the city shall have the powers of a police officer of the city while in actual charge of any bus, for the purpose of carrying out the provisions of the preceding section, and it shall be unlawful for any passenger to refuse or fail to take a seat among those assigned to the race to which he belongs, at the request of any such employee in charge, if there is such a seat vacant. (Code 1938, § 604.)

Sec. 12. Failure to carry passengers.

It shall be unlawful for any person operating a bus line in the city to refuse, without sufficient excuse, to carry any passenger; provided, that no driver of a bus shall be required to carry any passenger who is intoxicated or disorderly, or who is afflicted with any contagious or infectious disease, or who refuses to pay in advance the fare required, or who for any other reason deemed satisfactory by the recorder should be excluded. (Code 1938, § 699.)

Sec. 13. Smoking.

It shall be unlawful for any person to smoke a cigar, pipe or cigarette upon any bus in the city; provided, however, that

Illustration 7.2 Montgomery City Code. From: Alabama Department of Archives and History.

Illustration 7.3 Mug shot: Rosa Parks. Courtesy Montgomery County Archives.

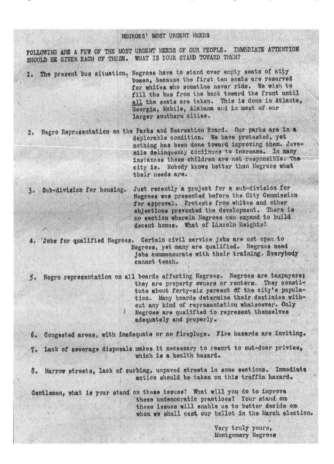

Illustration 7.4 Negroes' Most Urgent Needs. Alabama Department of Archives and History.

Stop and think. What did you learn from your study of primary resources? How can you utilize these resources to teach children about Rosa Parks? How will you introduce students to the notion of "primary" resources?

Examining Children's Literature

Take time to study children's literature related to the Civil Rights Movement. We encourage you to examine, compare, and contrast multiple biographies of Rosa Parks. Do not be surprised to find different selections of content and interpretations of the story. These comparisons can help you become more aware of the author's voice and of the selective process of making history. Can you imagine doing a similar activity with your students? For another, more extensive, comparison chart, see Myra Zarnowski's book, *History Makers: A Questioning Approach to Reading and Writing Biographies* (2003, pp. 35–37).

Investigating Children's Books about Rosa Parks

Title of Book: _____

Author/Illustrator of Book: _____

Audience: Is this book for a primary or intermediate audience? Why? Selection/Interpretation: Is there a table of contents? If so, what are the major events depicted in Rosa Parks' life?

Perspective: From whose perspective or voice is this book written? What makes you think so?

Primary Sources: Are primary sources (original documents, photographs, quotations) used in the book? If so, what sources are used? How are they presented?

Activism: Is there a special page or section devoted to activism, or to what Rosa Parks did to make a difference as a citizen? If so, what does it look like? What does it include?

Author's Note: Is there a note from the author that explains his/her research or his/her selection of noteworthy events? If so, what information can you gain from this exchange with the author?

Teaching Resources

Children's Literature

Tenor of the Times

Tillage, L. (1997). *Leon's story*. New York: Farrar, Straus, and Giroux. In this non-fiction autobiography, Walter Tillage recalls his childhood as a sharecropper's son in 1940s North Carolina. His tale is riveting, informative, and honest. It is easy for students to imagine the horrors of racism through his eyes. It is a great book to read as a prelude to studying the life of Rosa Parks.

Birtha, B. (2005). *Grandmama's pride*. Morton Grove, IL: Albert Whitman & Co. In this fiction story, two young African-American girls travel with their mother to visit their Grandmama down South, facing segregation for the first time. Their sense of exclusion is lessened by their grandmother's inventiveness and strong character. This book is a good read aloud for any age, with captivating illustrations that depict Grandmama's pride.

Johnson, A. (2005). *A sweet smell of roses*. New York: Simon & Schuster. In this fiction story, two children join a civil rights march. Simple yet powerful black-and-white drawings, marked by a spot of red (for roses) on almost every page, help portray the quiet strength of participants. The sweet smell of roses stands for the scent of freedom carried aloft by the winds of change. This book offsets the notion that only famous people, like Drs. King and Abernathy, led the fight for change.

Weatherford, C. (2005). *Freedom on the menu: The Greensboro sit-ins*. New York: Dial Books. This fiction book is based on real events. On February 1, 1960, four African-American students from North Carolina Agriculture and Technical College sat down at Woolworth's "whites-only" lunch counter in Greensboro, North Carolina, and asked to be served. Their actions spawned sit-ins all over the South. In this story, eight-year-old Connie watches as her older brother and sister take part in sit-ins. This book makes ideas of protest, freedom, and justice accessible to young audiences.

Rosa Parks' Life

Schaefer, L. (2002). *Rosa Parks*. Mankato, MN: Pebble Books. This "first biography" can be read by the youngest readers. We love the way the timeline of Rosa Parks' life is presented, as a horizontal line with one date that corresponds to one illustration on each page. The illustrations are photographs, introducing primary children to primary sources. A Words to Know section defines basic ideas such as *citizen* and *boycott* that are important to this story.

Ringgold, F. (1999). *If a bus could talk: The story of Rosa Parks*. New York: Aladdin Paperbacks. This fanciful story is historically based; the biography of Rosa Parks is told through the voice of a talking bus. A young girl gets on the strange-looking bus so she will not be late to school. The vehicle turns out to be a reincarnation of the Cleveland Avenue bus, the scene of Mrs. Parks' famous refusal to move to the back of the bus. In honor of Mrs. Parks' birthday, people from the days of the Montgomery Bus Boycott reappear on the bus to tell their story. Vibrant illustrations help bring a fairly detailed history to life.

Giovanni, N. (2005). *Rosa*. New York: Henry Holt and Co. This fiction story is historically based. It focuses on the fight for civil rights as a struggle on the part of many citizens. It is beautifully illustrated; one page folds out to show an enlargement of people marching. We read this book just before the creation of the "Citizens' Take Action" section of the biography; it reminds students that Rosa Parks was part of a battle for first-class citizenship.

Films

For years, we had our college students watch selections from the PBS film series *Eyes on the Prize* (http://pbsvideodb.pbs.org/resources/eyes/), particularly *Awakenings*, chapters 3 through 5. The film was highly informative, but more suitable for adults than children. We highly recommend *Mighty Times: The Legacy of Rosa Parks* (Carnes, 2002), a video obtained free of charge from Teaching Tolerance at the Southern Poverty Law Center (www.teachingtolerance.org). Children who are relatives of Rosa Parks play prominently in the narration of this story, heightening its power to help youth imagine themselves in the tumult of the times.

We also recommend *Rosa Parks: Modern Day Heroine* (Pointer, 2004), the first documentary ever done on the subject. The film focuses on big ideas that undergird the civil rights story: deeds that make people important, acts that create heroes or heroines, and examples of bravery and courage. Students are encouraged to consider what they would have done in Rosa Parks' shoes. A classic that is now on DVD, this film introduces the notion of outstanding citizenship, and Rosa Parks as the personification of it, to younger learners.

Songs

Eyes on the Prize is an obvious musical choice that helps students ponder what the prize is and why citizens kept their eyes (and hopes) focused on it. The lyrics follow:

> I know one thing we did right
> Was the day we started to fight
> Keep your eyes on the prize
> Hold on, hold on.

It Takes Courage is a song written in honor of Black History Month and sung by the Creek/Love first- and second-grade classroom of 2001 at Rogers/Binford Elementary School in Bloomington, Indiana (Lodge-Rigal, 2002).[2] The song recalls the struggles of Rosa Parks, Ruby Bridges, and Martin Luther King for equality and justice. The song translates courage into something children can do—"be the very best you." Lyrics for stanzas 1, 3, and 4 follow.

It Takes Courage

It takes courage to walk a mile in Rosa's shoes
Courage to sit down and simply refuse
To get up when you've worked all day
And you're tired of those old rules
It takes courage to walk a mile in Rosa's shoes
It takes courage to walk your days in Martin's shoes
Courage to speak up for justice, peace, and love
For me and you
We're all spokes on a wheel
Many fingers, one hand
It takes courage to walk you days in Martin's shoes
It takes courage to be the very best you
Courage to take a stand
For what you know to be true
Ask your questions and lend a hand
Listen well and understand
It takes courage to be the very best you (repeated three times).

TEACH!

Now we are ready to create a Cooperative Biography. We continue to speak to you as colleagues—teacher-to-teacher. Yet, at the same time, we encourage you to create your own text, learning the process from the inside out—as a *student* of biography. So, read *about* the engagement and *engage in it* as well.

Become Informed

Focus In: Mighty Times: The Legacy of Rosa Parks (a film from Teaching Tolerance)

Hook: What do you know about Mrs. Parks' life and times? Begin to construct a concept map of Rosa Parks' life. Save it and return to it, again and again, over the course of this

---

2 Funded by the school's parent–teacher organization, the children created a CD, *Higher Hopes*, which is available from Beth Lodge-Rigal at 812-333-7957. The song owes its inspiration to the melodic and lyric structure of Kiya Heartwood's song, *Higher Ground*.

task. This map can be used as an assessment tool; you (and your future students) can add to the map and easily see what you have learned. Try it now!

Focus Activity: Write terms, such as the following, on 4" × 6" index cards: BOYCOTT, SEGREGATION, JIM CROW LAWS, CIVIL DISOBEDIENCE, INTEGRATION, NATIONAL ASSOCIATION FOR THE ADVANCEMENT OF COLORED PEOPLE, and BROWN V. BOARD OF EDUCATION. Place them on the white board and ask students to choose one or two. We give teacher candidates (our students) a small data set (pages in a book, information from the internet, or a photo) that describes each term. We ask them to work in groups to learn a bit about their term and then share it with the class.

Watch the video: We then watch *Mighty Times: The Legacy of Rosa Parks*, asking learners to look for more information about these terms. Watch this film and see what you learn!

After the video: After watching the video, return to the terms. As a group, define them further. Last, outline the biography engagement, as per the sample task sheet above (p. 125).

Teach for Ideas: What makes a biography?

Hook: Ask students: What makes a biography? Read *Rosa Parks* by Lola Schaefer (see Children's Literature, p. 132), or another biography of your choice.

Example #1: Examine the organization and content of several biographies. Look to see if there is a chronological order to the book.

Example #2: Look for timelines of Rosa's life. Determine where they are located in the book. See how they are constructed.

Example #3: Reread the book. This time pay attention to the type of content included. Look carefully for ways in which Rosa Parks made a difference as a citizen. Imagine ways to spotlight this information.

Non-example: Read *Grandmama's Pride* by Becky Birtha. Ask students to think about why this book is NOT a biography. Explain: historical fiction is a story that depicts the times, but does so with fictional characters.

Assessment: Create a Connecting Web (see Chapter 3, p. 49). Ask students to compare biography with historical fiction.

Teach for Inquiry: Who was Rosa Parks?

Hook: Ask: Who was Rosa Parks? Read a biography of Rosa Parks, such as *Rosa* by Nikki Giovanni or *If the Bus Could Talk* by Faith Ringgold. Begin to make a conceptual mapping of Mrs. Parks' life.

Investigate: Remember that teacher Tarry Lindquist allows several week of reading/research time. Inquiries can't be hurried! Ms. Lindquist helps students learn to take notes, create mind maps, and make a Jeopardy-style game board to recall their research (Lindquist, 1997).

As noted in Chapter 6, we find the "retrieval file" quite effective in aiding student research. The retrieval file is a file folder in which pockets are glued. The pockets are large enough to hold 3" × 5" index cards. Each pocket is designated to hold information about some aspect of Mrs. Parks' life: Early Years, Life as a Grown-Up, Bus Boycott, and After the Boycott.

Organization of student research is a must! Select text passages, gather books, and duplicate primary documents for students' review. Mark pages to be read and provide directions for the examination of first-hand resources. Create a set of study materials. Avoid telling students to "go to the library and do research." Instead, support students as they conduct their inquiries. Help them become the investigators they will need to be as informed and active citizens!

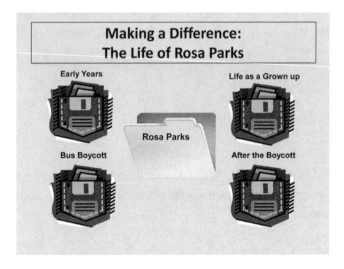

Illustration 7.5 Retrieval File: Rosa Parks.

 Note: Intermediate students usually can retrieve information on their own. For primary students, we suggest the creation of a "Class Retrieval Chart": read stories aloud, help students recall information, and construct a retrieval chart together. Try it out! Practice both forms of retrieving information.

Think It Through

Write to Learn: Composing the Biography

Review: Revisit the concept map of Rosa Parks' life. Add ideas and information to the map, as gleaned through research.

RAFT: Set the task of biography composition.

- Role: Author!
- Audience: Readers
- Format: A published book
- Topic: A biography of Rosa Parks' life

Pre**paration for Writing**

Developing Chapters

Reflect on your studies of Rosa Parks. Create a timeline, as a class, of her life. Circle events in the timeline that fit together; these groupings become chapters for the book. Give each grouping a chapter title, such as "Growing Up" or "Becoming an Activist."

Timeline

Growing Up:

- February 4, 1913:   Rosa McCauley born in Tuskegee, AL.
- 1918:   Enters school in Pine Level, AL.
- 1924:   Begins attending school in Montgomery.
- 1929:   Leaves school to care for grandmother.
- December 1932:   Marries Raymond Parks in Pine Level, AL.
- 1933:   Receives high school degree.

Becoming an Activist:

- December 1943:   Becomes secretary of the NAACP.
- ▪   Tries to register to vote and is denied.
- ▪   Put off bus for first time for not entering in the back.
- 1944:   Tries to register to vote and is denied.
- 1945:   Receives certificate for voting.
- Summer 1955:   Attends civil rights workshop at Highlander Folk School.
- August 1955:   Meets Dr. Martin Luther King.

Sitting Down to Stand Up:

- December 1, 1955:   Arrested for not giving up her seat on the bus to a white man.
- December 5, 1955:   Stands trial; found guilty.
      Montgomery Bus Boycott begins.
- November 13, 1956:   Bus Segregation declared unconstitutional by Supreme Court.
- December 21, 1956:   Rides in a position of honor in the front of the bus.

Continuing to Fight:

- 1957: Moves to Detroit, MI.
- 1965: Begins working for Congressman John Conyers in Detroit.
- 1987: Founds Rosa and Raymond Parks Institute for Self Development.
- 1988: Retires from work with Congressman Conyers.
- September 9, 1996: Receives Presidential Medal of Freedom.
- October 24, 2005: Dies in Detroit.
- October 31, 2005: Lies in state in U.S. Capitol Rotunda.[3]

Writing a Citizen's Take Action Page

As you learned from research, children often fail to connect people's deeds to the times in which they lived. Thus, they will not necessarily connect Rosa Parks' life to civic action for social change. Therefore, we include a "Citizens Take Action" page as part of our biography assignment. Use this page to highlight the ways in which a citizen made a difference, highlighting, perhaps as a sidebar, the impact of his/her times. What will you include on your Citizens Take Action page?

Creating Original Illustrations

Our pre-service teachers illustrate their biographies with original artwork, learning to make prints, create graphics, use media, and vary color to add meaning to the text. Recently, we added sidebars (spaces for quotations, songs, or important phrases) and captions (descriptions of the illustrations) to expand the means of conveying information (Zarnowski, 2003).

 Note: Sometimes, citizen actions, such as becoming informed and thinking it through, are not neatly sequential. Instead, they are interactive, with one enlightening the other. In order to construct biographies, we find it helpful to read a little, write a little, do a role play, sing a timely tune, and then read and write some more. Each approach deepens students' knowledge and enriches their writing. So, try a role play of the famous bus scene, then imagine using it with your own students. Next, chant *Keep Your Eyes on the Prize* or sing *It Takes Courage*. Consider what your students are likely to learn from similar exercises.

Teach through Drama: Refusing to Give Up her Seat

Hook: This role play simulates Rosa's refusal to give up her seat on the bus to a white man. The play helps youth recall the details of the bus episode and imagine what it was like to be there. Move chairs into a set-up reminiscent of a bus and count seats to ensure there is one less seat for a white passenger than needed. Use dimes or artificial coins to simulate payment for a ride.

3 This chronology was adapted from one found in the Appendix for *Rosa Parks: My Story* by Rosa Parks.

Set the Scene: Prior to the role play, examine primary documents in the Alabama Archives (www.archives.state.al.us/teacher/rights/html). They provide a real sense of the times. Utilize the resources provided above or find more at this archival website.

Roles: To involve 20 students, make role cards for the following characters:

- Narrator
- Bus driver James Blake
- Rosa Parks
- Nine white riders (only eight seats, two on each side of a "bus aisle")
- Eight Black riders (with eight seats behind a sign that reads "Colored Section")

Role Play: We have conducted this role play with pre-service teachers and with elementary students. At first, our "costumes" were "Black" and "White" cards, hung from ribbons, like a necklace. The cards designated the racial identification of bus riders. We found, however, that neither pre-service teachers nor elementary students talked during the "ride." They simply waited for the Rosa Parks character to be thrown off the bus.

We asked our students to contemplate what riders might have said—to each other, or to themselves, during the event. To help our students get into their roles and begin to act within the scene, we added dramatic prompts to the backs of the "Black" and "White" cards. For example, "You are a white passenger; you wish Mrs. Parks would just move from her seat. You do not want to be part of any trouble." We now freeze the action during the scene and ask students what they are thinking and feeling. This reflection seems to help students grasp the emotions of the day.

Assessment:

- Ask students to consider what it means to "sit down in order to stand up."
- Ask students why Rosa Parks is deemed an outstanding citizen.
- Ask students to imagine something they might protest in their own lives.

 It's your turn! Work cooperatively with your peers to compose a biography of Rosa Parks. Publish it by sharing it with your classmates and celebrating the completion of a major civic engagement.

ASSESSING THE BIOGRAPHY

Amazingly, you (and subsequently your students) have written a book! Let's return to the instructional objectives set for this engagement. Did you achieve your objectives? What did you learn? What are your future students likely to know and be able to do?

- Do you understand that biography is a person's life story?
- Do you understand that people live in particular places and times?

- Do you understand that people's stories illustrate multiple perspectives?
- Do you realize that a person can take action to improve democracy?
- Are you able to utilize data to develop a credible account?
- Are you able to construct a timeline of a person's life?
- Are you able to compose and publish a biography?

An authentic means of assessment is an examination of the book itself. You should determine, prior to the work, criteria for an excellent product. Then, you are ready to compare students' work to the pre-set criteria for performance. Try to develop a rubric which ascertains levels of mastery for your students. The rubric in Illustration 7.6 was used to determine the level of achievement for our pre-service teachers. For children, notions of mastery must be greatly simplified. Scores of fair, good, and excellent (or similar terms) can set three levels of achievement and acknowledge every effort children make. We discuss this rubric with our pre-service teachers before they develop biographies, and we invite revisions. So you too should invite your students to provide input on the tools by which they will be assessed.

Another form of assessment that demonstrates what children know and are able to do is the development of a concept map. As mentioned earlier, we typically create a concept map entitled "Rosa Parks: Life and Times" before and after the book-making activity. For younger children, this activity can be done jointly, as a class. For older children, the activity can be completed alone. As you can well imagine, the maps move from sketchy to comprehensive knowledge. Even our pre-service teachers surprise themselves with how little they knew and how much they learned about the Civil Rights Movement through this engagement.

Take Action

Civic Action: Teach about Rosa Parks

You (and your future students) have written a book! To "publish" a book is to make it public, to announce it, and, most of all, to share it. Let others know about this accomplishment and create ways to share students' learning. Plan a "reading." Make a public service announcement on the school's PA system to invite other students to the event. Set a dramatic scene: enlarge primary documents about the bus boycott, make an oversized bus as a classroom prop, and post the completed concept map about Rosa Parks' life. Be sure to highlight how Rosa Parks made a difference to our democracy through her example of personal courage. Commemorate the life of this outstanding citizen and, in so doing, celebrate the vitality of democracy! Remember, if democracy is a path that we all walk together, changing and improving it as we go along, then people like Rosa Parks lead us on that journey, exemplifying citizenship as a verb.

Cooperative Biography Evaluation Rubric

Names: _____ Total points: 100/4 for 25%

	Completeness (x10)	Quality of Content (x15)	Quality of Cooperation (x10)	Artistry in Book-Making (x15)
2	Biography includes title page, timeline, map, 4 chapters, Citizens Take Action page, dictionary, author's note, and illustrator's note.	Historic, geographic, and biographic content is accurate. Story is well-written and appropriate for either lower or upper elementary students. Content pays full attention to ways in which subject made a difference to democracy.	Work is well divided among group members. Book looks even and well integrated, like work of a coherent group.	Original artwork correlates strongly with the story. The same medium and techniques are used throughout the book. Art principles, such as color, line, shape, and/or texture, are used throughout the book.
1	Biography includes all assigned dimensions, but some look careless, sloppy, or hard to follow for elementary children.	Some historic, geographic, and biographic content is inaccurate. Story is fairly well written and mostly appropriate for either lower or upper elementary students. Little attention to ways in which subject made a difference to democracy.	It is not clear that work is well divided among group members. Book looks slightly uneven, as though the group did not meet to integrate their pieces well.	Original artwork correlates sometimes with the story. Medium and techniques are mixed in the book. Art principles, such as color, line, shape, and/or texture, are used sometimes in the book.
0	Some dimensions are missing. Some dimensions look careless, sloppy, or hard to follow for elementary children.	Some historical, geographic, and biographic content is inaccurate. Story needs editing. Some misspellings are noted. Story is too difficult or easy for intended audience. Little or no attention to ways in which subject made a difference to democracy.	It is not clear that work is well divided among group members. Some members did all the work. Book looks very uneven, as though the group did not meet to integrate their pieces well.	Original artwork correlates rarely with the story. There is no clear plan for medium and techniques in the book. Art principles, like color, line, shape, and/or texture are used rarely in the book.

Illustration 7.6 Cooperative Biography Evaluation Rubric

Teacher Review

Now, it is your chance to evaluate this civic engagement. Stand back and view this project from the point of view of the teacher you hope to become. Ask yourself the following questions, then discuss them with your classmates.

- To what extent does Biography Workshop push me to be a scholar, a teacher who is well versed in the subject he/she teaches?
- In what ways does Biography Workshop allow me to be a curriculum developer, a teacher who creates learning activities that are relevant to his/her students?
- In what ways does Biography Workshop assist my teaching of citizenship?
- To what extent does Biography Workshop teach citizenship as a verb?

Next, consider the extent to which this engagement incorporated principles of powerful teaching and learning. To what extent is Biography meaningful, integrated, challenging, value-based, and active? In what ways might you change this engagement to address these principles more robustly? Finally, contemplate the largest question of all: Will I use this engagement in my own classroom? Why or why not?

Making Connections

Why teach biography? Where does it fit into teaching citizenship as a verb, fostering citizens who are decision-makers and action-takers? How, if at all, does it support an inclusive, humanistic, culturally affirmative worldview? Biography, as mentioned earlier, is a form of History Mystery. Learning history is part of figuring out who we are as a people and how we might grow as a nation. But learning history for history's sake is not our intention. Remember, this book is about social studies, not social science, education. Learning history is fundamental to becoming informed, thinking it through, and taking action. Its study helps youth become vitally informed, rather than merely opinionated. Biography, as a special form of history, can tap into youth's attraction to people's histories and spotlight stories of outstanding citizenship as well. Biography can bring citizenship to life and exemplify what it means to make a difference. Making a difference is what citizenship as a verb is all about.

eight
Store
Making Everyday
Economic Choices

Economics is devoted to dealing with some of the big problems of human life, such as making a living, enjoying the better things, assigning value, apportioning resources, and planning for the future. These problems face all of us every day of our lives as people, families, communities, and countries, and every decision we make, and each action we take, has some kind of impact on us, others, and those far beyond our borders.

Economics is great for the elementary school because it can be a fun, motivating topic that can range from getting an allowance, to working for wages, to keeping a savings account, to donating money to worthy causes. Even the youngest children can grasp economic ideas, as they relate practically to their lives. In our experience, we've found that kindergartners can understand price, cost, wants, and needs pretty clearly and that first graders can learn ideas of supply and demand (as related to price) with no problem at all.

Economics also is vital for the elementary school because young people are big spenders. Recent data (The U.S. Kids Market, 2002, cited in Suiter & Meszaros, 2005) indicates that children 8–12 years old spend $40 billion a year! Additionally, kids are targets for advertising—in school and out. Programs such as *Read It*, sponsored by Pizza Hut, or *McDonald's McTeacher's Night* promote their products through rewards, discounts, and fundraisers (Consumers Union, 2005; Schor, 2004). Even the classic (and seemingly non-commercial) news magazine *My Weekly Reader* now includes advertisements geared to young people (Schor, 2004). Elementary students need to comprehend consumer culture, including their (valuable) place in it.

Long ago, Harold O. Rugg, an early proponent for integrated, issue-oriented social studies, proposed that, at heart, modern society is economic. In order to understand contemporary society, Rugg felt that youth should grasp its economic influences. His advice seems foresighted today. It is never too soon to develop children's knowledge of economic ideas, aims, principles, and institutions. In this chapter, we describe civic engagements that can guide your teaching of economic ideas, factors, and forces to children. We introduce the notion of money, simulate exchanges in a store, and assist in fundraising for a good cause. We approach money matters as real-world choices based on fundamental ideas of economics.

Store: What and Why?

Many people, as the saying goes, "have trouble balancing their checkbooks," but in spite of this negative sentiment, economics actually is an easy subject to teach and learn, and one that has a huge value in daily life. Deep down economics is a very basic subject with a dozen or so BIG ideas, such as opportunity cost and scarcity, that help with many other subjects such as history, science, and mathematics, while providing practical everyday guidance on buying, selling, saving, spending, investing, producing, and consuming.

Economics is very much a part of doing citizenship as a verb. Making wise choices about spending and saving, consuming and buying, can lead to positive effects personally and to good social ethics as well. For example, when a person drinks liquids that are healthful and inexpensive, such as milk, juice, and water, he or she is likely to be healthier, and others around him or her will benefit from fewer doctor or dentist bills. Alternatively, when an individual drinks soda, which is mostly sugar water, it can be expensive relative to both price and health.

Additionally, economics has a lot to do with mathematics. The consideration of most economic problems involves a variety of mathematical skills. Understanding and using money is a very basic skill. Addition, subtraction, multiplication, and division are all part of using money, as well as higher-order ideas such as proportions or ratios, and averages, including medians, modes, and means. Economics is everyday math, as well as civic decision-making.

There is a national movement to upgrade and enhance economic instruction and learning. The Excellence in Economic Education (EEE) Act (20 USC 7267) was authorized by Congress as a part of the *No Child Left Behind Act* (NCLB). The EEE program promotes economic and financial literacy among all students in kindergarten through grade 12. The National Council on Economic Education (NCEE) was awarded the first-ever federal grant for carrying out the goals of the EEE, and its outreach programs have been funded since 2004. The NCEE now offers academic standards, exemplary lessons, and teaching materials—inexpensively or free of charge. (Its website is described later in this chapter, as part of *Teaching Resources*.)

So, then, we hope you agree that playing Store—doing economics—is a very teachable subject for all ages and grades. Let's get busy learning big economic ideas and preparing to help youth make good fiscal decisions.

Learning from Research

Research on teaching economics to children has indicated that "if we teach it, they will learn" (Schug & Hagedorn, 2005). Not surprisingly, learning appears to be developmental; older students grasp economic ideas with more sophistication than younger students (Schug, 1993; Schug & Lephardt, 1992). Primary and early intermediate grades are good times to introduce fundamental economic concepts, such as scarcity, supply and demand, and opportunity cost. Notions of relationship, such as market system or international trade, may need to be taught later.

Research also indicates that children tend to see the world in literal, not relative, terms, leading to economic misperceptions (Kourilsky, 1987; Schug & Walstad, 1991). Children often confuse scarcity with rarity, tending to see scarcity as an absolute rather than a relative quantity. To them, scarcity is something fewer in number, regardless of whether there is any demand for it. So, if there are ten iguana eggs, but no one has any use for them, and 20 gallons of gasoline to meet a demand for 100 gallons, children still see the eggs, not the gasoline, as scarce. Also, children tend to see opportunity cost as the sum of all the options foregone, rather than the value of the one, next-best alternative. If a child purchases a candy bar, the cost to him/her is *all* the candies not chosen, not the other best choice. As teachers, you will need to find ways to tap into students' perceptions and to remedy their misconceptions.

There also is some evidence that children can learn economics through a variety of instructional methodologies, such as didactic teaching, video instruction, and inquiry-based simulations (Kourilsky, 1987; Schug, 1993; Schug & Hagedorn, 2005). However, inquiry-oriented, experience-based programs seem to hold a slight edge. In a review of her own research, Kourilsky (1987) reported that *Kinder-Economy* and *Mini-Society*, economic simulation programs, increased primary students' economic literacy, improved their attitudes toward learning, and enhanced their personal decision-making. Laney (1989) found that labeling concepts with children's own (invented) terms and participating in real-life decision-making situations improved their understanding of economic ideas. Morgan (1991) studied the effectiveness of the *Econ and Me* video program, and Schug and Hagedorn (2005) examined the value of the *Money Savvy Kids* curriculum—both focused on solving real-world economic problems. Students in both studies had higher post- than pre-test scores. Overall, research has shown that economic instruction, particularly if presented in a hands-on, active manner and focused on problem-solving and decision-making, produces significant learning gains in the understanding of basic economic concepts.

Other evidence underscores our call for teachers' scholarly knowledge—you can't teach what you don't know. Sosin, Dick and Reiser (1997) used a pre- and post-test model to investigate the effects of economic education for third- to sixth-grade elementary teachers, as well as their students. Teachers took a graduate class in economic education while simultaneously teaching economics to their students. Not surprisingly, the variable that explained student learning most was the extent to which concepts were taught. All grade levels scored significantly higher than the control groups on basic economic knowledge. Also, teachers gained in their positive views of economics and their enjoyment of teaching it. These findings suggest that, if teachers know it, they will teach it, and again that if taught, students will learn it.

What does this research suggest for your teaching? You, as teacher, can improve students' conceptual grasp of economics. You should start in the early grades to provide opportunities for students to progressively grasp and practice big economic ideas. VanFossen (2003) suggests four "best practices" for economic education that respond to this research: (1) use children's literature to teach economic concepts, (2) use internet resources to provide interactive experiences, (3) use simulations to provide direct practice in economic life, and (4) draw from pre-packaged curricula as a resource for exemplary, well-honed lessons. In the following pages, we attend to a number of these proposals.

Teacher's Scholarly Knowledge

The Voluntary National Content Standards in Economics (National Council on Economic Education, 1997) propose 20 BIG ideas (or content standards) that students should understand, in various degrees, at grades 4, 8, and 12. You can find a summary at www.ncee.net/ea/standards/. A kid-friendly translation of these terms is included in *Teaching Economics Using Children's Literature* by Harlan Day and his colleagues (2006, referenced below). We borrow from Day's format and cull from national standards to spotlight big ideas that can ground your teaching of Store. Several notes are in order.

 Note #1: Given the prevalence of a production/consumption economy in the U.S., it is easy to focus your teaching on consumerism. However, it is vital to emphasize saving, investing, and giving as beneficial economic options.

 Note #2: You are familiar with the strategy of *Teach for Ideas*. It is crucial that you define big economic ideas in advance, first, for your own understanding, and second, for youth, rephrasing ideas in child-friendly terms that children can grasp.

Illustration 8.1 Big Economic Ideas.

BIG Economic Ideas	Related Ideas

Big Idea #1: Scarcity

Teacher Knowledge: Productive resources (natural, human, and capital resources) are limited. People cannot have all the goods and services they want; they must choose some things and give up others.

Student Language: Scarcity means not being able to have everything we want. Scarcity forces us to make choices.

Example: Dogs that are trained to help people with disabilities are rare. It takes a lot of money and time to train them. People who want to help others decided to give money to an organization so it could train more dogs for more needy people.

Goods:
Teacher Knowledge: Goods are tangible things that people want.
Student Language: A good is something people want that they can touch and hold.

Services:
Teacher Knowledge: Services are activities that satisfy people's wants.
Student Language: A service is something that one person does for someone else.

Opportunity Cost:
Teacher Knowledge: The opportunity cost of a choice is the value of the best alternative given up.

Student Language: When you make a decision, the most valuable alternative that you don't choose is opportunity cost.

Big Idea #2: Cost/Benefit

Teacher Knowledge: Effective decision-making requires comparing the additional cost of alternatives with the additional cost of benefits. Most choices involve doing more or less of something: few choices are all-or-nothing decisions.

Student Language: A cost is what you give up when you decide to do something. A benefit is what satisfies your wants. A trade-off is getting a little less of one thing in order to get a little more of another.

Example: It is expensive to purchase a computer, but it is helpful for students' studies. Parents decide to buy a computer, but to wait for a sale so it will be cheaper.

Incentives:
Teacher Knowledge: People respond predictably to positive and negative incentives. Economic incentives are the rewards or penalties people receive from engaging in more or less of a particular activity. People make decisions based on the rewards or penalties that will accrue from their behavior.

Student Language: Rewards are positive incentives that make people better off. Penalties are negative incentives that make people worse off. Both positive and negative incentives affect people's choices and behaviors.

Illustration 8.1 Big Economic Ideas (continued).

BIG Economic Ideas	**Related Ideas**

Big Idea #3: Exchange and Trade

Teacher Knowledge: Exchange is the trading of goods and services for other goods and services, or for money. Voluntary exchange occurs only when all participants expect to gain. This is true for trade among individuals, organizations, or nations.

Student Language: Exchange is the trading of goods and services for money or for other goods and services. People exchange goods and services because they expect to be better off after the exchange.

Example: People trade things on the internet. Sellers are happy to sell things they don't want and buyers are happy to get them.

Supply:
Teacher Knowledge: The amount of goods or services available for use or purchase. When supply changes, market prices adjust, affecting ability to use or willingness to buy.

Student Language: Supply is how much there is of something you want. If there is more, the cost is less. If there is less, the cost is more.

Demand:
Teacher Knowledge: The level of desire for a good or service together with the ability to pay for it. When the demand changes, market prices adjust, affecting willingness to buy.

Student Language: Demand is how much you want something and what you are willing to pay for it. If something is popular, it is worth more. If it is unwanted, it is worth less.

Big Idea #4: Production

Teacher Knowledge: People try to effectively use natural, human, and capital resources to produce goods and services. In production these three resources are combined to produce goods and services.

Student Language: Production is the use of resources to make goods and provide services.

Example: When your mother or father cook dinner, he or she is a human resource who is producing a meal. He or she uses natural resources, like chicken or rice, to produce dinner. He or she might use a capital resource, which is a person-made tool or machine, to help cook the dinner.

Human Resources:
Teacher Knowledge: Human resources, or labor, represent the quantity and quality of human effort used in production.

Student Language: Human resources are people who work in jobs to produce goods and services.

Natural Resources:
Teacher knowledge: Natural resources refer to minerals, water, trees, and land. They are gifts of nature for production. They are present without human intervention.

Student Language: Natural resources are gifts of nature that are used to make things.

Illustration 8.1 Big Economic Ideas (continued).

BIG Economic Ideas	**Related Ideas**

Big Idea #5: Saving

Teacher Knowledge: Saving is the part of income not spent on taxes or consumption. Saving also can refer to economizing or cutting costs. A deposit account paying interest is often used to hold money for future needs.

Student Language: Saving is putting money in a safe place to use in the future. It is even better when savings earn a bonus, called interest.

Example: A child earns an allowance from her parents for doing chores around the house. She uses some to buy a ticket to a movie. She puts the rest in a piggy bank to save for a gift for her mother, or she puts it in her bank account and earns 5% interest.

Income:
Teacher Knowledge: Employers pay wages and salaries based on the value of employee's skills or services and on how productive the employees are.

Student Language: People earn income by exchanging their physical or mental work for money.

Interest:
Teacher Knowledge: The price paid for the use of borrowed money. A bank is a lender, loaning money to others. It draws funds from people with savings accounts, then pays these people a fee for the use of their savings for loans to others.

Student Language: Interest is a small fee paid to people who save their money or charged to people who borrow money.

Investment:
Teacher Knowledge: The purchase of a financial product or other item of value with an expectation of favorable future benefits. Also, commitment of time and energy, such as investment in a charitable cause.
Student Language: To put money into something of value to make a future profit. Or, to work for a good cause.

Reference: Voluntary national content standards in economics: NCEE.

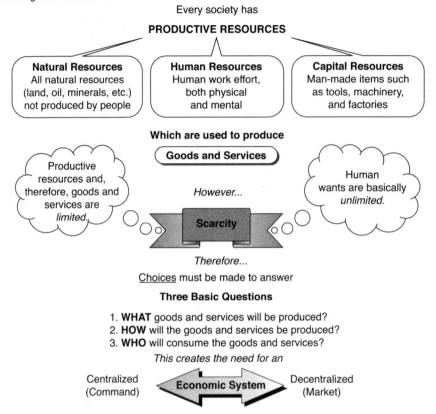

What Economics Is About

Economics is the study of how individuals and societies use their scarce productive resources to obtain goods and services.

Every society has

PRODUCTIVE RESOURCES

Natural Resources
All natural resources
(land, oil, minerals, etc.)
not produced by people

Human Resources
Human work effort,
both physical
and mental

Capital Resources
Man-made items such
as tools, machinery,
and factories

Which are used to produce

Goods and Services

Productive
resources and,
therefore, goods and
services are
limited.

However...

Scarcity

Human
wants are basically
unlimited.

Therefore...

<u>Choices</u> must be made to answer

Three Basic Questions

1. **WHAT** goods and services will be produced?
2. **HOW** will the goods and services be produced?
3. **WHO** will consume the goods and services?

This creates the need for an

Centralized
(Command)

Economic System

Decentralized
(Market)

The Basic Economic Problem: Every society must decide how to make the best use of its limited productive resources. Scarcity, with the resulting need to choose among competing alternatives, is the basic economic problem.

Illustration 8.2 What Economics is About. Redrawn from Day et al. (2006). *The Classroom Mini-Economy.* Courtesy the Indiana Department of Education.

Teaching Resources

Reference Books

Brophy, J., and Alleman, J. (2006). *Children's thinking about cultural universals.* Mahwah, NJ: Erlbaum. This text summarizes findings from interviews with K–3 students regarding their perceptions of cultural universals, or domains of human experience that have existed in all cultures, such things as food, clothing, shelter, family living, and money. This book offers insights into how children really think about fundamental aspects of their daily lives.

Day, H., Dolon, J., Foltz, M., Heyse, K., Marksbary, C., and Sturgeon, M. (2006). *Teaching economics using children's literature.* New York: National Council on Economic Education.

This reference book was written originally by teacher-authors as part of a project directed by the Indiana Department of Education in 1997. It is now available through NCEE from their online store: www.ncee.net. This book contains 24 economics lessons based on children's literature. A glossary of economic ideas, in adult and student language, is included.

Kielburger, M., and Kielburger, C. (2002). *Take action! A guide to active citizenship.* Hoboken, NJ: John Wiley & Sons. This book is a practical guide to real civic action for youth, by youth. The chapters on selecting worthy causes and raising funds are particularly relevant to economic decision-making.

Children's Literature

Bunting, E. (2004). *A day's work.* New York: Clarion Books. Francisco and his grandfather look for work as day laborers. Grandfather doesn't speak English, so Francisco joins him as translator. However, Francisco's desire for work leads to a lie, which causes trouble for his grandfather in the end. This book is suitable for primary children. It introduces ideas of labor, supply, and demand, as well as issues of immigration and work.

Maestro, B. (1993). *The story of money.* New York: Clarion Books. This non-fiction picture book offers a mini-history of money. Barter is shown evolving into trading money for goods and services. Currency's physical development is chronicled, from Sumerian coins to Spanish "pieces of eight." The history includes present-day usage of "cashless money," such as checks. This book is long and detailed and, probably, needs to be read in sections.

Mitchell, M. K. (1993). *Uncle Jed's barbershop.* New York: Simon and Schuster. Written in the first person, Mitchell tells the story of her great uncle Jedediah Johnson, the only Black barber in the county. The impact of segregation on making a living is told through this story. Regardless of racism, Uncle Jed did not give up on his dream of owning his own barbershop.

Smothers, E. (2003). *The hard-times jar.* New York: Frances Foster Books. This picture book is suitable for primary and intermediate students. It introduces the notion of scarcity and saving through the story of a young girl from a migrant family who loves to read and who wants, more than anything, a "store-bought" book. Eventually, she earns the right to a few quarters from her family's "hard-times jar" for doing the "hardest" thing, telling the truth.

Williams, V. (1982). *A chair for my mother.* New York: Greenwillow. A young girl, her mother, and her grandmother save coins in a jar in order to buy a much-needed easy chair after all their belongings are destroyed in a house fire. Suitable for primary learners, this book showcases the returns from long-term saving.

Zimelman, N. (1992). *How the second grade got $8,205.50 to visit the Statue of Liberty.* Morton Grove, IL: Albert Whitman & Co. A second grade sets out to earn money for a class trip. The story is written as a report from the class treasurer of profits and expenses from class jobs. The uproariously funny adventures of the class present budgeting in a humorous but effective way. This book is a must-read prior to a fundraising project.

Internet Sites

National Council for Economic Education (NCEE): www.ncee.net. You can download Voluntary National Content Standards in Economics from this site. Look under "resources" for online lessons, organized by grade level. The online "store" sells a book on creating a classroom mini-economy, a simulation that we draw from here. You can download a sample lesson from the book free of charge.

EconEdLink: www.econedlink.org/lessons/. This site is a wonderful resource for economics lessons. Lessons are aligned with national standards. Our favorite lessons include "A Favorite Pet" and "Toys for Me: A Lesson on Choice."

Financial Fitness for Life: www.fffl.ncee.net/. This program borrows its terminology from physical fitness, calling its lessons "workouts" and encouraging wise money management throughout life. Lessons are categorized according to grade level. For grades 3–5, lessons focus on big ideas for economics, such as earning an income, saving, spending, borrowing, and managing money.

Curricular Programs

Money Savvy Kids: www.msgen.com. This program offers sets of eight lessons for elementary grade levels. Students learn economic ideas and put them to work solving real-world issues. The lessons center on the "Money Savvy Pig," a four-slotted bank that helps children learn to make choices among saving, spending, investing, and donating. This curriculum is not, however, free of charge. Reusable packets of materials must be purchased by schools.

The Classroom Mini-Economy: www.ncee.net. This program was developed by the Indiana Department of Education with the help of teacher-authors. The third edition of this program was supported by NCEE, and it is available through their website. The book provides instructions to create a classroom mini-economy and use it to teach economic ideas. Chapter 3, "How to Start a Mini-Economy", can be downloaded freely from the NCEE website. This chapter outlines five easy steps to initiate a mini-economy in your classroom.

Films

Herschel's World of Economics, created by the Indiana Council for Economic Education, 2007. This DVD contains six ten-minute lessons that teach big economic ideas: goods and services, producers and consumers, productive resources, scarcity, trade and money, and opportunity cost. The lessons are child-friendly and fun, presented through the character of Herschel, a dog puppet who makes everyday decisions based on economics. The DVD is inexpensive, and it can be purchased at www.kidseconposters.com.

TEACH!

Become Informed

Focus In: The Story of Money by Betsy Maestro

Hook: Money, as an idea, can be a great topic to introduce economic notions such as value, cost, purchase, and trade. Ask students: What has value? List the students' ideas. Help students consider which, if any, of these items can be used as money. A prime requirement is that money is scarce, durable, portable, and divisible. As examples, a house may be worth a lot, but it is not easily moved around or traded. Jewelry can be worth a lot, and it is easily carried and traded.

Focus Activity: Write four or five key facts from the story on sentence strips or chart. Before reading, ask students: Do you agree or disagree with these statements? Why?

 Note: This book is long and complicated. We suggest reading it in two sittings. Use the first questions to focus in on pages 1–25; the second to focus in on pages 26–43.

1 Barter is a way to trade without money.
2 Salt is a good form of money.
3 Metal coins are a good form of money.
4 Traders thought that paper was not valuable enough to be a good form of money.

_____

5 The first money made in the United States was the penny.
6 A mint is more than a candy. It is a place to make money.
7 People all over the world now value paper money for itself.
8 Electronic credit cards are like cashless money.

Reading: *The Story of Money* by Betsy Maestro

After Reading: Return to the Focus Activity. Reconsider: Do you still agree or disagree with these statements. Why? Why not?

Teach for Ideas 8.1: What is Money?

Hook: The oldest form of standardized money was most likely the coin. Show students some old and some new coins—fronts and backs. Discuss their shape, form, symbols, date, and probable value. Compare and contrast ancient and modern coins in the illustration below.

Illustration 8.3 Comparison of Coins.

Example #1: Compare two Roman coins and two U.S. coins. Ask:

Who is on one side? Is it a man or a woman? Is the figure posed looking at you or sideways? What numbers, if any, are on the coin? Are there any dates, words, animals, and other items? Why are coins generally small in size? Are the ancient and modern coins pretty much alike or different? How, why, and can you point out details?

Example #2: Compare paper money and promissory notes (IOUs). Ask: Does each form of money have value? Which form is most widely accepted? Why?

Example #3: Credit Card. Ask: Are credit cards money? Why would people like to use credit cards for money?

 Note: Technically, a credit card, though very common nowadays, is NOT money. Why? It is issued by a bank, company, or store, but not by the government, and it is not backed by the government. In addition, when you sign your credit card bill you are taking out a loan from a bank, and you are promising to pay it back, with interest if you are overdue, and with a penalty if you can't pay. So, a credit card is not like cash, which is always legal payment backed by the government, and which has the face value stated on the paper bill.

Create a new example: Hold a contest to create a currency for your classroom. Ask students to design paper currency that can be used later in Store.

Assessment: Ask students to define what money is in their own words.

Teach for Ideas 8.2: What is Scarcity?

Hook: Read *The Hard-Times Jar* by Ethel Smothers. Ask students: What was scarce in Emma's family? What did it mean when Emma's mother said there would be "no extras"? How did Emma's family deal with scarcity? Make a three-way chart comparing scarcity, rarity, and plenty, and point out the differences. Next, compare and contrast examples of *scarcity* and *plenty* from *The Hard-Times Jar*. Ask youth to draw posters illustrating their comparisons.

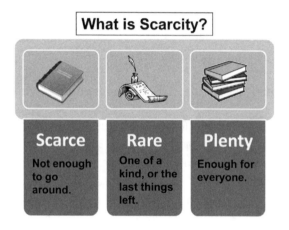

What is Scarcity?		
Scarce	**Rare**	**Plenty**
Not enough to go around.	One of a kind, or the last things left.	Enough for everyone.

Illustration 8.4 What is Scarcity?

Scarcity is . . .

Scarcity	Plenty
• No-extras • Not enough money for all the things the family needs • Using home-made things instead of store-bought things because they cost less	• Having extras • Enough money to buy the things the family needs and buy books for Emma • Buying things you at the store, even if they cost more

Illustration 8.5 The Hard-Times Jar.

Study Example #1: Watch the program *Scarcity* from the video, *Herschel's World of Economics*. In the program, Herschel, a dog puppet, uses a special recipe to make dog biscuits. His friends like them so much, there is not enough to go around. As Herschel decides what to do, ideas of scarcity and choice are illustrated.

Study Example #2: Present real-life examples of scarcity that children encounter every day. Here is one example: your family is going on a trip. There is scarce or limited space in the car. Ask students to decide between taking one thing and another. If they take the picnic basket, for example, they will have lunch, but if they take their basketball, they will have something with which to play. There is not room for both. Explain that scarcity means life is about "This OR That", not "This AND That." Every person, child or adult, rich or poor, has to deal with scarcity because no one can have everything he or she wants.

Create a new example: Ask students to describe an example of something that is in limited supply or scarce in their own lives.

Assessment: Ask students to describe what scarcity is in their own words.

 It's your turn! Practice Teaching for Ideas! Develop activities to teach about opportunity cost. Here are some ideas to get started. Remind students that every person has to make choices because of scarcity. Utilize *Herschel's World of Economics* as a teaching resource. In the DVD, Herschel, a dog puppet, wants two candy bars, but he only has enough money for one. Help Herschel make his decision using the Decision Tree below. Then, tackle other everyday decisions that involve opportunity cost.

What we will get . . .   What we will give up . . .

Economic Problem:
What choice should we make?

Illustration 8.6 Opportunity Cost: Decision Tree.

Teach for Inquiry: What Should I Do with My Money?

Hook: Ask students what they think is happening in this classic Norman Rockwell painting. Ask them for ideas about what they would do with the money earned from selling lemonade.

Illustration 8.7 Lemonade Stand: Norman Rockwell. Norman Rockwell Gallery Collection. Courtesy the Norman Rockwell Family Agency.

Ask an Essential Question (EQ): What am I going to do with my money?

Elicit hypotheses: Ask students to fill out the following survey. Discuss their responses.

What am I going to do with my money? Viewpoints

How to earn money: jobs, allowances, errands, sales, trading.
- Allowances
- Odd jobs/work
- Street sales: the Lemonade Stand

If you had $20 to keep, would you:

Strongly agree (SA); agree (A); can't decide (CD); disagree (D); or strongly disagree (SD)

Save most of it?	SA	A	CD	D	SD
Spend most of it?	SA	A	CD	D	SD
Save a little of it?	SA	A	CD	D	SD
Spend a little of it?	SA	A	CD	D	SD
Save all of it?	SA	A	CD	D	SD
Spend all of it?	SA	A	CD	D	SD

Give students evidence, one bit of data at a time. Ask them to consider each clue, then to revise their responses to the EQ.

Clue #1: *Spending.* Create an economic problem. Tell students winter is coming. What, if anything, will they purchase? Why? Show an illustration of a basic item, such as clothing, and a luxury item, such as a popular toy. Tell students they have only $60.00 to spend.

Transformer Movie Helmet: $30.   Leapster Learning System: $60.   Winter Coat: $60.

Illustration 8.8 Spending Options.

Clue #2: *Saving.* Read *A Chair for My Mother* by Vera Williams. Before reading, ask students what they would do to get a special chair for their mother: buy one, save for one, or find one that someone wants to give away? Invite students to explain their reasoning. After reading: Consider the decision to save for a chair. What were the good points and bad points of that decision?

Clue #3: *Giving.* Describe the mission of the American Humane Society. Focus on pet adoption. Illustrate levels of donation: $10, $25, and $50. Suggest giving of time as well. See this organization's website at www.americanhumane.org. Create an economic problem: You earn $2.00 a week in allowance. You can earn $2.00 a week for watering your neighbor's plants while she is gone. What level of money will you donate? How long will it take you to save it?

 It's your turn! Review the clues we provide. Now, write Clue #4 on your own.

Clue #4: Introduce a mixed approach to the utilization of money: *some spending, some saving, some giving.* **Write your own example!**

Conclusions: *Revise hypotheses.* Answer the EQ: What am I going to do with my money?

Think It Through

Teach through Drama 8.1: Store

Store is a role play involving the setting of value or price in order to sell goods or services. Store provides opportunities to discuss price and determine value. Students can consider "why" an item is priced high or low: is it popular or disfavored, valued or unappreciated, available or scarce? Concepts of value, supply, demand, production, and profit can be taught through this exercise.

Hook: Display the following items: a sack of apples, a new toy, and a popular but broken toy. Ask students to determine what should cost more and to explain why. Invite them to play Store, buying and selling products. Give each student a "secret" product wrapped in an opaque paper bag. Tell them to peek inside and, then, decide if they can charge a lot, some, or a little for their item. Distribute play money to students so they can make bids on products. (You can also print out cards for services, like "doing your homework for you for a week," and place them in bags.)

Roles: Not everyone gets to sell the same things or even the same type of things. To make this work really well, you, the teacher, have to collect a range of products for students to sell. This range should include produce (unprocessed foods, e.g., broccoli, apples, tomatoes), processed or restaurant foods (e.g., pizza, bag of potato chips, jar of apple sauce), and finished products, such as toys and games (e.g., a board game, an art set, a robot, or a jump rope). It is important to include a desirable but broken item. Assign students to buying/selling groups.

Role Play: Instruct students to look in their bags without letting other groups see what's inside. Within the group, discuss the value of the good or service and set a price for it. Students will conduct their own sales. Give them a minute or two, in which they set a price (a lot, some, or a little) and offer their product for sale. Students should offer a reason for others to purchase their item, but not show what's in the bag. The other kids in the class use their play money to make bids and try to obtain what's inside. Once a group accepts a price, another group can "buy" it. The second group looks inside the bag and then tries to resell the good or service, raising or lowering the price in the bargain. You will see students develop a sense of value and set a price, based (whether they can articulate it or not) on their sense of cost, supply, and demand factors.

We have done this a number of times with classes as young as first grade and almost never have students been found to ask for a lot for, say, a head of broccoli. They clearly think they can only ask for a little or they won't be able to sell it. On the other hand, few ever ask a little for something like an art kit, or a favorite toy, because they sense they can charge a considerable amount and their audience will pay. Also, students rarely think they can charge a lot for a broken toy, unless it can be easily mended, or works reasonably well, though broken.

After everyone has sold their product and bought another's (once or twice), debrief the activity. Ask students who they think made the best buying and selling decisions and why they think so. Go around the room and see who has the most money left—the kids who bought basic products or those who wanted the finished and more costly items.

As your students reveal their economic reasoning, point out the market ideas embedded in their examples, such as price, costs, supply, and demand. In this way, you can introduce key economic ideas to the youngest children, and reinforce their sense of market forces, in which they are daily participants.

Conclusions: Raise questions about the bidding process: Which items do you think are worth more or less? What would you do if your parent says, "Sorry, it costs too much," or "it isn't worth it"? When are our decisions personal? When are our decisions social, affecting many others?

Assessment: Ask students to describe in their own words *value, price, supply* and *demand*.

Teach through Drama 8.2: Classroom Mini-economy

The classroom mini-economy has been around for some time, and is well known as an effective way to teach economic ideas and practice economic decision-making (Day et al. 2006). For this activity, students earn money through work in class jobs, redeeming their earnings for goods or privileges in a classroom "store." In the process, they put all sorts of ideas related to employment to work. For younger students, the mini-economy can be quite simple, focusing on classroom jobs. For older students, the economy can be more complicated, including things such as the purchase of insurance for unforeseen school problems, or the payment of taxes for the use of classroom space.

 Note: A *token economy* is earning money primarily for the purpose of classroom management. In this case, you reward students for good conduct, or quality school work. Although students can earn extra money in this way, economic education, not classroom management, should be the central aim of this experience.

Hook: Read aloud: *How the Second Grade Got $8,205.50 to Visit the Statue of Liberty* by Nathan Zimelman. Ask students: Have you ever earned money? What did you do? How much did you earn? Invite students to earn money in their classroom, by doing classroom jobs and by exhibiting desired classroom behavior. Explain that students will be able to spend their money in the classroom store for tangible items and class privileges.

Roles: Every student should have a job, though some might want to hold more than one! Post job descriptions, listing the necessary qualifications. Create a job application and encourage students to apply for jobs. Conduct a job interview, if you like. You can pay the same amount for all jobs, or differentiate the pay, depending on the effort and skill required. Wages are a reflection of a person's training and productivity, so you can offer training for better-paying jobs.

Types of classroom jobs:

- Accountant: Keeps class monies straight. Needs math ability. Requires a lot of training.
- Class Messenger: Takes messages to other rooms. Needs to be responsible and quick, but requires little training.
- Attendance Officer: Takes daily attendance. Needs regular school attendance, but requires little training.
- Playground Equipment Supervisor: Keeps track of playground equipment. Needs to be well organized. Requires some training.
- Pet Caretaker: Takes care of class pets. Needs to like animals. Requires some training.
- Librarian: Keeps books shelved correctly. Needs to alphabetize. Requires a lot of training.
- Homework Monitor: Keeps track of assignments for absent students. Needs to be organized. Requires some training.
- Courtesy Director: Greets visitors. Needs to be friendly. Requires little training.

Jobs that relate directly to Store:

- Payroll Clerk: Helps distribute pay. Needs to be organized. Requires some training.
- Store Keeper: Runs class store. Needs to be organized. Requires a lot of training.

 It's your turn! For a class of 20 students, you need ten more jobs. Make a list of possibilities.

Types of desired behaviors:

- Clean desk or cubby
- All work done on time
- Studying quietly
- Helping a classmate with a task
- Serving as a leader for projects

Determine what money each job or behavior will earn. Then, decide what items and privileges earnings will buy. Set up a store that is open a regular time (or times) each week.

Try to get saleable items donated, of course! Or, operate a "Swap Shop:" trade one item for two items children bring from home. You will take in more items than you give out.

Items:

- Pencils, pens, and erasers
- Free books from book clubs
- Used CDs
- Used clothing or athletic equipment
- Used books or games

Privileges:

- Lunch at a restaurant with the teacher (Expensive!!)
- Lunch at school with the teacher (Less expensive!)
- Time on the computer
- Buying back a "no name" paper
- Buying an option to skip a quiz

Role Play: This role play takes some time. Classroom mini-economy can operate for weeks or months. You will need to manage the following processes: job postings, job interviews, job assignments, supervision of employment, payment for work and behavior, and operation of the store. If the role play is ongoing, you will need to provide some mechanism for changing jobs. Kinds of purchases might grow "old" as well; items and privileges must remain something students truly value. Additionally, it will be necessary to set prices for store items. You can involve students in setting prices; as you can see in the photograph below, pre-service teachers in a second grade classroom had to put privileges "on sale" when students thought they cost too much!

Illustration 8.9 Store: Second Grade.

Conclusions: Hold a class discussion of the economic ideas and practices involved in this scenario. Consider notions such as labor, productivity, value, income, and consumption.

Assessment: Ask students to define basic economic ideas, such as employment, productivity, job training, income, and spending.

 It's your turn! Modify this engagement. Add other ways to earn money, such as the operation of classroom businesses, as means to spend, save, or invest money. Include businesses that provide goods and services. Imagine what a rental or insurance company might do. Use your imagination! Next, consider ways to use children's literature as a hook to motivate interest in your classroom mini-economy. Read and envision uses for several of the books listed in Teaching Resources, e.g., *A Day's Work* and *Uncle Jed's Barbershop*.

Take Action

Teach for Deliberation: Saving or Spending?

Thus far, our activities have focused on teaching BIG ideas and on making choices—fundamentals of economics. However, we do kids a disservice if we do not also help them consider the larger, consumer-oriented culture of which they are a part. We offer the following data to provoke your thoughts about teaching children to spend and save wisely.[1]

- The typical first grader already has an unprecedented number of possessions, with an average of 70 toys per year.
- Children are becoming shoppers at an earlier age. Six- to twelve-year-olds are estimated to visit stores two times a week, putting six items into the shopping cart each time they go.
- One in four kids make trips to stores alone before they enter elementary school, often buying for family needs, particularly in single-parent households.
- Children aged four to twelve directly influenced over $300 billion in adult purchasing in 2004. Spending by children this age exceeded $40 billion in 2004.

Hook: Show students the *Money Savvy Pig* (mascot of the Money Savvy Kids curriculum). Ask them for examples of things they can do with their money: save, spend, donate, or invest. Tell them they are going to consider what's best to do with the money they earn.

---

1 Sources: Juliet Schor's book *Born to Buy* (2004), James McNeal's *The Kids Market* (1999), and the 2005 report of the Consumers Union, *Captive Kids* (2005).

Illustration 8.10 Money Savvy Pig. Money Savvy Kids: www.msgen.com.

Raise an essential question (EQ): Should we save or spend the money we earn?

Discussion Web: Write the EQ on the board. On either side write *Yes* or *No*. Write *Reasons* above the question. Write *Conclusions* below the question (see Illustration 2.1 on p.26). Ask students to silently answer the question and to think of a reason for their answer. Ask students to share their thinking. Write students' names and reasons under the appropriate *Yes* or *No* columns.

Readings/Discussions: Ask students to read *Save* or *Spend* readings (see Table 8.1) in small groups, according to their own initial responses.

TABLE 8.1 Spend or Save?

Spend	Save
▪ We earned our allowance for doing chores. We should be able to spend it as we like. ▪ There are a lot of things I want. I can use my allowance to buy them. ▪ My parent(s) will not let me buy candy unless I use my own money. ▪ I want to have the kind of things my friends have. ▪ It's really fun to go shopping! ▪ I go shopping with my mom a lot and I see things I want in the store.	▪ Some things cost a lot so I have to save until I get enough. ▪ It's not good to spend everything because you have nothing left for an emergency. ▪ Saving teaches us to wait patiently. We don't get everything we want immediately. ▪ Saving is good citizenship because then we have money to do good things, like go on a field trip, or help a worthy cause. ▪ Saving helps us learn to manage our money so we don't have to borrow from others.

Switch readings, so that all students read both sides. Mix student groups, including *Save* and *Spend* views in the same group. Ask students to share their views and reasons for holding them.

Add a new reading for the mixed group to consider the story of *the Ant and the Grasshopper*. Ask students to try to find a mutually agreeable solution to the problem.

Share as a class.

Conclusions: Ask students if anyone changed his/her mind, and, if so, why? If not, why not?

The Ant and the Grasshopper*

In a field one summer's day a Grasshopper was hopping about, chirping and singing to its heart's content. An Ant walked by, grunting as he carried a plump kernel of corn. "Where are you off to with that heavy thing?" asked the Grasshopper. Without stopping, the Ant replied, "To our ant hill. This is the third kernel I've delivered today." "Why not come and sing with me," said the Grasshopper, "instead of working so hard?" "I am helping to store food for the winter," said the Ant, "and think you should do the same." "Why bother about winter?" said the Grasshopper; "we have plenty of food right now." But the Ant went on its way and continued its work. The weather soon turned cold. All the food lying in the field was covered with a thick white blanket of snow that even the grasshopper could not dig through. Soon the Grasshopper found itself dying of hunger. He staggered to the ants' hill and saw them handing out corn from the stores they had collected in the summer. Then the Grasshopper knew:

It is best to prepare for the days of necessity.

*This story was originally part of Aesop's Fables.

 It's your turn! Create your own Discussion Web. Here are some ideas to help you get started. EQ: Should the school be an ad-free zone? Invite students to be "Advertising Detectives." Locate and display examples of the advertisements that surround students in their school day. Examine two common incentive programs, "Book It", sponsored by Pizza Hut, and McDonald's "McTeacher's Night." Consider: What is sold to kids as they read or support their schools?

Take Action

Civic Action: Organize a "Buy Nothing Day"

Hook: Introduce *Take Action! A Guide to Active Citizenship* by Marc and Craig Kielburger. Explain that it is a guide for active citizenship written by students for students. Post the Seven Steps for Social Involvement. Briefly explain each. Invite students to take action based on their new economic knowledge. They can remind their friends that happiness is not defined by how many material things one has. Organize a "Buy Nothing Day"![2]

2 The idea for a "Buy Nothing Day" is borrowed from Kielburger & Kielburger (2002).

Seven Steps to Citizen Action

- Step 1: Choose an issue.
- Step 2: Do your research.
- Step 3: Build a team.
- Step 4: Call a meeting.
- Step 5: Make a plan of action.
- Step 6: Take action and then review.
- Step 7: Have fun!

Illustration 8.11 Seven Steps to Citizen Action.

STEP 1: CHOOSE AN ISSUE: CONSUMERISM, OR ADULTS AND KIDS BUY TOO MUCH

STEP 2: DO YOUR RESEARCH

Inquiries for teachers: There are quite a few websites that provide information on mass marketing to kids. These sites primarily serve an adult audience, so you, as teacher, will need to scan them for pertinent information, then rewrite it for kids to read. Be aware: these websites promote a particular perspective—that there is too much marketing of products to youth, encouraging spending over saving. Check out these websites.

Campaign for Commercial Free Childhood: www.commercialexploitation.com
Citizens' Campaign for Commercial Free Schools: www.scn.org/ccsc/resource.html
Consumers Union: www.consumersunion.org

Inquiries for kids: Students can talk to experts, the school principal, a marketing strategist, a community leader, and/or a concerned parent about marketing to kids. They can do research on themselves, taking a survey of their buying habits, recent purchases, and number of toys. Although this inquiry can seem oh-so-middle-class, even children from economically stressed homes can desire expensive, name-brand articles. Additionally, students can examine the advertising they see around them in schools, looking for ads in news magazines, on book covers, on posters, and on prizes they earn for academic achievement.

STEP 3: BUILD A TEAM

Your classroom is a built-in team. However, citizen action is a voluntary thing, a personal motivation to change something for the better. You might decide to encourage only those students who are stirred by the issue to participate in the project. They can involve the entire class in the actual event, and they can learn from their peers' review of it.

Be sure to elicit assistance from the principal. He or she, too, might struggle with conundrums related to the commercialization of schools. Or, the principal might be a parent, grappling with materialism at home. At the very least, the principal can share resources and provide counsel on the action effort itself.

Family and friends always are important. Enlist parents' help with the home-survey of buying and spending.

STEP 4: CALL A MEETING

Help students determine a place and make a plan for a get-organized meeting. Assist their completion of the following tasks:

- Define the goal: Organize a "Buy Nothing Day."
- List people who will help: Teacher, parents, principal, and/or classmates.
- Develop a strategy: What will you do? What role will each person have?
- Map out actions on a calendar: What will you do and when will you do it?
- Plan media coverage or education: How will you get the word out about the effort?
- Create a budget: What supplies, transportation, or money will you need?

STEP 5: MAKE A PLAN OF ACTION

STEP 6: TAKE ACTION AND THEN REVIEW

- Turn your ideas into reality.
- Work as a team!
- Take responsibility!
- Look back: How did we do? What could we improve upon next time?

STEP 7: HAVE FUN!

- As teammates, inspire and encourage one another.
- Be positive about your work for change.

Service Learning: Raise Funds for a Good Cause

In Chapter 10, "Engage," we consider service learning at length. Here, our emphasis is on fundraising and budgeting, rather than on the cause itself. Any cause that is of value to your students and their community will do. Service to the cause matters too; donation is just one possibility, as we take up later. For now, we spotlight the task of raising money for worthy work.

STEP 1: CHOOSE AN ISSUE

Select a worthy program or agency for a donation, in effect, giving to a charity: "Save the Whales", or "Save the Children," or one popular with your neighborhood, community, or class.

Illustration 8.12 Fundraising for a Cause.

Review the notion of investing in a good cause: it is giving of time, money, and/or energy for efforts that will benefit others. Consider the benefits of giving (for others and for yourself) to a good cause, like your local Humane Society (as did some of our prospective teachers above).

STEP 2: DO YOUR RESEARCH

Inquiries for teachers: Learn more about the issue the students choose. Carefully examine the organization with which they will work. Seek out its perspectives and positions. Make sure the organization is genuine; in the case of animal welfare, for example, some groups that support radical animal control measures masquerade as humane societies. Identify leaders of the organization who are willing to work with students.

Inquiries for students: Learn more about the issue of your choice. Visit the library, search the internet, watch appropriate videos, and talk to people who know a lot about your concern. Get in touch with the organization you will serve and determine what resources or assistance people really want or need.

STEP 3: BUILD A TEAM

Find others who share your concern. Get them involved! Make sure to include leaders from the organization of your choice. They should participate "from the ground floor up" in planning.

STEP 4: CALL A MEETING

As noted above, teachers should provide direct assistance in planning for and conducting the meeting.

This is a fundraising effort, so focus on ways to raise money. Explain to students that money can be raised to pay for their operating expenses, as well as to fund the projects they champion. There are many ways to raise money, but, in our opinion, selling items is overused and problematic. This strategy often places students in uncomfortable (and potentially dangerous) situations, at the doors of strangers, and encourages them to market items, such as candy, of questionable worth. Instead, encourage students to raise money through odd jobs or fundraising events.

Take Action! A Guide to Active Citizenship by Marc and Craig Kielburger offer a list of *Top Ten Crazy Fundraisers*, as well as *101 Fundraisers*. As educators, we like the following school events that involve teachers making a little fun of themselves for money.

1   For $1, students can throw a pie or water balloon at a willing teacher during lunch hour.
2   Weigh a willing teacher on a scale. Collect his/her weight in dimes, nickels, and quarters. If your teacher weighs 150 pounds, collect 150 pounds of coins.
3   Organize a car wash in which teachers agree to participate in a water fight.
4   Hold a contest in which participants pay a fee to match baby pictures with current photos of your teachers. The winner gets a prize (try to get the prize donated).
5   Hold a contest in which the lucky winner receives one day free from homework.

Here are a few more of our favorites that practice good citizenship and build school spirit, while raising money for a worthy cause.

1   *Concert.* Ask your school band or choir to donate their time by performing a benefit concert for your cause.
2   *Spelling bee.* Organize a spelling bee. Have participants and spectators pay fees to join in.
3   *Puppet show.* Make puppets. Write a story. Set a time and place for the show. Sell tickets.
4   *Plant a tree.* Then, get people to sponsor the tree (with appropriate recognition) for a fee.
5   *Hug-a-gram.* Sell a hug for a fee. Children can buy a hug for a friend. After a member of your group delivers the hug, give the person a card with a message from his/her friend.

Help students develop a simple budget for their fundraising efforts. Ask them to think about the activities they will do, the income they will earn, the expenses they will incur, and the profit that will remain. Will they earn enough to make their efforts worthwhile? What level of donation are they likely to make? Here is a sample budget for your teaching.

TABLE 8.2 Sample Budget

Item	Income (how much you will make)	Expenses (how much you will spend)	Profit (income less expenses)
Band concert: $1.00 per person	$50.00		
Posters to advertise for concert	donated		
Spelling bee: $1.00 per participant or spectator	$50.00		
Set up/Clean up of library for spelling bee		$15.00/hour for custodian. 2 hours of work for $30.00 total	
TOTALS	$100 income	$30 expenses	$70 profit

Teacher Review

Let's ascertain what you learned from this engagement. When teachers are uninformed about or uncomfortable with economic ideas and decisions, they tend to disregard them. Did this chapter raise your comfort level? Can you see that economics is about learning big ideas and solving real-world problems?

Economics is, arguably, at the heart of social understanding. Do you agree with this claim? Why or why not? To what extent can economic instruction help youth understand today's society? Is raising the consciousness of kids about marketing tactics part of your responsibility?

Store, by its nature, focuses on ideas and practices of buying and selling, earning and spending. A real-world simulation of Store can teach a host of big economic ideas. Is this emphasis sufficient? Where does instruction in saving, investing, and giving fit into the picture?

Economic issues and problems are encountered by all of us each day of our lives. As a budding social studies teacher, how will you prepare young citizens of the world for the economic dilemmas and pressures that they will face?

Making Connections

In developing activities for Store, we focused on the provision of tools for economics-related decision-making. Understanding the everyday impact of economic realities is very much part of doing citizenship as a verb. Students need to learn about, deliberate, and act upon issues in our consumer culture, including our targeting of them as a potential market. One of the ten themes of the standards for the National Council for the Social Studies (NCSS) is Production, Distribution, and Consumption, and you will find attention to economics in many state academic standards as well. However, in our view, more than economic "literacy," or basic knowledge, is at stake. The application and analysis of economic ideas and issues also matter. Store highlights the economic nature of decisions we make as citizens, including our decisions to save, spend, donate, or invest, and possibly to support social causes that we, and our students, hold dear.

nine
Explore
Investigating Place and Space

Where is something? Why is it there? How did it get there? How does it interact with other things? These questions are asked by geographers as they explore our place and space on Earth (Bednarz et al., 1994). Children are natural geographers; they are curious about their world. They want to understand where they are, learn about fascinating people, and figure out why places grow, change or decline. Even the youngest children have a concept of the world drawn from stories, travel, news, and other sources, often surprisingly accurate, and sometimes oddly distorted. Our aim, in this chapter, is to help you tap into children's inherent inquisitiveness, spurring their sense of exploration about their world.

Geography is about natural features, such as mountains, plains, islands, and oceans, and physical systems, such as climate, weather, and water flow; but it is also about much more. Geography is about people, especially our perceptions and actions, actions that can transform the earth and sky above us. It is about how we view the world and our place in it, and about what choices we make regarding the use, adaptation, abuse, or preservation of the Earth we all inhabit. As noted in the National Geography Standards, "geography is not a collection of arcane information. Rather, it is the study of spatial aspects of human existence" (Bednarz et al., 1994, p. 18). Geography is more than filling in a map or naming states, countries, and capitals. According, again, to the Standards, it "has much more to do with asking questions and solving problems that it does with rote memorization of isolated facts" (1994, p. 18).

As a school subject, geography has morphed over time. In the early 1900s, it was perceived as the "mother of all sciences" (Schulten, 2001, p. 92), embracing all sorts of physical sciences, such as botany, geology, and meteorology, in studies of the Earth. In 1918, aims for education turned toward practical ends, partly as a result of the *Report of the Commission on the Reorganization of Secondary Education*, which included the famous *1916 Report* (see Chapter 1). Educators aimed to prepare youth not as scholars but as hard workers, responsible citizens, and worthy home members. Geography became a social science, rather than a hard science, helping youth grasp their world and their place in it.

Today, geography is perceived as a broad subject. It incorporates political, cultural, and historical components—all necessary to understanding space, place, and people's impact upon them. It crosses easily into hard sciences, such as botany, geology, and meteorology to explore biome zones, landform shifts, or climatic patterns. Additionally, environmental or ecological studies are often included in geography as bases for grasping and responding to issues that face our planet.

In the National Geography Standards (Bednarz et al., 1994), the following six broad elements have been defined as the essence of geographic education:

1 The World in Spatial Terms
2 Places and Regions
3 Physical Systems
4 Human Systems
5 Environment and Society
6 The Uses of Geography

Geographic education should teach students to see the world in spatial terms, looking at Earth in terms of its dimensions, directions, locations, and boundaries. It should acquaint students with places and regions, both as physical settings and as human creations. It should help students understand human systems of population, settlement, cooperation, and conflict. It should alert students to human interaction with Earth, such as our use of natural resources or our pollution of the environment. Last, but certainly not least, it should help students get from place to place, understand why people act as they do, and make decisions about the place we call home (Shearer, 2007).

Geography includes not only subject matter, but skills and perspectives as well. Its special skills include asking (and answering) geographic questions, and finding, organizing, and analyzing geographic information. Its two main perspectives are spatial and environmental. Students can look at a place in terms of "whereness," or its location, or "connectedness," or its living and non-living components. Notably, memorization of place names or features is NOT highlighted as a geographic aim, skill, or result. Instead, as in History Mystery, a *sense of discovery* about Earth as a physical space and human place is emphasized.

Geography, then, is the study of Earth, as physical ecosystems, human environments, and the interactions between them. It is a broad, complicated, integrated subject that draws from hard and social sciences. Most of all, it is a study that should not be ignored because it is the *exploration* of the place we, humans, call home.

Geographic Literacy

The National Assessment for Educational Progress, which is the basis for the "Nation's Report Card," reports geography scores, for grades 4, 8, and 12, at three levels: Basic, Proficient, and Advanced. According to the latest (2001) figures for this measure, fourth and eighth graders showed improvement from an earlier assessment (1994); still, only 21% of fourth graders scored at or above Proficient level, indicating geographic literacy is far too low (NAEP, 2001). Interestingly, teacher preparation mattered. In 2001, more teachers reported that they felt prepared to teach geography than in 1994.

A recent, national survey of geographic literacy also showed cause for concern (*National Geographic*–Roper Public Affairs, 2006). In regard to world affairs, six in ten young Americans, ages 18–24, could not find Iraq on a map of the Middle East, despite intense news coverage since the Iraq War began in 2003. Three quarters could not find Indonesia, even after televised images of the Tsunami. A majority believed that English is the most commonly spoken language in the world (it is Mandarin Chinese). In regard to national geography, one third could not find Louisiana on a map, even after Hurricane Katrina. Fewer than half could identify the state of New York, even though it is the third most populous state in the union.

Concern with geographic illiteracy is nothing new. Its continuity, perhaps, is most alarming. After World War I, criticism of Americans' lack of knowledge of international politics, nation creation, and trade issues was commonplace (Schulten, 2001). There was a sense that Americans were not ready to serve as leaders for a new globally interdependent world. Then, as now, talk turned to the development of "world citizenship" and schools' role in it. Today, there are new worries that geography is being "left behind"—identified as a core academic subject within NCLB, but not tested or federally funded (Daly, 2003). It is likely that many students are not getting the geographic education they need.

Ways of Knowing

We see geography as contributing at least three vitally important moorings for young people growing up in our increasingly smaller world. These anchoring points follow our citizenship model of becoming informed, thinking it through, and taking action. The engagements in this chapter exemplify these ways of knowing.

1 Knowing Earth as a natural, physical, and territorial space, settings, situations, locales, and regions—locally, nationally, and globally.
2 Knowing Earth as a human place, as a creation of environments in which to live, work, interact, and enjoy life. Knowing Earth as a human place means grasping

cultural diversity, especially the development of accurate understandings of other people and places, rather than stereotypic images of what is found there.

3   Viewing Earth as a series of local and global interconnections between and among humans, animals, technology, natural resources, and ecological systems, as something alive, dynamic, and purposeful, as something of which we are all a part and can impact for good or ill.

Explore: What and Why?

In this chapter, we outline three civic engagements: *World Address*, *Newlandia*, and *Focus*. Yes, it is a lot for one chapter! Our aim is to provide three options for teaching place and space. *World Address* focuses on geo-spatial thinking, and *Newlandia* puts that thinking to work in a settlement simulation. *Focus* centers students' attention on intriguing people and places. All three engagements are intended to kindle children's curiosity and stimulate their exploration of the world.

 Note: All three projects enact our curriculum framework (i.e., Becoming Informed, Thinking it Through, and Taking Action), but the emphasis differs across them. *World Address* exemplifies "becoming informed" and "thinking it through" and utilizes most of the outstanding teaching strategies, including the making of a folk-art map. *Newlandia,* alternatively, mainly illustrates "thinking it through" with dramatization and negotiation. *Focus* highlights "becoming informed" as students work independently at a learning center. All three engagements can motivate civic action or service learning related to people, places, and issues worldwide.

World Address

Throughout this text, we suggest ways to foster world-mindedness, or a feeling of connectedness to Earth and her peoples, near and far. *World Address* promotes world-mindedness by having students make a graphic depiction of their planetary address as: home, neighborhood, town/city/borough, state, nation, continent, and world. World Address can be a single activity, using a children's book, such as *Me on the Map* (see Teaching Resources), to identify one's planetary address, or it can involve a series of engagements with geo-spatial location. We take this latter course, providing a set of correlated activities to help students investigate and illustrate their world.

Newlandia[1]

The aim of *Newlandia* is to develop student's geographic thinking by engaging them in a simulation of human/environmental planning. *Newlandia* is an imaginary place

---

1   Newlandia was created by Jack Zevin in 1989 as Transforma, a middle/high school-level simulation. Zevin revised and adapted it many times. The role play presented here was adapted from his fall 2005 version and rewritten for the elementary level.

containing many biospheres—landforms, resources, climate conditions, and habitats—that can sustain human activities of different sorts. Students' task is to settle and resettle *Newlandia* in role groups, such as hunters, farmers, herders, factory owners, and super-technology users. First, students decide upon the best place for settlement, for their role group alone. Second, they consider the needs and demands of other groups, possibly changing their settlement plans in the process. Choices for settling and developing *Newlandia* are based on what students think is best for their group. The fun is in deciding how to resolve multiple claims on the same space; compromise, migration, trade, and warfare are all human possibilities!

Newlandia is meant to be interactive, active, and artistic, giving student groups the opportunity to study and draw maps while deciding where they will hunt, settle, build factories, construct cities, erect airports (if they wish), and, above all, deal with other human beings who have lesser or greater skills than themselves. *Newlandia* is designed for upper elementary students, but it can be simplified to foster geo-spatial thinking among younger students as well.

Focus

This project involves the creation of a learning center focused on a space and place. In the center, students learn all about a special place, its location, natural features, physical systems, and remarkable attributes, by completing activities, such as reading, writing, drawing, and sculpting. *Focus* can be a "standing" center: one that remains all year, changing only in its point of emphasis.

Why a learning center? A learning center allows you to "teach smart." This phrase is one we hear often in elementary schools today; it means teaching more efficiently, or getting more done in less time: literally, doing two or three things at once! The integration of subjects, so that one enhances the other, is one method for teaching smarter. Independent study is another. A learning center is a means for independent study, allowing children to work on their own to learn geography, while you are busy teaching something else.

In our exemplar, we highlight Nigeria, as an important African country with a rich history and a special trade relationship with the U.S. Why Africa? Many students (and adults) in North America know little about Africa; worse yet, we tend to misperceive it as a land of jungles, tribal warriors, and wild animals. Unfortunately, stereotypes and misperceptions of Africa have a long history in the United States, dating back to the late 1800s (Schulten, 2001). We want to disturb this trend by providing accurate, positive examples of African culture and history. Just as easily, we could have focused on Asia or South America—additional places that U.S. citizens tend to find "exotic," or "unknown." Our point is to challenge cultural ethnocentrism and national egotism, attitudes that constrain the development of a worldview, as noted in Chapter 5.

Learning from Research

Most of the research on learning geography centers on learning about maps (Gregg & Leinhardt, 1994). The investigations focus either on developmental capacities or cognitive processes. Developmental studies explore degree of performance on tasks, such as finding an object using a map. Cognitive studies examine mental processes, such as perception, recognition, and memory, needed to read maps. Developmental studies are the most pertinent to teaching and learning geography, and, thus, our focus here.

Piaget's studies are classic developmental inquiries. He investigated how children perceive space, e.g., horizontal and vertical components, of an area they live in (Piaget & Inhelder, 1956). In a famous "sandbox experiment" Piaget and his colleagues asked students to arrange objects in spatial relationships to each other, calling upon them to understand distance and direction in a familiar environment, like the route from home to school. In effect, students were creating a sandbox map, using objects to indicate aspects of places they knew.

Piaget and his colleagues found that younger children could not coordinate landmarks or provide reasons for their distribution of objects on a map, whereas somewhat older children could group and coordinate objects around a street or center. Those a bit more advanced in age could coordinate their objects to mimic the actual environment, and they understood the concept of centrality and organization, although not always in accurate proportions to each other (Piaget, Inhelder, & Szemiska, 1960). Hart refined Piaget's study, setting up three categories, or stages, of understanding: egocentric (roughly ages 2–7), fixed (roughly ages 7–8), and abstract (ages 8–12) (Hart, 1981). In the egocentric phase, space revolves around the child, whereas in the fixed phase, objects and places correspond to what is actually there. In the abstract phase, children have a more comprehensive grasp of directions, territory, and symbols.

In another classic developmental study, Bluestein and Acredolo (1979) found that children as young as three could read a map, with their performance level increasing dramatically by age five. In this study, researchers asked youngsters to find a stuffed elephant through its position on the map. More than half of the three-year-olds could find the elephant when the map was inside and horizontally aligned with the room, and all of the five-year-olds could do so. When researchers moved the map outside the room, similar developmental progress occurred. It was more difficult for children to read the map when it was rotated, but still almost all could do this task by age five.

Though age definitely makes a difference, some researchers have challenged stage-based progressions as simplistic, artificial, or narrow. Even Hart, described above, noted wide variations in his three categories, with some students demonstrating abstract thinking much earlier than others, and with great unevenness in performance, particularly at the middle stage. As another example, Stoltman (1976) found wide variation in the students' development of abilities to describe territorial concepts such as city, county, state, nation, and world, even in countries such as Scotland, that have strong programs of geographic education for *all* youth.

More recent studies have focused on students' mental maps and perceptions of space, territory, and distance, and concluded that human beings tend to see places subjectively, as well as objectively (Gould & White, 1986; Schmidt, 2008). Schmidt found that secondary students "read" a place, like they might read a book. They are attentive to color, decorations, organization, and what people do in a place. Their identities, such as good student or sociable teenager, impact their "reading" of their surroundings, determining whether a place is hospitable or inhospitable for them. Relatedly, Gould and White found that students' worldviews shape their descriptions of their communities, nation, and world, producing judgments of belonging, value, and safety. Students from three different income levels in Los Angeles, for example, drew very different maps of their city, more detailed maps from the upper-income students and less detailed from the lower-income students.

Studies of mental mapping, webbing, and perceptual worldviews have grown out of these earlier studies. Many of these studies have provided interesting suggestions for ways in which teachers can promote a sense of space and place with students through assigning hand-drawn maps, and by calling upon students to develop world maps of places they view as historically or personally important to them (e.g., Tobin, 1990).

Some studies suggest that students lack geographic vocabulary and misunderstand fundamental geographic ideas (e.g., Shin & Henning, 2007; Gregg & Sekeres, 2006). The common practice of looking up words in the dictionary is ineffectual because definitions do not provide enough information for students to grasp concepts with any complexity. Instead, constructive, conceptually based teaching holds promise. According to one report, the use of multiple examples and experiences, such as examining models, studying photographs, and doing experiments, as well as reading and writing about ideas, helped third graders develop extensive sets of meanings for rivers, their parts and processes (Gregg & Sekeres, 2006). This case justifies our claim for the power of teaching big ideas, and supports integrated, interdisciplinary studies.

The Arizona GeoLiteracy Program, a series of 85 K–12 lessons, developed by teachers in partnership with the Arizona Geographic Alliance, is another successful example of an integrated geography/language arts curriculum. In a pre-/post-test study involving over 2,500 third through eighth graders, investigators found that even minimal geography instruction (three to five lessons) boosted reading comprehension, particularly for grades 5 through 8 (Hinde et al., 2007). For all grades, teaching geography did not hurt reading; there were no negative impacts on comprehension scores. There seems to be no reason to cut social studies in order to stress reading, as reading-in-the-content-area enhances both.

A final area of interest is the utilization of Geographic Information Systems (GIS), computerized layers of spatial information, in geography education. In a number of studies, researchers found that elementary and middle school students' attitudes, self-efficacy, motivation, and achievement improved with the addition of GIS technologies to their geography lessons (Baker & White, 2003; Keiper, 1999; Shin, 2007; Wiegand, 2003).

Students tended to find GIS systems "cool," interesting, and fun, though some frustration with the technology was reported. The use of GIS technology tended to shift geography from the memorization of places to the practice of skills and the solving of problems. Although child-friendly GIS technologies are not yet readily available, researchers shared the conclusion that GIS can be an invaluable resource for extending and enriching geographic instruction.

What does this research mean for you, as geography teacher? Geographic understanding appears to have a strong developmental component, which suggests a powerful role for you, as teacher. You can plan experiences of exploration that promote spatial understanding. You can help even the youngest children orient themselves in their worlds, making and decoding mental and physical maps. As in all of your teaching, you should pay attention to students' developmental capacities; however, based on this research, you should expect some variation, even among children of the same age. Interestingly, you can personalize geography, asking students to "read" or describe places and to consider differences and similarities among their descriptions. Since perceptions of places can derive from worldviews, you can help youth distinguish their personal, affective views from real, physical attributes of places near and far (possibly debunking stereotypes in the process). Additionally, you can aid children's grasp of geographic ideas through the provision of multiple examples and experiences. The integration of geography and reading can be fruitful, especially as a planned interface, such as reading a book about an interesting place, rather than a coincidental "add-on," such as pinpointing a place from a story. The use of GIS technology can play into all of these impetuses, helping to develop and utilize a keener sense of place and space.

Teacher's Scholarly Knowledge

Here is a little secret: we, teachers, are part of the problem (as well as part of the solution) in geography education! Traditionally, we have not been well versed in geographic knowledge. You can't teach what you don't know!

In the 1970s and 1980s, several inquiries documented mediocre levels of knowledge among pre-service teachers. In a study of almost 500 pre-service teachers, researchers found multiple weaknesses related to map and globe skills, such as determining whether a map or a globe is the more appropriate teaching tool in certain circumstances, or using a map legend to determine the meaning of symbols, or reasoning with longitude and latitude (Green & Clark, 1983). In several other studies (e.g., Giannangelo & Frazee, 1977; Schneider, 1976), prospective teachers took the same standardized achievement tests as their students—and made similar errors! Teachers found questions relating to latitude, longitude, earthly rotation, and elevation particularly troublesome. In response to such findings, in 1986, the National Geographic Society helped to build the "Geographic Alliance," a state-based, national network of K–12 teachers, college geographers and educators, school administrators, and others, dedicated to improving geography education. Each state alliance offers teacher development workshops, geography conferences, outreach events, and an array of resources, such as lesson plans or consultation. The Geographic Alliance Network has provided training for more than 100,000 teachers, like you.

 Stop for a moment and consider your preparation to teach geography to elementary students. Do you fall in the category of teachers who have shaky knowledge of mapping terminology and skills? Have you traveled widely and gained a cosmopolitan worldview? Do you feel capable of integrating GIS technology into your teaching? If your answer to any of these questions is "no," or "maybe," then reading this chapter and doing these activities is not enough! Begin to think about ways to supplement your geographic knowledge. Look it up: is there an office for the Geographic Alliance in your state?

Big Powerful Ideas

- **Place:** A physical and relative location, but, even more so, a cultural, economic, political creation by people of landscapes, buildings, parks, schools, sites of worship, highways, and homes; things they want, believe in, need, and use.
- **Space:** A natural setting on earth; a locale, region, country, or continent; represented by such things as maps, globes, and photographs; measured by distance, scale, or relief, and identified by coordinates, such as latitude and longitude.
- **Geographic Features:** Landforms, such as mountains, plains, coastal regions, islands, and oceans; as well as specially preserved or protected areas, such as preserves or wetlands; and resources, such as oil, coal, iron, fertile soil, or fresh water.
- **Physical Systems:** Seasons, climate, weather, water systems, as well as phenomena that result from them, such as floods, storms, and drought.
- **Human–Environment Interaction:** The interplay between people, places, and spaces. People use land: farming, developing cities, and constructing highways; they consume water, build dams, disrupt ecosystems, pollute air, replant forests, and landscape homes. In the process, people change their environments, for better or worse, over the short and long term.

Map and Globe Terms

- **Representation:** A likeness or image of something; maps and globes represent the earth. A globe is a small model of the earth. Satellite photographs are not representations, but real depictions of earth.
- **Projection:** The transfer of information from a globe to a flat map is called projection. In thinking about the meaning of map projection it is helpful to imagine a globe with a light source placed at some definite point with respect to it, projecting features onto a surface. No projection is accurate; rather, it is the result of a mathematical formula for the depiction of direction, distance, and area. Projections reflect the

intended use of the map. The Mercator projection, invented by Gerardus Mercator in the sixteenth century, oversized Europe and undersized Africa, but was excellent for navigation by sea, then the order of the day. The Peters projection, published in 1974, was developed to correct the biases of the Mercator map. Developed with the aid of computers, this map accurately portrays size, so Africa appears much larger than on the Mercator map. The Winkel projection currently is preferred by the National Geographic Society. This projection does not eliminate area, direction or distance

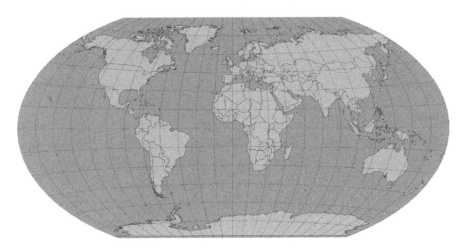

Illustration 9.1 Winkel Projection. Image constructed by: Denis Dean, PhD, Professor and Head, Geospatial Information Sciences Unit, University of Texas at Dallas. Courtesy Dennis J. Dean.

distortions; rather, it tries to minimize the sum of all three. It is a slightly curved view of the world, approximating the globe itself!

- **Latitude and Longitude:** Any location on Earth is described by two numbers—its latitude and its longitude. Latitude lines run horizontally on a map. Each degree of latitude is approximately 69 miles apart; there is variation due to the fact that the earth is slightly egg-shaped. Degrees of latitude are numbered from 0° to 90° north and south. 90° north is the North Pole and 90° south is the South Pole. Three of the most significant imaginary lines running across the surface of the earth are the Equator, the Tropic of Cancer, and the Tropic of Capricorn. The Equator is located at 0° latitude. The Equator is the longest line of latitude on the Earth. The Equator divides the planet into the Northern and Southern Hemispheres.

On the globe, lines of longitude (or meridians) extend from pole to pole, like segments of a peeled orange. They converge at the poles and are widest at the equator (about 69 miles apart). Zero degrees longitude is located at Greenwich, England (0°). The degrees continue 180° east and 180° west where they meet and form the International Date Line in the Pacific Ocean. The Prime Meridian and the International Date Line divide the earth into the Eastern and Western Hemispheres.

The Eastern Hemisphere consists of Europe, Africa, Asia, and Australia; the Western Hemisphere includes North and South America.

- **Elevation:** The elevation of a place is its height from a reference point, usually mean sea level. Mean sea level is the average height of the sea, as calculated through hourly observation of the sea on an open coast over a 19-year period. According to this definition, Mt. Everest is the highest point on earth, and Mt. Kilimanjaro is the highest mountain in Africa. Elevation is often shown through contour lines on a topographical map or by height on three-dimensional plastic-molded maps. The elevation of a place is calculated through survey techniques, such as aerial photography. Close contours indicate a steep slope, and wide contours indicate a shallow slope. Climate is related to elevation, with lower temperatures at higher elevations.

- **Scale:** On maps, things are necessarily smaller than in real life. Scaling is reducing things on the map by the same amount; say half as big as in reality. Maps should show relative size as accurately as possible; for example, a three-story building is taller than a home. On maps, legends define the scaling process used, often as a linear, graphic scale of inches to miles.

Teaching Resources

Children's Literature

Books for World Address

Cherry, L. (1994). *The armadillo from Amarillo.* New York: Voyager Books. An unlikely voyager, Sasparillo the armadillo, wants to find out more about his world. He walks north through Texas, then hitches a ride on an eagle's back to go further—from Amarillo to the universe. Along the way, Sasparillo writes postcards to his cousin, Brillo, describing the places he's been. This book is just the right thing to introduce a travelogue of the United States, and sharing information about places through the mail.

Hartman, G. (1993). *As the crow flies.* New York: Aladdin Paperbacks. In this book, animals' ground-level views of their trails are translated to bird's-eye views, as used in maps. Notions of map-making, scale and symbols are introduced in simple ways. This book is appropriate for young learners' explorations and map-making.

Leedy, L. (2000). *Mapping Penny's world.* New York: Henry Holt and Co. In this book a young girl draws maps of places her Boston terrier, Penny, goes. Real places are translated into maps, much like *Me on the Map.* This book includes more sophisticated map codes, such as scale, compass rose, symbols, and legends. Its attention to scale is quite unusual. Use as a follow-up to *Me on the Map,* or with older children.

McCurdy, M. (2002). *Trapped by the ice! Shackleton's amazing Antarctic adventure.* New York: Walker & Co. This book tells the tale of Robert Shackleton's ill-fated Imperial

Trans-Antarctic Expedition, which was brought to a halt when their ship, *Endurance*, was gripped by the Weddell ice pack. For almost two years, 22 men survived on an icy island while their captain and crewmates traveled hundreds of miles for help. This book focuses on a little-known part of the world, Antarctica. It is suitable for intermediate grade students.

Sweeney, J. (1996). *Me on the map.* New York: Dragonfly Books. A child introduces maps with a map of her bedroom, then moves out to her town, state, nation, continent, and world. At each juncture, she shows where she is on the map. A perfect fit for World Address, especially for younger students.

Williams, V. B. (1988). *Stringbean's trip to the shining sea.* New York: Mulberry Books. In this book, Stringbean Coe writes postcards to his family as he and his older brother travel in an old truck across the country from Kansas to the Pacific Ocean. The book is small, sort of postcard size, and should be read individually or in small groupings. It is a great resource for a travelogue/mapping activity.

Books for Newlandia

Cherry, L. (1992). *A river ran wild.* San Diego: Harcourt Brace & Co. This environmental history tells the story of the decline and reclamation of the Nashua River in Massachusetts. It describes the different impacts that Indian people, settlers, and factory owners had on the river, sustaining, utilizing, or polluting it. This book is a wonderful introduction for a role play about different lifeways and land use.

Zimmerman, W. Frederick. (2006). *The world is flat: Not!* Ann Arbor, MI: Nimble Books. In this book, maps of the world show layers of information, comparing the location and abundance of people, crops, and animals over time in 1700, 1800, 1900. The maps are simple, but relatively small, so multiple copies of the book might be needed. This book can introduce the notion of layers of information, necessary for *Newlandia*.

Books for Focus: Nigeria

Giles, B. (2007). *Countries of the world: Nigeria.* Washington, DC: National Geographic Society. This non-fiction book has the look of a *National Geographic* magazine, complete with yellow borders. It explains the history, culture, government, and economy of Africa. It describes the slave trade that originally linked the U.S. to Nigeria, as well as the oil trade that links us today. This book is suitable for upper elementary students.

MacDonald, F. (1998). *Ancient African town.* London: Franklin Watts. This non-fiction book offers a tour of Benin City, once the center of the great West African empire, Edo. The book provides glimpses of life and work, differentiating among skilled workers, farmers, and leaders. The book is factually full, with pictures of detail; it is suitable for individual study. It is complementary to *Newlandia* and appropriate for a learning center.

Oluonye, M. (2008). *Nigeria*. Minneapolis, MN: Lerner Publications Co. This appealing, readable, non-fiction book introduces Nigerian land and life, in all its variety. Photographs of people and places invite the reader to "see" this country. The book includes sidebars with tasks students can do. This book is suitable for all grades.

Onyefulu, I. (1995). *Emeka's gift: An African counting story*. New York: Puffin Books.[2] In this book, Emeka, a little boy from Ibaji, a village in Southern Nigeria, dreams of a gift to give his grandmother when he visits her. He counts things that are customary aspects of his life. Each person, place, or thing is illustrated with a beautiful photograph. This book is suitable for primary children.

Onyefulu, I. (1997). *Chidi only likes blue*. London: Frances Lincoln Children's Books. In this book an older sister introduces her little brother to his colors. Each color represents something in Nigerian life, from foods, to homes, to clothing, and more. The book is written for primary level children, but, since it tells a great deal about Nigerian life, it can be used in a learning center for upper grades too.

Onyefulu, I. (1998). *My grandfather is a magician: Work and wisdom in an African village*. London: Frances Lincoln Ltd. In this book, the author describes the work her family does in Eastern Nigerian, from healing, to law, to baking, to art. She focuses on the worthy work of her grandfather, a traditional herbal healer. This book seamlessly blends traditional and present-day jobs. This book is easy to read, but the content is suitable for all grades.

Internet Sites

Google Earth: http://earth.google.com. This site provides satellite imagery of the world. The software can be downloaded free of charge. This program can zoom in from Earth to a neighborhood address and back again.

National Standards for Geography: www.nationalgeographic.com/xpeditions/standards. This site is a MUST for teachers! It includes remarkable lessons and activities, aligned with the six elements of geography and students' levels of understanding. The *Xpeditions* or explorations particularly are suited to an active, inquisitive view of learning. Click on the Atlas link to find printable maps from around the world.

Map Machine: http://plasma.nationalgeographic.com/mapmachine. This National Geographic website provides satellite, physical, and thematic maps. The theme maps present issues such as human population density and environmental threats. These maps can be used to support geographic reasoning, particularly through the strategy of Discussion Web.

2 Nigerian author Ifeoma Onyefulu has earned many book awards for her appealing, easy-to-read, authentic travelogues. Her books are "must-reads" for any learning center on Nigeria. These books represent a selection from her work; look for others as well.

TEACH!

Become Informed: World Address

Focus In 9.1: Me on the Map by Joan Sweeney[3]

Hook: Use Google Earth to show children an image of the world. Zoom in from the globe to your school address. Use the "fly to" prompt, to type in, first, United States, then, your state, city, and school address. Ask Essential Question (EQ): What is your world address?

Focus Activity: Select four or five important generalizations to consider before and after the reading. Ask students to consider the generalizations; predict whether they are true or false (or use yes/no comparisons for primary-age students). Here is an example for *Me on the Map*.

1 A bird's-eye view is how a place looks from up above it.
2 Maps are drawn from a bird's-eye view.
3 An address is the place where you live.
4 You live in the United States and in the world at the same time.
5 Your world address includes outer space.

Reading: Read the entire book. Do not stop to ask more questions of students. You want their attention to remain on the generalizations noted in the Focus Activity.

After Reading: Return to the Focus Activity. Revisit each generalization. Adjust or affirm predictions as needed. Discuss reasons for changes or verifications.

Going Further: Think about what it means to map a place from a "bird's-eye view." Show students an aerial photograph of a well-known local place. Ask questions such as:

1 Why do we call this type of picture a "bird's-eye" view? Would you like to be a bird and fly over the world?
2 What can you learn from a bird's-eye view that you couldn't know from a car, bus, or train? What kind of machine would give you a bird's-eye view?
3 Could you draw your own bird's-eye view of your neighborhood, town, or state, or would it be pretty difficult? Explain.

Going still further: The format below illustrates one's planetary location. It can be used as an introduction to and/or culmination for the activities in *World Address*, demonstrating changes in students' perceptions. When our pre-service teachers identified their world

---

3 This book probably is too simplistic for intermediate students. Try using *Where Do I Live?* by Neil Chesanow for a more complicated narrative, or acknowledge the simple text of *Me on the Map* with students, but point out that it introduces a complicated idea: where one lives in the world.

address, some found the graphic helpful as an ever-enlarging depiction of their personal location, from home to world. Others drew their home, country, and planet vividly, with the rest fading into anonymity. Still others "zoomed in" on their most significant address, emphasizing this place. In any case, it is likely that you and your students will redraw this conventional view of *World Address* into something far messier. Give it a try right now. What will you draw? Where in the world are you? How do you identify your *World Address*?

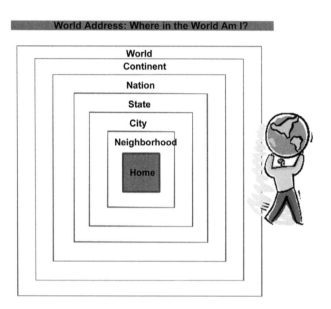

Illustration 9.2 World Address.

Teach for Ideas 9.1: What is an explorer?

Hook: Ask students: What is an explorer? What made Christopher Columbus an explorer? Are explorers still alive? Can you be an explorer? Read: *Mapping Penny's World* by Loreen Leedy. Ask students to think about the exploration of their neighborhood. What makes it special?

Example #1: Explore the school. Brainstorm special people, places, and things in the school. Go on a school walk. Encourage students to make careful observations of special features and faces in the school. Older students can take a notebook and record sights and sounds.

Example #2: Share observations. List, group, and label outstanding aspects of school.

Example #3: Make a mental map of the school. Denote special people, places, and things. Share and compare.

Assessment: Answer the EQ. Pinpoint the following: characteristics of an explorer and stages for an exploration. For example, an explorer is a traveler who is inquisitive, observant, brave, and persistent. Exploration is journeying, searching, investigating, recording, and recounting.

Going Further: Ask students to ponder: What does exploration have to do with geography? How, if at all, can exploration help us learn about our world?

Teach for Inquiry 9.1: Explorations

This inquiry involves exploration outside school, on students' own time. Students can work alone or, better yet, with a travel partner or an exploration crew. Several potential explorations are suggested here. Students should map the place of exploration, record their observations (with notes, pictures, or diagrams), and select a means to share their adventures (e.g., a diary, journal, letter, storyboard). Mental mapping is a good first step, followed, if possible, by adjustments based on revisiting the place. Observation steps or reminders should be provided to assist students in recording their search. Formats for recounting the exploration should be developed, discussed, and selected.

Hook: Ask students to draw a mental map of the most special place in their neighborhood. Share. Ask students to pinpoint what makes the place special. Raise the EQ: What can we learn from exploring our world?

Hypotheses: Ask students to predict what fascinating things an explorer might find in their homes, neighborhoods, or local stores. List and save for future reference.

Get Ready to Explore: Read *As the Crow Flies* by Gail Hartman.[4] Discuss how the animals' journeys were illustrated as maps. Ask students draw mental maps of their neighborhoods in a minute or two. Share and compare the maps. Consider the following queries: In what ways were the maps similar (i.e., recorded the same places, businesses, streets, homes, etc.)? In what ways did the maps differ? Were any of the maps drawn from a particular point of view (e.g., an interest in parks, stores, houses, people, dogs, or cats)?

Compare students' maps with a satellite photo of their neighborhood from Google Earth. Determine what students recalled or overlooked. Point out that Google Earth, although detailed, is still a photograph from afar. It cannot capture interesting people, beautiful parks, ugly spots, favorite places, or momentary changes in students' neighborhoods. But students, as on-the-spot observers, can do just that! Invite students to undertake one of the following explorations.

EXPLORE 9.1A: INSPECT YOUR HOME

Our homes are designed to create an *inside* divided from an *outside*. Yet the outside is often a part of our inside, in the form of houseplants, pets, and uninvited guests such

4 *As the Crow Flies* introduces the notion of seeing, then mapping, a place. It is a useful guide for self-mapping by students. However, it might be too simplistic for upper-grade youth. *Trapped by Ice!*, the true story of Sir Ernest Shackleton's perilous Antarctic expedition, can serve as a substitute that emphasizes a sense of exploration and utilizes journal entries as a means of recording one's adventures.

as dust, ants, spiders, and surprises! Get a piece of blank paper and map out your living space or building. Start at one far corner of your home or building, whether it is an apartment, house, or other dwelling, and draw a map of all of your discoveries, including people, places, plants, and animals. Be sure to note, color, or pencil in the location of your discovery on the map you create. And remember to make a legend to guide others to your discoveries. Write a journal or diary or letter about what you found. What did you find? Did you uncover anything new? Did you discover any horrors? Did you stumble upon any surprises?

EXPLORE 9.1B: GO SHOPPING

Decide on a shopping goal. Identify something you want or need, such as clothing, school supplies, books, ice cream, broccoli, or toys. Plan an expedition to a destination you know. Record the path you take with a paper and pencil, or with a disposable camera. Pay special attention to the store you are visiting and to the stores and businesses along the way. What kinds of businesses did you discover? Where were the businesses located? What did you find in the store you chose? Were there different departments, such as clothes, tools, or toys? Was it a gigantic or tiny place? Draw a map of your destination. Include a key or legend for others to read. Did you encounter any difficulties? See any weird things? Have any adventures?

EXPLORE 9.1C: TAKE A TRIP

Read some travel brochures or travel books. Take a trip by car, plane, boat, or train; or on foot is OK too. Go somewhere you've never been at all, accompanied by a responsible adult of course. Keep a travel log, writing down what you see every ten minutes or so, noting where you are when you write your entry. Keep a diary too. Write in it every day, remembering your experiences. Has your trip led to any discoveries, have you learned anything you didn't know before? Have you met any interesting people? Do you feel lonesome or surrounded by friends? Do you feel lost or are you comfortable? Why do some places seem nicer than others? Yes or no, why or why not? Did the travel brochures and books give accurate information about the place you visited?

EXPLORE 9.1D: IMAGINE AN ADVENTURE

Take an imaginary trip to an exotic place. Stop by a travel agency and ask for free pamphlets, books, or pictures of the place you want to go. Or look on the internet for photos of places such as Tahiti, or Thailand, or Timbuktu. Find out more about where you'd like to go, read books or look at a map or both! Find an adult who would like to go along, and ask him or her to help you with your research (you can ask your teacher too!). Take travel notes of all the information you find. Make up an adventure story that happens in your fascinating place. (It is OK to add you own ideas, even to include a hero or heroine, maybe you, if you like.)

Recount Explorations: Share and celebrate students' projects.

Revise Hypotheses: Revisit predictions about results of explorations. Discuss the expected and, especially, the unexpected!

Conclusion/Assessment: Answer the EQ: What can we learn from exploring our world?

Think It Through

Teach through Art: 3-D Map Project[5]

Hook: Ask students: Does it surprise you that most people (even adults) can't locate all 50 states? Are you one of those people? Try it now: Where is New York? Texas? California? Alaska? Here is your chance to identify and investigate several states in the U.S. and to make new friends in the bargain!

Explain the Project (Correlate with Write to Learn: RAFT below).

- **Make a 3-D Map.** Focus on the United States. Include important information about your state(s) on the map. Use everyday items, such as spools from thread, ribbons, yarn, buttons, Hershey's Kisses, M&Ms, beans, or shells, to stand for mountains or rivers, or to show crops, or to mark cities. Think in three dimensions. Be creative, have fun!
- **Reading:** Read books about the states. Find out something special about people or places, in the past or now, and figure out a way to exhibit this information on the map.
- **Writing:** Write to school classes in other states. Ask them for information about their school, community, and state. Make a booklet or display of the information to share with others.
- **Cartography:** Include the following information on your maps.

  1 The name of the state and its capital, marked with a star.
  2 Mountains, lakes, forests, and other geographical features.
  3 Major cities, clearly labeled.
  4 Natural resources, such as coal, oil, rivers, iron ore, etc.
  5 People, places, or events that make this state special.

---

5 In place of a role play, this folk art map project utilizes the arts to illustrate cultural, physical, and historical aspects of place. This map project should be completed in conjunction with Write to Learn: RAFT below (p. 194). Our focus here is on the U.S., but you can easily select other interesting places (such as Antarctica!) to map. This map project is adapted from an activity originally developed by Mr. Michael Burr from Lawrence Central High School, Indianapolis, Indiana.

Hook: Tell students they will have a chance to locate a new toy store in town. Ask: where do you think it should go? Why? Raise the EQ: *What is geo-spatial thinking?*

Example #1: Place a large white sheet (or white shower curtain) on the floor of the classroom. Hand out containers of M&Ms. Tell students that they will create a community, then gather geographic (or spatial) information about it. Explain features the candies stand for.

- Blue: water
- Green: parks
- Brown: factories
- Orange: fast food restaurants
- Red: fire stations
- Licorice: roads

Ask students to gently toss different colors of M&Ms on the map. Note that each color adds a layer of information about the community. When all the colors have been tossed, look for any concentrations. Discuss where roads should go and add them with licorice (or the teacher can add the streets by fiat).

Explain that the spatial information can be used to make decisions. Ask students where they might put a school or market and why. Last, ask them to locate the new toy store and justify its location according to geographic information, as represented by M&Ms and licorice.

Example #2: Invite students to serve as cartographers, mapping M&Ms Community. Ask them to create a mental map. Include layers of information. Develop a legend or map key, and include a compass rose.

Example #3: Show layers of information on a real map. The book *The World is Flat: Not!* by W. Frederick Zimmerman can be used as one such exhibit. Another option is to locate local GIS information. The following map is posted on Access Indiana, a state government website, by the Indiana Geographic Information Council. When you click on features, they are added to the map, showing a layering of information about the state. Encourage students to consider the ways that geographic information can help in decision-making.

Conclusions/Assessment: Answer the EQ: What is geo-spatial thinking?

Illustration 9.4 Indiana GIS Map: Geographic Information Council. Retrieved from: www.in.gov.igic. Courtesy Indiana Geographic Information Council.

Think It Through

Teach through Drama: Newlandia

Hook: Ask students what might happen if people with different lifeways and land needs, such as hunters, farmers, herders, and city folks, had to share the same areas and resources. Make a list of "what ifs." Read *A River Ran Wild* by Lynne Cherry. Return to the list and add to or subtract from it. Invite students to play *Newlandia* and explain the gist of the game.

Illustration 9.5 Map of Newlandia.

Newlandia: Basic Information

 Plant and animal resources

- Fish, near the delta, in and around the harbor, and in the lakes and rivers (if they are not polluted).
- Antelope and wild chicken in the grasslands.
- Deer, nuts, and fruits in the deciduous (broad leaf) forests.
- Elk, bear, and berries in the evergreen forests.
- Rabbits and wild birds in the desert.
- Turkey and pheasant in the southern hills.

 Mineral resources

- Oil, near the middle of the desert.
- Iron ore in the mountains on the north side of the map, near the evergreen forests.
- Coal in the hills by the north fork of the river.
- Gold and uranium in the far northern hills near the lake.
- Potash deposits (good for fertilizer) in the desert, near the bend of the river.

 Climate

	Desert	Grasslands	Hills	Mountains
Rain	0–5"	5"–15"	15"–25"	25"–40"
Snow	0	1"–2"	2"–5"	5"–10"
Summer Temp.	90°–110°	80°–95°	75°–85°	65°–75°
Winter Temp.	40°–50°	20°–40°	15°–30°	0°–20°

To turn on/off the map features and labels you want to see on your map, click Update Map below. If you do not click Update Map, your changes will not show up.

	Layer	Label
Counties	☐	☐
Cities	☐	☐
Major Highways	☐	☐
Major Rivers and Lakes	☐	☐

Illustration 9.6 Newlandia: Basic Information.

Roles: Basic information about *Newlandia* and group characterization follows.

Hunters and gatherers

Population: 50–300

Technology: Men hunt, usually with bows, arrows, spears, and axes. Women gather nuts and berries. Men and women use tools made by hand to cook food, build homes, and sew clothing.

Wealth: Based on skills, like the best hunter has more; also based on barter, such as giving tools to get furs.

Food: Hunt deer and antelope; gather nuts and berries. Move from place to place to find food. Build temporary shelters where food is found.

Work: Men hunt. Women care for children and gather food. Men and women work together to cook food.

Social groups: Men and women have separate "secret" groups with special meanings. A few people, like healers and tribal leaders, make decisions and teach the children tribal ways.

Values: Think highly of people who share food, tools, and furs. People are very proud of hunters. They have great respect for animal life.

Play your role as a **hunter-gatherer.**

Remember: You need to hunt wild animals and gather nuts and berries in order to live well. Fish are a possible source of food, but learning to fish will require difficult changes for your people.

Illustration 9.7 Newlandia: Hunter-Gatherers

Herders

Population: 100–600

Technology: Wood-working, leather-working, sheep-shearing. Make carts or wagons. Sell or trade animals and animal products.

Wealth: Based on animals; the one who has more animals is richer. Also products from animals, such as wool rugs, nicely made jewelry or wooden objects, and things gained by trading, count as riches.

Food: Goats, sheep, and cows are used for meat and milk, and their skins or wool are used for clothing. Group moves as new grazing lands are needed. Belongings are carried in wagons. Some meats are dried and saved for winter.

Work: Men care for animals, do leather work, and build wagons. Sometimes they fight with other groups. Women make clothes, care for children, and prepare food.

Social Groups: Chiefs or leaders make decisions with the advice from a few respected people. Those who are sick or old are cared for by families. One religion is directed by a priest-like leader. Parents teach skills to children.

Values: Think highly of people who are skilled at herding animals or good weavers. Good musicians are enjoyed too. People are proud of good warriors.

Play your role as a **herder.**

Remember: You need to find grazing lands for your animals to live well. You could learn to farm, but it would be a difficult change for your people.

Illustration 9.8 Newlandia: Herders.

Farmers

Population: 1,000–6,000

Technology: Family farming. Each family or group of families raises many kinds of crops and animals. Farmers use plows, hoes, and hand tools. They weave clothes and make pottery. They rotate crops, dig irrigation canals, and build small bridges.

Wealth: Based on land and livestock. The one who has more and better of each is richer. Crops, farm products, and hand-made items count as riches.

Food: Crops of grains, vegetables, fruit trees, and animals, such as cows, sheep, goats, pigs, and chickens.

Work: Men and women share many chores. Men are more responsible for animal care, plowing, and heavy chores. Women are more responsible for care of the home, raising children, and food preparation.

Social Groups: There are two religions; most people belong to one or the other. Decisions are made by families or meetings of people living in the same area. There are a few schools and stores. Elderly or sick people are cared for by relatives.

Values: People think highly of those who work hard, manage their lands and animals carefully, take part in group meetings, and help others when needed. Robust animals or finely crafted items, such as quilts or jellies, are highly prized.

Play your role as a **farmer.**

Remember: You need land and water suitable for farming to live well. You could learn to work in factories, but it would mean many difficult changes to your way of life.

Illustration 9.9 Newlandia: Farmers.

Factory Owners

Population: 10,000–50,000

Technology: Manufacturing from cotton and wool (textiles), paper production, ship-building, bridge-building, steel-forging, and gun-making; horse-drawn harvester, telegraph, sewing machines, wool carder, and loom; farming on a larger scale.

Wealth: Based on ownership of land, buildings, and factories. People have jobs, but factory jobs don't pay much. There is some investment in companies and banks.

Food: Farming larger areas of land with machines allows fewer farmers to grow more. There is a variety of meats, dairy products, vegetables, and fruit (in season).

Work: Men build and own factories. Men and women hold factory jobs. Men usually work in steel production, ship building, forestry, mining, or weapon-making. Women usually work in textile factories or stores. Farming is shared by men and women.

Social Groups: There are several religions. Elected officials run the towns. Usually, people who are richer or more educated have more power in decision-making. Schools are available; those who have more money can go to school longer. Some sick or older people are offered help, such as group housing, by religious groups.

Values: There is strong interest in earning more money and getting more things. People also want a formal education. Schools to teach reading and writing to all, have been set up. Medical care by doctors and in hospitals is seen as beneficial.

Play your role as **factory owners.**

Remember: You will need oil, coal, iron mines, railroad tracks, roads, harbors, farmlands, and medium-size towns to live well.

Illustration 9.10 Newlandia: Factory Owners.

Super-technology Users

Population: 20,000–100,000

Technology: Computers, internet communication, cell phones, iPods, cars, airplanes, submarines, tractors, harvesters, and rockets; plastics, aluminum, nuclear power, gasoline, water and solar power.

Wealth: Based on ownership in homes and land; investments, amount of money and credit. There is widespread ownership of small businesses.

Food: Farming on large farms by very few people. Lots of varied foods; some shipped from other countries. Foods are pre-made to meet needs of busy workers.

Work: Very complex: men and women hold similar jobs in factories, medicine, law, and education. Women are almost equal to men in pay. Most jobs are in offices or services for people. Factories are becoming automated; machines do a lot of the work. Highly skilled and educated people hold the best jobs.

Social Groups: There are a variety of religions. Government is democratic; one person can represent thousands of citizens. Schooling is required for all children to age 17. A welfare system helps older people, poor people, or homeless people.

Values: There is strong emphasis on earning more money. People want more technology to provide jobs and make life easier. There is some interest in controlling factories for pollution and preserving the environment.

Play your role as **super-technology users.**

Remember: You will need inexpensive energy sources, highly automated factories, a good airline system, a rapid communication network, pollution controls, large farms, many services, and big cities to live well.

Illustration 9.11 Newlandia: Super-technology Users.

Role Play: The simulation takes place in two or three rounds—four if you include a full discussion or debriefing of the game, which we recommend.

- Round #1: The first round is one of orientation and discovery. Ask students what they notice about the topography of Newlandia: its hills, mountains, forests, and rivers. Encourage them to think geographically about where they would like to live and why. Use the data sheet to add information in layers: first plants, then animals, then mineral resources. Use different colors to represent this information and make a legend to code it. Ask students to reconsider their original preferences in light of this new information.
- Round #2: The second round calls upon students to form groups, with four or five students to a group. The groups are: hunters and gatherers, herders, farmers, factory owners, and super-technology users. Each has a list of skills, customs, and populations to manage, and each is unlike the others. The groups must utilize or develop Newlandia, according to their needs and to the requirements of the game, which are: settle on a favorite area in which to live; decide which land is best for your group; be ready to explain your decision.

 Note: Each group may NOT settle in more than one third of Newlandia.

Each group talks it over and uses maps of Newlandia to color in the areas they want, and to draw the farms they will establish, or the herds they will drive, or the cities they will build. (Enlarged copies of the map should be made to enable each group to present their choices, and reasons for them, to their classmates.)

Next, each group (holding their symbol cards) presents its maps to the class, reporting on how they used their piece of land in Newlandia. Each group should be allowed to give a fairly detailed presentation, holding up their map work, and sharing it with other groups, who will come to realize that nearly everyone likes pretty much the same places and that conflict is likely unless all are very cooperative.

- Round #3: A third round calls upon student groups to visit each other and negotiate (if they can agree) on where all can live in Newlandia without getting in each other's way. Ask that consensus be reached, if possible, but if not, and the play goes on too long, then ask for reports from each group explaining how far they got in trying to reach agreements.
- Round #4: A fourth round focuses on the discussion of conflict and cooperation. At issue are how people of varying skills and technologies use the land, and how this choice affects natural resources and other peoples. Ask students questions about why they settled in certain locations and how their lifestyles impacted the earth. Also, encourage a discussion of "getting along with others," particularly with those different from you (e.g., how can herders live with farmers, farmers with factory owners, and what happens to hunter-gatherers as technology takes over)?

Conclusions/Assessment: Ask students to share what they learned by playing *Newlandia*, especially about human–environmental interaction—how people shape and are shaped by their environments. You might find it interesting to poll them on which groups they would MOST want to belong to in real life, or in the game, and why (one choice only, sorry!).

FOCUS: NIGERIA

Focus is an independent study, organized by a learning center. It is an engagement that reinforces and enriches understandings and skills gained throughout Explore. Students can continue to learn about their *World Address*, investigating countries world-wide, particularly those outside a normal Eurocentric view. Students can carry on their reading about special places, creating folk-art maps of their outstanding characteristics. As in *Newlandia*, students can apply GIS-like strategies, studying layers of information, and practice geo-spatial thinking, responding to real-life problems. Most of all, students can keep on approaching geographic studies through the eyes of an explorer.

Learning Center Checklist

So, how does a learning center work? Learning centers have been around for a long time. They evolved from impetuses to individualize learning in the latter 1970s and early 1980s (e.g., Kaplan, Kaplan, Madsen, & Taylor, 1973). Often called literacy work stations, centers are frequently used by primary teachers to differentiate and enhance reading instruction. A geography center is, basically, another iteration of the work station approach. Similar to work stations, the center should be a *learning* place, not an optional, free-time, fun space. The following checklist can help you envision this end.

At learning centers:

- Tasks should be clearly identified.
- Tasks should be differentiated, including reading, writing, listening, and/or experimenting, and allowing for self-pacing and more advanced work.
- Tasks should be self-directing, giving students clear directions for their work.
- Materials should be available, organized, and easily replenished.
- Charts to record self-progress should be provided and understood.

Notably, learning centers, like any other instructional method, should be taught. You, as teachers, should introduce the center, describing its contents and use. You should check in with students, monitoring their progress. And, if appropriate, you can teach a follow-up lesson, reinforcing center activities. Moreover, you should manage the center. You should provide a plan for using and resupplying the center and discuss behavioral expectations for independent work.

Learning Center Materials

Think carefully about books, maps, and other materials you will need for *Focus*. In order to foster a sense of place and to practice geo-spatial thinking, you will need items such as:

- Computer with Google Earth software.
- Maps with layers of information about Nigeria: its land, people, history, and resources.
- Children's books about Nigeria, such as the series by Onyefulu.
- Photographs of Nigeria, such as those found in National Geographic books and magazines.
- Artifacts, such as gourd bowls, fez, palm leaf, chalk rock, carved wood, bead necklace, and colorful cloth, like that made in or native to Nigeria.

 Think about it: *Focus* relies on independent study. A probable benefit is that *Focus* can fit into a highly constrained schedule, providing more time for geographic learning. However, a potential downside is that activities can seem extracurricular, diminishing their educational value. This problem can be solved! What can you, as teacher, do to support the *Focus* center as a *learning* place? How can you respond to students' learning in the center? How can students exhibit the real work accomplished at the center?

TEACH!

Become Informed

Focus In 9.2: Emeka's Gift by Ifeoma Onyefulu

Hook: Invite children to learn about Nigeria. Ask questions such as: Where is Africa? Where is Nigeria? Have you ever played okoso? Have you ever been to an outdoor market? Can you imagine saving rain water to use in the dry season? Did you know that chalk can be used to write wishes for children? Let's learn about Nigeria, a fascinating African nation! Use *Google Earth* to locate Africa, then, to home in on Nigeria.

Focus Activity: Select four or five generalizations to consider before and after the reading. Ask students to predict whether they are true or false. Here is an example for *Emeka's Gift*:

1 A village is like a small town in Africa.
2 A market in Nigeria is like a shopping mall in the United States.
3 Water is a very valuable thing in Nigeria.
4 A typical family in Nigeria includes three generations: grandparents, parents, and kids.
5 Chiefs help to make important decisions for the village.

Reading: Read *Emeka's Gift*, stopping to point out interesting aspects of the real-life photos.

After Reading: Return to the Focus Activity and revisit children's predictions.

Going Further: Teach (or introduce) the learning center. For years, we have utilized a phrase from *Changes for Children* (Kaplan et al., 1973) to spark children's interest: "At this center you can . . ." At the Nigeria center students can:

- Locate Nigeria in Africa and on the globe.
- Use geo-spatial thinking to figure out questions about settlement in Nigeria.
- Put layers of information about natural resources on a map of Nigeria.
- Read and write about life in Nigeria.

At this center you can . . .

Investigate Nigeria with Maps

- The nation of Nigeria is nearly 100 years old. But African kingdoms and city-states existed long before that and there are still kings and emirs. Figure out what the present-day capital, Abuja, has to do with ancient times. Find an ancient city that still exists!
- The vegetation in Nigeria includes rain forest, coastal area, river delta, plateau, mountains, and savanna or grassland. Figure out where farming, fishing, and oil production take place and why.
- Nigeria's population is growing quickly. Imagine: in 2000 half of the population was under 15 years old! About one in five Nigerians live in cities. Figure out where most of the cities are located and why.
- Investigate a map of ancient Nigeria. Find the kingdoms, city-states, and culture of Nok. Make a good guess about why the modern capital, Abuja, is located where it is. Read *Ancient African Town*. Find the ancient city described in the book.
- Investigate a map of the vegetation of Nigeria. Identify where you would live if you were a farmer, forester, or oil worker, and tell why.
- Investigate a map of the population of Nigeria. Compare it with a map of oil resources. What did you find?

Illustration 9.12 Investigate Nigeria with Maps.

Emphasize that the center is a LEARNING place. Familiarize students with the center's activities. Walk through the lessons below. Provide guidance for the independent work to come.

Teach for Ideas 9.3: What is Nigeria?

Hook: Pinpoint the poster *Investigate Nigeria with Maps*. Ask children: How old is the nation of Nigeria? What is the environment like in Nigeria? Where do most people live in Nigeria? Invite children to do the activities in this part of the center to find out.

Example #1: Investigate a map of ancient Nigeria. Find the kingdoms, city-states, and culture of Nok. Make a good guess about why the modern capital, Abuja, is located where it is. Read: *Ancient African Town*. Find the ancient city described in the book.

Example #2: Investigate a map of the vegetation of Nigeria. Identify where you would live if you were a farmer, forester, or oil worker, and tell why.

Example #3: Investigate a map of the population of Nigeria. Compare it with a map of oil resources. What did you find?

Assessment: Post your findings in the special place designated for "My Work."

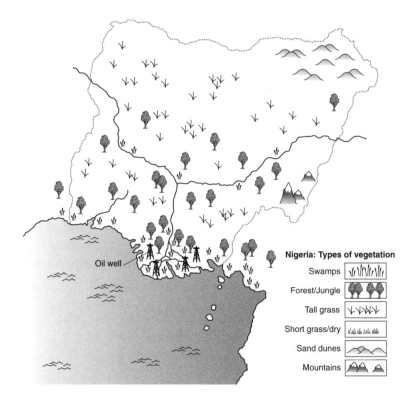

Illustration 9.13 Map of Nigeria.

Teach for Inquiry 9.2: What is Life Like in Nigeria?

Hook: Pinpoint the poster *Imagine Life in Nigeria*. Raise the EQ: What is life like in Nigeria? Invite students to read and find out! To pique children's curiosity, do a "picture walk," or show selected illustrations from books by Ifeoma Onyefulu and Mary Oluonye.

Hypotheses: Make a "Detective's Notebook" for children to independently record and revise their hypotheses as they work through the following "clues."

Clue #1: Read *Nigeria* by Mary Oluonye. Make a four-flap book. Name the major population groups, and then draw pictures and give facts about their lives.

Clue #2: Read *Chidi Only Likes Blue* by Ifeoma Onyefulu. Make a color wheel. Draw pictures from Nigerian village life to illustrate the wheel. White is the color for . . .

Clue #3: Read *My Grandfather is a Magician* by Ifeoma Onyefulu. Write an "I am" poem as if you were a healer like grandfather. While you are at it, make a list of other jobs in Eastern Nigeria.

Revise Hypotheses: Record your conclusions in your Detective's Notebook.

Assessment/Conclusions: Answer the EQ. Write it down in your Detective's Notebook.

Teach for Inquiry 9.3: How Does Oil Affect Life in Nigeria?

Hook: Pinpoint the poster *Think about Nigeria's Oil Billions*. Raise the EQ: How does oil affect life in Nigeria? Show photographs of oil fields, fires, and pollution from books such as *Countries of the World: Nigeria* by Bridget Giles. Encourage students to, once again, pull out their Detective's Notebook and start investigating!

Hypotheses: Remind students to record their initial thoughts and change them later, as evidence rolls in.

Clue #1: Study the chart "Trading Partners" (see Table 9.1). Identify Nigeria's biggest trading partner. Think about: What else, beside oil, could Nigeria ship to the U.S.? How can oil riches help other industries to develop? Write down your thoughts and post them next to the chart.

Clue #2: Read *Nigeria* by Mary Oluonye or *Countries of the World: Nigeria* by Bridget Giles. Notice all the interesting things that a tourist would like to see. Make a travel brochure to encourage tourism as another industry in Nigeria.

At this center you can . . .

Imagine Life in Nigeria

- Long ago, different groups of people ruled parts of Nigeria. Each group had its own language and history. The Hausa and Fulani lived in the north. The Yoruba lived in the southwest. The Igbo lived in the southeast. Find out how these groups live today.

- Almost one half Nigerian people live in cities, but many still live in villages. People make things by hand and play games from long ago. Find out more about village life.

- A healer is an important person in Nigerian villages. He or she knows a lot about plants that can heal sick people. Some people think a healer has magic powers. Learn more about a healer and see what you think.

- Read *Nigeria* by Mary Oluonye. Make a four-flap book. Name the major groups, and then draw pictures and give facts about their lives.

- Read *Chidi Only Likes Blue* by Ifeoma Onyefulu. Make a color wheel. Draw pictures from Nigerian village life to illustrate the wheel. White is the color for . . .

- Read *My Grandfather is a Magician* by Ifeoma Onyefulu. Write an "I am" poem as if you were a healer like grandfather. While you are at it, make a list of other jobs in Eastern Nigeria.

Illustration 9.14 Imagine Life in Nigeria.

TABLE 9.1 Trading Partners

Country	% Exports
United States	52.5% (oil)
Spain	8.2%
Brazil	6.1%
All others combined	33.2%

Other possible exports: rubber, cacao.
Other possible industry: tourism.

Resource: Giles, B. (2007). Nigeria. Washington, DC: National Geographic.

Clue #3: Examine a photograph of oil spills and fires in Nigeria. (You will find one in the Giles book.) How would you feel if your country looked like this photograph? What could you, as a citizen, do? Write a newspaper editorial about the oil situation in Nigeria.

At this center you can . . .

Think about Nigeria's Oil Billions

- Nigeria is oil-rich! See how Nigeria's coastline bulges into the Atlantic Ocean? That bulge is the Niger Delta, and in 1956 oil was discovered there. Now, oil rigs dot the skyline and oil pipes cross the land.
- Many Nigerians are moving to cities in the south. Cities are growing because of jobs in the oil industry.
- Many Nigerians live in poverty, regardless of oil riches. Corrupt politicians or military rulers took oil profits for years. The Niger River is becoming polluted.
- Oil is 95% of Nigeria's exports, and half of it is shipped to the United States.
- Study the chart "Trading Partners." Identify Nigeria's biggest trading partner. Think about: What else, beside oil, could Nigeria ship to the U.S.? How can oil riches help other industries to develop? Write down your thoughts and post them next to the chart.
- Read *Nigeria* by Mary Oluonye or *Countries of the World: Nigeria* by Bridget Giles. Notice all the interesting things that a tourist would like to see. Make a travel brochure to encourage tourism as another industry in Nigeria.
- Examine a photograph of oil spills and fires in Nigeria. (You will find one in the Giles book). How would you feel if your country looked like this. What could you, as a citizen do? Write a newspaper editorial about the oil situation in Nigeria.

Illustration 9.15 Think about Nigeria's Oil Billions.

Revise Hypotheses: Record your thoughts in your Detective's Notebook. Change your initial impressions as needed.

Assessment/Conclusions: Answer the EQ. Explain how your detective work shaped your response.

Note: While a learning center is meant to foster independent work, it can also prompt deliberative activities and propel service learning. Imagine making a simulation, like *Newlandia*, to extend student learning at the Nigeria center. Upon completion of their work in the center, students will be prepared to ponder competing land claims by, say, foresters, farmers, and oil workers. Or, envision service learning projects that can spring from independent work. Although Africa is a fascinating continent, many of its nations struggle with poverty, violence, disease, and water and food shortages. In the next chapter, we highlight two children's books, *Beatrice's Goat* by Page McBrier and *Ryan and Jimmy and the Well in Africa that Brought Them Together* by Herb Shoveller, which can be utilized to initiate service activities relevant to African nations.

Teacher Review

Where is something? Why is it there? How did it get there? How does it interact with other things? Do you feel comfortable facilitating explorations that will help children answer these questions? Can you see that geography is as much about how humans influence space as the space itself? Can you imagine geography as a series of questions about where and how we live on Earth? Respond to this question: why is this chapter entitled "Explore"?

As teachers, review the three teaching engagements presented here: *World Address*, *Newlandia*, and *Focus*. Consider: to what extent does each pay attention to the six broad themes for geography education? As a reminder, here they are:

1 The World in Spatial Terms
2 Places and Regions
3 Physical Systems
4 Human Systems
5 Environment and Society
6 The Uses of Geography

Next, reflect on the three "Ways of Knowing," orientations that we proposed as central to children's grasp of geography. Are these orientations embedded in the engagements outlined here? If so, how are they included? If not, how would you alter these projects in order to help children develop human–environmental interactive views of geography? As a reminder, here are the Ways of Knowing proposed earlier:

1 Knowing Earth as a natural, physical, and territorial space, settings, situations, locales, and regions—locally, nationally, and globally.
2 Knowing Earth as a human place, as a creation of environments in which to live, work, interact, and enjoy life.
3 Viewing Earth as a series of local and global interconnections between and among humans, animals, technology, natural resources, and ecological systems, as something of which we are all a part and that we can impact for good or ill.

Finally, consider the three teaching engagements, just for their sense of exploration, adventure, and downright fun. Do you think *World Address* will capture children's imaginations? Do you think *Newlandia* will spur geographical thinking? Do you think students will gravitate toward a *Focus* on faraway places, such as Africa, or Asia, or South America? Why? Why not?

How will you teach space and place? Can you foster earthly exploration? What will you, as teacher, do?

Making Connections

Teaching about place, space, and people's use or abuse of them is inherently interconnective. A place, such as Nigeria, is special because of its rich history, diverse people, and economic resources. Thus, *Focus* can be approached as a History Mystery, a biography project, or a study in international trade. Moreover, *World Address* and *Focus* readily enlarge and enhance worldview, offering students chances to envision their world and their role in it. Making wise decisions—approaching citizenship as a verb—is what this book is all about. Our students simply need to know more about their world—its interesting places, natural resources, human conflicts, and environmental dilemmas—in order to make informed decisions and take wise actions that impact their planetary home.

ten
Engage
Living One's Civics

"Community civics" was proposed as a startling new idea almost 100 years ago! As noted in Chapter 1, community civics was more than the "study of government forms and machinery" (Dunn, 1915, p. 8); it was the *exercise* of citizenship. Community civics, as taught in the Indianapolis public schools, was adopted, almost without revision, into the *1916 Report*, which, as you know, was a foundational document for social studies. In this chapter, we focus on service learning, a contemporary means of *living one's civics*, which is gaining in popularity.

When the phrase was coined, what did it mean to "live his [sic] civics" (Dunn, 1916, p. 22)? We provided some examples in Chapter 1 (p. 6). Now, we reiterate its meaning, quoting its developer, Arthur William Dunn:

> The pupil as a young citizen is a real factor in community affairs . . . Therefore, it is the task of the teacher to cultivate in the pupil a sense of his [sic] responsibility, present as well as future. If a citizen has an interest in civic matters and a sense of his personal responsibility, he will want to act. Therefore, the teacher must help the pupil express his conviction in word and deed. He must be given an opportunity to *live his civics*, both in the school and in the community outside. (1916, p. 22)

Arguably, this proposal is as alive today as it was in 1916! It challenges you, as teachers, to kindle, in students, a sense of civic responsibility, right now, in the present, guiding them in civic matters, and allowing them to act. This charge can seem ambitious for elementary students, but, on this point, Dunn offered important advice: "the class has the essential characteristics of a community. Therefore, the method by which the class exercises are conducted is of the utmost importance in the cultivation of civic qualities and habits" (1916, p. 23). So, how can you promote democratic dispositions in your class-room? You can hold classroom meetings and foster classroom discussions, as detailed in Chapter 4. You can organize your classroom as a mini-economy, as outlined in Chapter 8. Also, you can foster service learning, our focus here.

The idea behind service learning is that students serve to *learn*; their community work is related to their school studies, and they reflect seriously upon their efforts, gaining insights into local matters. Service can, of course, be an offshoot of any subject, but it is particularly suited to social studies as a format for teaching citizenship. Unfortunately, service can be seen as apolitical, that is, disconnected from government policies, citizens' preferences, or struggles for equality (e.g., Battistoni, 2000). Moreover, civic learning does not automatically accrue from service experiences. Activities must be developed that teach the arts and crafts of citizenship, teaching values, like tolerance, or practicing skills, such as letter-writing, public speaking and fund-raising. Additionally, service can be seen as a mission of uplift for the less fortunate, prompting a sense of superiority on the part of the giver. Susan Henry (2005) challenges service learning practitioners, such as you, to upset binaries between "server" and "served," finding ways to recognize the contributions of both parties to community engagements.

In response to these concerns, Harry Boyte (e.g., 2004) prefers to think of service learning as "public work" in which students plan and take action on public problems, such as school violence, racial prejudice, or environmental pollution. In Boyte's Public Achievement projects, students are seen as "society-makers," or co-creators of a common world, rather than as "service-providers," or benefactors to others.

How can children take action? What, if anything, is the difference between service learning and civic action? How, if at all, can children serve to learn arts and crafts of citizenship? Responding to such questions is becoming increasingly important. In the last decade, community service and service learning have gained in popularity. In 2004, researchers from The State of Service-Learning Project surveyed almost 1,800 K–12 prin-cipals. They found that high schools are more likely to provide service opportunities than middle or elementary schools. Still, the trends are impressive: 60% of elementary schools offer community service and 22% provide service learning (Scales & Roehlkepartain, 2004). Further, service programs exist in every state of the union, with California and Maryland establishing service goals for *all* learners.

Unfortunately, almost "anything goes" in regard to service; often, it is not carefully defined or effectively practiced. Service learning is criticized, somewhat truthfully, as "a mile wide and an inch deep" (Kielsmeier, 2000, p. 655). Kielsmeier calls for more attention to "north star" (p. 655) principles, or guiding tenets, for service learning, par-ticularly for service practitioners, such as teachers. In the following section, we provide "north star guidance" for learning through service.

such as mail boxes, telephone access, or job training, which are provided by the facility. You arrange to speak with people who are homeless to hear their stories.

- Finally, you *Teach for Deliberation*, inviting students to consider how they can help. You read aloud *The Can-do Thanksgiving* by Marion Pomeranc. You ask students to consider the benefits and limitations of a canned food drive.

- Now, you plan to *Serve and Learn*. Your students decide to organize a Donation Day at school to collect things needed by the community center. You help them educate their school-mates first, making posters, visiting classes, and podcasting information about homelessness. They post items needed prominently; canned foods are on the list, but, so are many other things. Students label donation boxes for different items and place them in the school lobby. Then, the big day comes, and they provide "people power" for the donation process. Here is a typical listing of needed items.

Donations Needed*

- Bus tickets
- Laundry detergent
- Toiletries (e.g. soap, shampoo, deodorant, disposable razors, toothbrushes, toothpaste, and shaving cream)
- Socks
- Diapers and baby wipes
- Sleeping bags and blankets
- Spices and sugar
- Tea and coffee
- Institutional-size canned food
- Disposable salt and pepper shakers

For our Spanish Population
- Refried beans
- Tostadas (round crunchy tortillas sold in plastic bags)
- Masa harina (flour for making tamales and tortillas)
- Dry pinto beans
- Chiles (canned or dried)
- Rice
- Corn husks (for making tamales)

*Shalom Community Center, Bloomington, Indiana.

- The Donation Day was a success! Next, you organize a trip to the community center, allowing students to see first-hand where their donations will go.

- Finally, you reflect with students on the process. Help them consider what they learned about poverty, homelessness, and taking action.

 Think about it! Is this project community service or service learning? What kind of service is it? Who benefits most, the youth or the community? Why? Does this effort enact the Principles for Social Justice-oriented Service Learning? Why or why not? If yes, how; if no, what is missing? How can you improve this effort?

Scenario 10.2: Intergenerational Biography Project[4]

You realize that intergenerational bonds are important for children and for seniors. Youth can make meaningful connections with older adults, learn about the past, and understand aging. Seniors can share their skills and life stories and develop friendships with young people. While some of your students enjoy older relatives who live close by, others visit them rarely. A senior care center is within walking distance of your school, so you decide to work with the center and with your students to develop a worthy service project. Last year, you organized several visits to the care center. Students sang to residents, gave them gifts, and ate lunch in their dining hall. As you reflected upon the effort, you realized that your students learned little about the seniors, overlooking their years of accumulated wisdom. This year, you decided to improve the project, linking it more to language arts and social studies curricula and aiming to work with, not for, care center residents.

- You invite your students to think of elders as living historians, asking: What can we learn about the past from people who lived it? You press forward, seeking to link a previous Biography Workshop to this endeavor. You ask things such as: Could elders be or have been outstanding citizens? What do you think it meant to be of help in your grandparents' day? You raise the idea of making biographies of elders' lives, including times when they helped others or made a difference in their communities or cities.
- You arrange a planning meeting at school between a selected group of seniors and children. Children show the biographies they made earlier. They work with seniors to develop a list of questions about their lives. You encourage students and seniors to include a question or two about helping and making a difference. Seniors remind students that they can't remember too many questions at once, so they decide together to conduct two interviews. They also decide to have some informal get-togethers to become friends before the interviews.
- You work with the care center director and seniors to assign buddies for kids and residents. Together, you plan several meaningful buddy visits.

---

4 This scenario draws from actual elementary projects as reported in Wade (2007b) and in Parker (2006).

- Next, you teach your students about oral history. You read aloud *Aunt Flossie's Hats (and Crab Cakes Later)* by Elizabeth Fitzgerald Howard (see Focusing In for Chapter 2) and *Grandma's Baseball* by Gavin Curtis, in which a grandmother teaches her grandson family history through an autographed baseball. You help students write oral history questions, and assist them in role playing an actual interview.
- Now, you organize the research. You make notebooks with students, putting a question on top of each blank page. For added assistance, you ask parents for their help and a cadre goes along on the interviews.
- Next, you begin the process of making biographies of the seniors' lives. You make sure to include a "Making a Difference" page!
- Pretty soon, the biographies are ready to share with seniors, and you begin to plan a celebration event. You invite your care center partners to help showcase ways in which both seniors and students served and learned.

Think about it! To what extent did this project integrate language arts and social studies? Did this service activity provide charity, foster civic education, or advocate for change? How, if at all, can you orient the activity more toward advocacy, especially for senior's issues, such as healthcare, housing, or companionship?

Prepare-a-Project

In the United States, we rarely think about a shortage of fresh water. We just turn on our faucets and get potable water, quickly and easily. Yet, the world's supply of fresh water is limited. Already many people lack safe drinking water and, in such places as Africa, they walk miles every day to get it. As we mentioned in Chapter 9, the children's book *Ryan and Jimmy and the Well that Brought Them Together* by Herb Shoveller is a true story of the efforts of an elementary school boy to build a well and make a difference. This book easily can inspire a service learning project that addresses a real, growing world problem: water shortage. We use it as the centerpiece of the exemplar below.

Become Informed

Focus In: Ryan and Jimmy and the Well that Brought Them Together by Herb Shoveller

Hook: Allow the children to get a drink from the school's water fountain. When they return, ask them to imagine what it would be like to lack access to clean, safe water—to drink or bathe in. Instead, you would walk miles to get water, or drink polluted water and, possibly, become quite ill. Find a website that offers information about the world's water crisis, such as the Ryan's Well Foundation website (above) or WaterAid (www.wateraid.org). We like a site hosted by BBC News because it provides a map of the worldwide water shortage: http://news.bbc.co.uk/hi/english/static/in_depth/world/2000/

world_water_crisis/. Some African nations, such as Nigeria and Uganda, face severe water shortages, as do other places in the world, such as Turkey, China, and Mexico.

Focus Activity: Propose four or five statements for children's consideration. Ask them to predict whether they are true or false. Here are some possibilities.

1 It is a luxury to have clean drinking water.
2 In many places, including Africa, water is smelly, brown, and makes you sick.
3 Children can spend their days walking miles to get water and then back home.
4 A second grader can help solve the world's water shortage.
5 It takes a lot of people working together to make a difference.

Reading: Read Parts One and Two of *Ryan and Jimmy*.

After Reading: Return to the Focus Activity, revise predictions, and discuss points.

Go Further: Invite children to participate in a service learning project to build a well and learn about the world's water crisis.

Teach for Ideas: What is the water crisis?

Hook: Show photos of drought and polluted rivers. Display a globe. Tell children that although two thirds of the world is covered with water, most of it is too salty to drink. Go to the website www.census.gov, which shows the world's population—up to the minute. Explain that the world's population is growing, but the availability of fresh water is not.

Example #1: Continue to read *Ryan and Jimmy*; Part Three.

Example #2: Display a map of Africa. Show the major rivers that water depends on: the Nile, Zambezi, and Niger. Explain that when water levels drop, whole nations suffer.

Example #3: Explain climate, seasons, and rainfall in Africa. There are basically two seasons in Africa: wet and dry. Some places in West Africa, on the edge of the Sahara, such as Mali, get very little rainfall all year, whereas others in East Africa, such as Kenya, get a lot of rain, but only during the rainy season. Very few African nations get rain all year, as we do in the U.S. Make and discuss a chart of rainfall. Or show a climatic map of Africa. We like to use the Map Machine website listed in Chapter 9 as a resource for "thematic maps": those that show things such as climate, natural resources, and population. See Map Machine at http://plasma.nationalgeographic.com/mapmachine.

Example #4: Make and display a chart of national statistics related to health. These statistics are available from the Human Development Report (HDR) of the United Nations: www.hdr.undp.org/en/reports/global/. According to the HDR for 2006, 60% of the population of Uganda has access to clean water and 43% has adequate sanitation coverage. The infant mortality rate is 140/1000, or 14 of every 100 children.

Non-Example: Compare Jimmy's life in Uganda to your children's life in the United States. Note differences such as having plenty of water for drinking, bathing, and even swimming.

Teach for Inquiry: What can children do to reduce water shortage?

Hook: Display and discuss the Ryan's Well Foundation website: www.ryanswell.ca. Note especially the number of wells Ryan's foundation has built: as of this writing, almost 400 wells in 15 countries! Ask the EQ: What can we (children) do to reduce the water shortage?

Hypotheses: Ask children to imagine what they can do to help people get fresh water. List.

Clue #1: Read Part Four of *Ryan and Jimmy*.

Clue #2: Play the "Motivate Video" on the Ryan's Well Foundation website. This five-minute video invites youth to act and shows ways to make a difference.

Clue #3: Study the "education" link on the Ryan's Well Foundation website. You will find ongoing projects that are in need of help.

Clue #4: Study the "ripple effect" link on the Ryan's Well Foundation website. Look especially at all the ways schools have made a difference. Make a list of possibilities, such as a Walk-for-Water, Used Toy Sale, or Wave-of-Hope Campaign.

Revise Hypotheses: Reconsider the EQ. What do children think now?

Conclusions: Answer the EQ in children's own words.

Think It Through

It's your turn! *Teach for Deliberation.* Select three or four ways to support Ryan's Well Foundation. Draw from the Ryan's Well Foundation website. Provide information to small groups of students, pointing out pros and cons of each choice. Hold a class discussion. (Look back at Chapter 4 for points on holding a discussion.) Always hold out the possibility that some youth might choose NOT to participate. This conundrum calls for another decision! Should the whole class offer service to this cause, or only those most interested?

Take Action: Serving to Learn

Remember, no two service projects are alike, but quality efforts attend to "north star" guiding principles. Now is the time to review "Service Learning: What and Why?" Make a "short list" of imperatives. Here is our "short list"; how does it compare to yours?

- Learn from service. Continue to learn and consider the world's water crisis throughout this effort. Study root causes to determine wise actions.
- Work *with* people *as partners*. Ryan's well Foundation (and other non-profit organizations, such as Heifer International) assists you, as teacher, with this step, at least for causes with worldwide impact. However, it's up to you to create friendly relationships and build equal partnerships with people close to home.
- Teach civic dispositions and skills. Write letters, give speeches, develop budgets, and make decisions! Try podcasting, described below, as an innovative way to broadcast the actions of your class.
- Talk about tough issues. Discuss inequality or unfairness. Why do some people live in poverty? Lack water? Struggle with disease? How can we, as citizens in a wealthy nation, help our neighbors, close to home and a world away?

Podcasting Democracy

Podcasting is like radio for kids by kids. It is an innovative way to publicize information, such as alerting schoolmates to service learning projects and inviting their participation. Students, basically, create audio broadcasts, reporting on their learning and sharing their ideas in a public space. In the place of more conventional announcements, students publish their reports (to a potentially worldwide audience) online via the internet. With little more than a computer and freely available software, even elementary students can create audio content, complete with sound effects!

Podcasting emerged in 2004 as a means of cataloging and downloading audio and video programs. A podcast has a news feed that allows it to be cataloged in directories such as iTunes. Audio podcasts are the most common, but podcasts can be enhanced with images as well. As of this writing, podcasting is more of an individual initiative than a groundswell, but, given the prevalence of digital communications, it is likely to gain popularity quickly.

Podcasting can be a vital tool for activism. The very act of publication can be considered a public, civic activity. Moreover, students can educate others about issues, advance causes, announce events, and/or invite civic participation. On *Radio Willow Web* (www.mpsomaha.org/willow/radio/index.html), the voice of Willowdale Elementary School in Omaha, Nebraska, students, school-wide, are invited to address issues that concern them. Here is the call for participation:

Is there something in this world that is bothering you?

Do you have a solution to a problem?

Is there something you would do differently?

Tell Radio Willow Web listeners what you think!

Here are some sample topics:

Cell phones in school

School lunch

Number of school days

Amount of recess

Amount of homework

Illustration 10.9 Do It Differently. Source: Radio Willow Web.

We can only imagine the lively interchange such requests engendered! Additionally, *100% Kids* (www.bazmakaz.com/100kids/), a podcast series from a second-grade classroom, tackles all kinds of vital issues, such as global warming, animal welfare, and environmental protection—in both English and Spanish!

In our college classes, we experimented with podcasting as a form of information for service learning. Pre-service teachers became podcasters, undertaking roles and tasks just as their future students might do. As part of their Seven Steps to Citizen Action, they chose an issue, investigated it, created and recorded a podcast about it, and then took action, raising funds for their cause. Through the use of simple, free recording software (http://audacity.sourceforge.net), pre-service teachers recorded their messages, and then uploaded them to space on our university's website. All of us were pleasantly surprised by the feedback from other members of our school community. People heard our podcast, attended our events, and donated to our causes! Podcasting is, essentially, a public forum for service learning. Contrary to community service, which puts the emphasis on service, podcasting allows teachers and students alike to put the emphasis on learning.

Teacher Review

So, how can students "live their civics"? Let us count the ways . . . Civic action and service learning are two major forms of citizen engagement. As you look back, can you answer the following questions?

- What are the differences between community service and service learning?
- What types of service can my students do?
- What kind of citizenship aligns with what kind of service?
- Who is empowered by service and why does it matter?
- What, if anything, is the difference between taking action and service learning?
- What is the difference between taking action, abstaining, and apathy?

Next, try to make a checklist for a quality service learning project. What would you add to a customary effort to make it a justice-oriented endeavor? Review our lists. What did your list include or exclude that ours did not?

Why do these questions and exercises matter? Remember, there is no blueprint for service learning. There is, instead, a set of fundamental ideas and valuable guidelines. It is in your power to make of service this or that, and its quality and learning vitality hang in the balance. As we have asked throughout this book, what will you, as teacher, do?

Making Connections

You can help your students *serve to learn* and *learn to serve*. Children can serve to learn about a history of local injustice, investigating and publicizing a case of discrimination. They can *serve to learn* about biographies of local citizens, writing life stories of older relatives or friends. They can serve to learn to raise funds, financing their plans for civic action. Additionally, they can *learn to serve*, developing an ethic of service, becoming more humane, tolerant, compassionate, and activist in the process. If you think about it, you can create service projects that buttress all of the civic engagements highlighted in this book. In fact, serving to learn is, arguably, a central form of civic engagement in and of itself.

APPENDIX A
Lesson Plan Formats

Focus In

Name of Lesson: Grade Level:

State or National Social Studies Standard(s):
- State the standard(s) that the lesson supports.
- Describe briefly how this lesson supports the standard.

Objectives:
- The students will demonstrate their knowledge/understanding of . . .
- The students will be able to . . .

Materials Needed:
- What materials/supplies, books, artifacts, and computer equipment are needed for the lesson?
- List titles and authors of all books.

Engage Student Interest:
- How will you motivate the students?
- Describe your "hook."

Focus Activity:
- Identify central ideas that you want to emphasize in the passage that students will read.

- Choose facts or ideas that will likely be new for students.
- Write the ideas to fit a true/false or agree/disagree response.
- Include a "before the reading" and an "after the reading" column for responses.

"Get Ready for Reading"
- Older students (grades 4 thru 6):
  - Tell students that you would like to find out what they already know about a topic.
  - Give students Focus Activity as a handout.
  - Have students decide whether statements are true or false. Discuss their reasoning.

- Younger students (grades K thru 3):
  - Read Focus Activity aloud to the students.
  - Have students decide whether the statements are true or false. Discuss their reasoning.

Read the social studies text or trade book.
- Older students—select pages for reading from textbook or trade book.
- Younger students—select pages to be read aloud to students.

After reading/assessment:
- Revisit statements and change to true or false as needed.
- Ask students what new information they gained from their reading.

Teach for Ideas

Name of Lesson: Grade Level:

State or National Social Studies Standard(s):
- What state social studies standard(s) does this lesson support?
- How does this lesson support the state standard?

Objectives:
- What will the students learn?
- What will the students be able to do?

Materials Needed:
- What materials/supplies, books, artifacts, computer equipment are needed for the lesson?
- List titles and authors of all books.

Engage Student Interest:
- How will you motivate the students?
- What is your "hook"?

Concept Formation:
- What is your Essential Question? (In this case, it should be a question of meaning.)
- What examples (at least two) of the concept (idea) will you present?
- What new example (or non-example) of the idea will you present?
- How will you help students compare and contrast examples?
- How will you apply students' understanding of the idea?

*Consider how you will present examples to emergent readers/conventional readers. For example, emergent readers can study photographs, whereas conventional readers can read descriptions.

Assessment:
- How will you test students' understanding of the idea?
- Create a graphic organizer (such as a Connecting Web or Conceptual Map) to document students' knowledge.

Teach for Inquiry

Name of Lesson: Grade Level:

State or National Social Studies Standard(s):
- What state social studies standard(s) does this lesson support?
- How does this lesson support the state standard?

Objectives:
- What will the students learn?
- What will the students be able to do?

Materials Needed:
- What materials/supplies, books, artifacts, computer equipment are needed for the lesson?
- List titles and authors of all books.
- Provide "data sets"*—a collection of information for students' research.

*You must have data sets ready for students. Copy passages, mark textbooks, locate children's literature as needed.

Engage Student Interest:
- How will you motivate the students?
- What is your "hook"?

Teach Inquiry Process:
- Raise essential question. (What happened—or why?)
- Elicit hypotheses (good guesses or predictions).
- List possibilities on board.
- Ask students to jot down hypotheses they think might be true (on a 3" × 5" card).
- Examine evidence. Give students information, one clue at a time. (Use data sets.)
- Consider information. Between each clue, ask students to revise hypotheses on the board.
- Ask students to return to their own hypotheses. Revise as needed.
- Share conclusions. Ask students to read their conclusions to class.

Assessment:
- Recall steps of inquiry.
- Ask students what new information might cause them to change their conclusions.

Teach through Drama

Name of Lesson: Grade Level:

State or National Social Studies Standard(s):
- Identify the state standard(s) that the unit supports.
- How does this lesson support the state standard?

Objectives:
- What will the students learn?
- What will the students be able to do?

Materials Needed:
- What materials(s)upplies, costumes, or set-ups are needed for the lesson?
- List all materials (costumes can be as simple as role cards worn around the neck).

Engage Student Interest:
- How will you motivate the students?
- What is your "hook" for the dramatization?

Roles:
- What roles are pertinent to the topic?
- How will you prepare students for their roles?

Role Play:
- Keep it simple, extemporaneous, and unrehearsed.
- Do the play several times so all students can participate.
- Set the scene. Discuss possible actions, feelings, and dialogue.
- Invite students to play out their roles.

- Stop and "freeze frame" in the midst of the play. Ask students to share how their character is feeling right now.
- Switch roles and do the play again. Freeze frame several times.

Assessment:
- Discuss the actions and feelings of the characters. Consider why they acted as they did.
- Ask students to share what they learned from participation in the role play. How will the students choose the format for their writing?

Write to Learn

Name of Lesson: Grade Level:

State or National Social Studies Standard(s):
- Identify the state standard(s) that the unit supports.
- How does this lesson support the state standard?

Objectives:
- What will the students learn?
- What will the students be able to do?

Materials Needed:
- What materials/supplies, books, artifacts, computer equipment are needed for the lesson?
- List titles and authors of all books.

Engage Student Interest:
- How will you motivate the students?
- What is your "hook" for your topic of study?

Review:
- Writing to Learn reviews prior learning.
- How will you recall the facts, ideas, and questions from previous lessons?

RAFT
- **R: Role of the writer**
  How will students select their role?
- **A: Audience**
  How will students choose their audience?
- **F: Format of the writing**
  How will the students choose the format for their writing?
- **T: Topic**
  How will the teacher introduce the topic?

Assessment:

- How will the students share their writing?
- What criteria will be used to assess their writing?

Teach for Deliberation

Name of Lesson: Grade Level:

State or National Social Studies Standard(s):

- Identify the state standard(s) that the unit supports.
- How does this lesson support the state standard?

Objectives:

- What will the students learn?
- What will the students be able to do?

Materials Needed:

- What materials/supplies, information sets, and computer equipment are needed for the lesson?
- List all readings*, books, and photos.

*You should have yes and no (pro and con) readings ready for students. Create two folders: Yes Readings and No Readings. Create one more folder: Additional Readings (these readings offer all students additional information).

You should develop readings that are appropriate to students' reading levels.

Engage Student Interest:

- How will you motivate the students?
- What is your "hook" for the discussion?

Discussion Web:

- Raise an Essential Question (EQ) about a topic that is controversial and interesting to children.
- Write the EQ on the board. On either side write *Yes* or *No*. Above the question write *Reasons*; below it, write *Conclusions*.
- Ask students to silently answer the question and to think of a reason for their answer.
- Ask students to share their thinking. Write students' names and their reasons on the board under the appropriate *Yes* or *No* columns.
- Ask students to read the *Yes* or *No* readings in small groups, according to their initial responses.

- Switch readings, so that all students read both sides.
- Mix student groups, including *Yes* and *No* views in the same group. Ask students to share their views and reasons for holding them. Ask students to try to find a mutually agreeable solution to the problem.
- Share as a class.
- Add conclusions to the web on the board. Ask students if anyone changed his/her mind, and, if so, why? If not, why not?

Appendix B

Illustration A.1 Guggenheimer & Weil Building in the Baltimore Fire of 1904. Library of Congress: LC-US262-45624.

Illustration A.2 1904 Fire East from Charles and Lexington. The Maryland Historical Society.

Illustration A.3 US Army Infantry Troops: African American Unit, marching northwest of Verdun, France, in WWI. Library of Congress: LC-US262-116442.

Illustration A.4 Recruitment of African American Soldiers: WWI. National Archives: 165-WW-127 (121).

Illustration A.5 Colonel Charles Young. Library of Congress: LC-US262-62353.

Illustration A.6 True Sons of Freedom: Created by Chas. Gustrine, 1918. Library of Congress.

Illustration A.7 Chief Justice John G. Roberts, Jr. Supreme Court Historical Society.

Illustration A.8 Interview with Chief Justice John Roberts.

The Interview: Chief Justice John G. Roberts, Jr.

From: Scholastic News, Online Edition, September 14, 2006. Copyright © 2006 by Scholastic Inc. Reprinted by permission.

Scholastic News: Why was the Constitution considered such a remarkable revolutionary document when it was written more than 200 years ago? Was there anything like it before in human history?

Chief Justice John G. Roberts, Jr.: The people who wrote our Constitution recognized that those who governed countries—typically kings and queens, up to that time—often abused their power, so that the people suffered. The drafters of our Constitution had themselves been the victims of such abuse of power by King George III. So they took the revolutionary step in the Constitution of dividing power among the different branches of government—legislative, executive, and judicial—so that no one would have unchecked power that they might abuse. Ideas along these lines had been talked about before, but our Constitution was the first to put them into practice by setting out written rules establishing a new government.

SN: What about the Constitution gives it the longevity to remain relevant after 219 years?

Chief Justice Roberts: Our Constitution, adopted almost 220 years ago, on September 17, 1787, is the oldest written constitution of any nation in the world. It is not very long—seven short sections, called "Articles," plus 27 Amendments—but it lays out the structure, powers, and limitations of our government. One of the reasons it has remained relevant for such a long time is that it can be changed, or amended. For instance, under the original Constitution, slavery was allowed in the United States. After the Civil War, in December 1865, the 13th Amendment was ratified, making slavery illegal everywhere in the United States. Another example is that when our Constitution was adopted, women were not allowed to vote. It was not until 1920, when the 19th Amendment was ratified, that all states were required to allow women to vote.

SN: How does the Constitution work in the lives of ordinary Americans today?

Chief Justice Roberts: By ensuring that no one in government has too much power, the Constitution helps protect ordinary Americans every day against abuse of power by those in authority. The Constitution gives those who serve in public office the authority they need to govern effectively, to protect Americans from the threats we face in the world today, and to promote policies to make our lives better. At the same time, the Constitution limits the power of public officials and safeguards the rights of Americans, to secure the blessings of liberty for us all.

SN: How does the Constitution affect the lives of kids?

Chief Justice Roberts: There is no better gift a society can give children than the opportunity to grow up safe and free—the chance to pursue whatever dreams they may have. Our Constitution guarantees that freedom.

SN: Why do you think it's important for children to learn about the Constitution? What is the most important thing kids should know about the Constitution?

Chief Justice Roberts: A document written long before the invention of the automobile, the airplane, the computer, and the Internet may seem so old that students might think that they today don't need to know about it. But our Constitution will only work if people learn about it and actively participate in our democratic form of government. You can't fight for your rights if you don't know what they are. And you can't participate in our democracy if you don't know how it works. I think the most important thing children should know about our Constitution is that it applies to them, just like school rules apply to them. If children do not understand the Constitution, they cannot understand how our government functions, or what their rights and responsibilities are as citizens of the United States.

SN: At what age did you first become interested in and realize the importance of the Constitution? What was that experience like?

Chief Justice Roberts: In grade school I learned about how our government was organized—how we had local, state, and federal government offices; how the Constitution divided power among the different branches so that the President, Congress, and the courts shared authority; and how the Constitution protected the liberty of every individual. Learning about that helped me understand what it was we celebrated every year on the

Fourth of July—the freedom we as Americans enjoy and have defended over the years.

SN: As an interpreter of the Constitution, where do you go for guidance and information on the document?

Chief Justice Roberts: I have a copy of the Constitution on my desk and the first thing I do when I have a case involving the Constitution is read what it says. I also have a copy of the *Federalist Papers*—a series of essays by the Founding Fathers that helps explain what the Constitution means. For over two hundred years, the Supreme Court has been interpreting the Constitution by writing papers, called "opinions," in individual cases. Those opinions say what the Court has decided and explain what particular parts of the Constitution mean. Every one of the Court's opinions is published in a book. All of those books of opinions together take up almost 100 hundred [sic] feet of space. I will go and find previous opinions of the Court that have interpreted the part of the Constitution at issue in a particular case, and I will read those opinions.

SN: Briefly describe how your role as Chief Justice differs from that of an Associate Justice.

Chief Justice Roberts: As Chief Justice I have one vote, just like every Associate Justice. So I really do not have much greater authority than anyone else on the Court. One thing I do get to do is decide who should write the opinion of the Court, explaining why we decided a case the way we did. I get to do that whenever my vote is with a majority of the Justices. I also have the responsibility to make sure the Court runs smooth—that we get the decisions out on time.

About the Authors

Marilynne (Lynne) Boyle-Baise is a Professor in the Department of Curriculum and Instruction at Indiana University, Bloomington (IUB), and a John Glenn Scholar in Service Learning. She teaches Curriculum Studies and Social Studies, with a special focus on elementary social studies. She has published widely on social studies, service learning, and multicultural teacher education. Her first book, *Multicultural Service Learning: Educating Teachers in Diverse Communities*, won the Critics' Choice Award from the American Educational Studies Association in 2003. She won the Martin Luther King Jr. Legacy Award for the Banneker History Project in 2005, and the Trustee's Teaching Award for outstanding teaching in 2006.

Dr. Boyle-Baise has served on the Board of Directors for the National Council for the Social Studies (NCSS), as well as on Editorial Boards for *Theory and Research in Social Education* and the *International Social Studies Forum*. She is a Consulting Editor for *The Social Studies*. She is past-chair of the College and University Faculty Assembly (CUFA) for the NCSS. She has served as a Faculty Fellow in Service Learning for IUB.

Lynne lives in Bloomington, Indiana, with her husband, Michael, and their Portuguese Water Dogs: CH DoMarco's Boston Tea Party (aka Tea) and MBISS CH DoMarco's My Cuppa Tea (aka Lipton). When she leaves the computer behind, Lynne enjoys talking with her husband, playing with her dogs, and showing dogs with her sister, Brytt, especially when Lipton wins!

Jack Zevin is a Professor in the Department of Middle and Secondary Education at Queens College/City University of New York, a senior advisor, and a former chairperson.

He also directs a Resource and Training Center for Economic Education at the college and co-directs a civic education program under the auspices of a small foundation, The Taft Institute for Government. Obsessed with inquiry teaching and thought-provoking curriculum, Jack has taught methods for many a year, publishing several books on instruction, including *Creative Encounters in the Classroom, Teaching Creatively* (both with B. G. Massialas), and his own methods book, *Social Studies for the 21st Century*, now in its third edition. He won the Presidential Teaching Award at Queens College in 1996, as well as other awards for instruction and service.

Jack has ranged widely across fields and levels, working on a number of elementary, middle school, and secondary topics, for example "The Treatment of War and Conflict in Young Adult Literature" in the 1993 NCSS publication *Children's Literature and Social Studies,* and served for many years on the Children's Book Council. He and his children have a great love of children's books, and he now has the opportunity to relive these readings with his grandson. He has also done a great deal of curriculum work, on political science, geography, anthropology, and economics, as well as history, from the early years of the New Social Studies movement to recent days, and is currently working on a curriculum for teaching 9/11, with Professor Michael Krasner (Political Science) for the World Trade Center United Family Group.

Dr. Zevin has served in the leadership group of CUFA (the College and University Faculty) within NCSS, and has also served on many committees and conducted many clinics over the years, his current favorite being "Teaching History as Mystery." He is also a consulting editor for *The Social Studies*, and has been for *The Record* (NYS Council for the Social Studies) and the local ATSS/UFT bulletin. In general, Jack is very active in social studies and history associations, including NCSS, NCEE, AHA, and OAH. He is also very active in developing, implementing, and promoting in-service teacher training through grants supported over the years by the NSF, NEH, US Office of Education, and other agencies and organizations, and is currently directing a Teaching American History program in New York City, working with regions 3 and 4 to promote the improvement of instruction in this area.

Jack lives in Queens, New York, an outer borough of the city, with his wife, Iris, also an active social studies teacher, and his son Alex, who is technically at home while studying in Paris and will soon embark on a history Ph.D. program. In a house filled to the brim with books, articles, papers and other scraps, as well as lots of crumpled lesson plans, escape consists of taking advantage of the wonderful cultural resources of New York, in the form of music, film, art, literature, and further education. No dogs, sorry, but does an interest in bird-watching, nature, and travel into the wilderness qualify?

References

Scholarly Works and Reports

Adler, S. (2001). The NCSS Standards: A response to Anna Ochoa-Becker. *Social Education, 65* (5), 315–318.

Akujobi, C., & Simmons, R. (1997). An assessment of elementary school service learning teaching methods. *NSEE Quarterly, 23* (2), 19–28.

American Historical Association (AHA) (1899). *The study of history in the schools* (Report of the AHA Committee of Seven). New York: Macmillan.

—— (1909). *The study of history in the elementary schools* (Report of the AHA Committee of Eight). New York: Charles Scribner's Sons.

Ammon, M. (2002). Probing and promoting teachers' thinking about service-learning: Toward a theory of teacher development. In S. Billig & A. Furco (Eds.), *Service-learning through a multi-disciplinary lens* (pp. 33–54). Greenwich, CT: Information Age Publishing.

Anderson, F. L. (1979). *Schooling for citizenship in a global age: An exploration of the meaning and significance of global education.* Bloomington, IN: Social Studies Development Center.

Angell, A. (1998). Practicing democracy at school: A qualitative analysis of an elementary class council. *Theory and Research in Social Education, 26* (2), 149–172.

—— (2004). Making peace in elementary classrooms: A case for class meetings. *Theory and Research in Social Education, 32* (1), 98–104.

ASLER. (1993). *Standards of Quality for School-based Service Learning.* Chester, VT: Author.

Baker, T., & White, S. (2003). The effects of GIS on students' attitudes, self-efficacy, and achievement in middle school science classrooms. *Journal of Geography, 102* (6), 243–254.

Banks, J. A. (1997). *Educating citizens in a multicultural society.* New York: Teachers College Press.

Banks, J. A. (with Clegg, A. A.). (1990). *Teaching strategies for the social studies: Inquiry, valuing, and decision making* (4th ed.). New York: Longman.

Barber, B. (1984). *Strong democracy.* Berkeley, CA: University of California Press.

Barton, K. (1994). *Historical understanding among elementary children.* Unpublished doctoral dissertation, University of Kentucky.

—— (1997a). "Bossed around by the Queen": Elementary students' understanding of individuals and institutions in history. *Journal of Curriculum and Supervision, 12* (Summer), 290–314.

—— (1997b). "I just kinda know": Elementary students' ideas about historical evidence. *Theory and Research in Social Education, 25* (4), 407–430.

Barton, K., & Levstik, L. (1996). "Back when God was around and everything": Elementary children's understanding of historical time. *American Educational Research Journal, 33* (2), 419–454.

Battistich, V., Watson, M., Solomon, D., Schaps, E., & Solomon, J. (1991). The child development project: Program for the development of prosocial character. In W. Kurtines & J. Gewirtz (Eds.), *Handbook of Moral Behavior and Development* (Vol. 3, pp. 1–35) Hillsdale, NJ: Lawrence Erlbaum.

Battistoni, R. (2000). Service learning and civic education. In S. Mann & J. Patrick (Eds.), *Education for civic engagement in democracy* (pp. 29–44). Bloomington, IN: ERIC Clearinghouse for Social Studies/Social Science Education.

Beck, T. (2003). "If he murdered someone, he shouldn't get a lawyer": Engaging young children in civics deliberation. *Theory and Research in Social Education, 31* (3), 326–346.

—— (2005). Tools of deliberation: Exploring the complexity of learning to lead elementary civics discussions. *Theory and Research in Social Education, 33* (1), 103–119.

Bednarz, S., Bettis, N., Boehm, R., deSouza, A., Downs, R., Marran, J., Morrill, R., Salter, C. (1994). *Geography for life: National Geography Standards.* Washington, DC: National Geographic Research & Exploration.

Bellah, R., Madsen, R., Sullivan, W., Swidler, A., & Tipton, S. (1985). *Habits of the heart: Individualism and commitment in American life.* New York: Harper & Row.

Berman, S. (1997). *Children's social consciousness and the development of social responsibility.* New York: SUNY.

Berti, A., & Andriolo, A. (2001). Third graders' understandings of core political concepts (law, nation-state, government) before and after teaching. *Genetic, social, and general psychology monographs, 127* (4), 346–377.

Bigelow, B., & Peterson, B. (1998). *Rethinking Columbus: The next 500 years.* Milwaukee, WI: Rethinking Schools.

Billig, S. (2000, May). Research on K–12 school-based service-learning: The evidence builds. *Phi Delta Kappan, 89* (9), 658–664.

—— (2004). *Heads, hearts, and hands: The research on K–12 service-learning.* National Youth Leadership Council. Retrieved from www.nylc.org

Billig, S., & Salazar, T. (2003). *Earth Walk environmental service-learning program interim evaluation.* Denver, CO: RMC Research Evaluation.

Bluestein, N., & Acredolo, L. (1979). Developmental changes in map-reading skills. *Child Development, 50* (3), 691–697.

Bohan, C. H. (2004). Early vanguards of Progressive Education: The Committee of Ten, The Committee of Seven, and social education. In C. Woyshner, J. Watras, & M. Smith Crocco (Eds.), *Social education in the twentieth century* (pp. 1–19). New York: Peter Lang.

Boulding, K. (1988). *Building a global civic culture: Education for an interdependent world.* New York: Teachers College Press.

Boyle-Baise, M. (1999, Summer). "As good as it gets?" The impact of philosophical orientations on community-based service learning for multicultural education. *The Educational Forum, 63,* 310–320.

—— (2002). *Multicultural service learning: Educating teachers in diverse communities.* New York: Teachers College.

—— (2003). Doing democracy in social studies methods. *Theory and Research in Social Education, 31* (1), 50–70.

—— (2007). Learning service: Reading service as text. *Reflections: Writing, service-learning, and community literacy, 6* (1), 67–85.

Boyle-Baise, M., Hsu, M., Johnson, S., Serriere, S., & Stewart, D. (2008, March). *Putting reading first: Teaching social studies in elementary classrooms. Theory & Research in Social Education,* 36(3), 233–255.

Boyte, H. (2004). *Every day politics: Reconnecting citizens and public life.* Philadelphia: University of Pennsylvania Press.

Brophy, J. & Alleman, J., (2005). *Children's thinking about cultural universals.* Mahwah, NJ: Erlbaum Publishers.

Brophy, J., VanSledright, B., & Bredin, N. (1992). Fifth graders' ideas about history expressed before and after their introduction to the subject. *Theory and Research in Social Education, 20* (4), 440–489.

Burroughs, S., Groce, E., & Webeck, M. L. (2005). Social studies in the age of testing and account-ability. *Educational Measurement: Issues and Practice, 24* (3), 13–20.

Butin, D. (2003). "Of what use is it? Multiple conceptualizations of service learning within educa-tion, *Teachers College Record 105,* 1674–1692.

Campbell, S. (2008, March). *A critical view of history: Fifth grade students' process of construct-ing a critical historical perspective.* Paper presented at the annual meeting of the American Educational Research Association, New York, NY.

Carbone, P. (1977). *The social and educational thought of Harold Rugg.* Durham, NC: Duke University Press.

Case, R. (1993). Key elements of global perspective. *Social Education, 57,* 318–325.

Center for Civic Education. (1988). *We the people.* Calabasas, CA: Author.

Center on Education Policy. (2008, February). *Instructional time in elementary schools: A closer look at changes for specific subjects.* Retrieved from www.cep-dc.org

Character Counts (2007). *The six pillars of character.* Retrieved December 21, 2007, from www.charactercounts.org

Connell, R. (1971). *The child's construction of politics.* Melbourne, Vic.: Melbourne University Press.

Consumers Union. (2005). *Captive kids: A report on commercial pressures on kids at schools.* Retrieved from www.consumersunion.org/other/sellingkids/summary.htm

Correia, S. T. (1994). Thomas Jesse Jones—Doing God's work and the 1916 Report. In M. R. Nelson (Ed.), *The social studies in secondary education: A reprint of the seminal 1916 Report with annotations and commentaries* (pp. 93–119). Bloomington, IN: ERIC Clearinghouse for Social Studies/Social Science Education.

Daly, R. (2003). *"No geographer left behind": A policy guide to geography education and the No Child Left Behind Act of 2001.* College Station, TX: Geography Education National Implementation Project.

Deans, T. (1999). Service-learning in two keys: Paulo Freire's critical pedagogy in relation to John Dewey's pragmatism. *Michigan Journal of Community Service Learning 6,* 15–29.

Dewey, J. (1916/1944). *Democracy and education.* New York: Macmillan.

Dewey, J., & Dennett, T. (1935). Education and our society: A debate. *Forum, 93* (6), 334–345.

Dilworth, P. P. (2003–4). Competing conceptions of citizenship education: Thomas Jesse Jones and Carter G. Woodson. *International Journal of Social Education, 18* (2), 1–15.

Downey, M. (1994, April). *After the dinosaurs: Elementary children's chronological thinking.* Paper presented at the annual meeting of the American Educational Research Association, New Orleans, LA.

DuBois ,W. E. B. (1918, September). *The Crisis.*

Dunn, A. W. (1915). *Civic education in elementary schools as illustrated in Indianapolis* (U.S. Bureau of Education, Bulletin No. 17). Washington, DC: Government Printing Office.

—— (1916). *The social studies in secondary education: Report of the committee on social studies of the Commission on the Reorganization of Secondary Education.* Washington, DC: National Education Association.

Engle, S. (1994). Introduction. In M. R. Nelson (Ed.), *The social studies in secondary education: A reprint of the seminal 1916 Report with annotations and commentaries* (pp. 93–119). Bloomington, IN: ERIC Clearinghouse for Social Studies/Social Science Education.

Engle, S., & Ochoa, A. (1988). *Education for democratic citizenship: Decision making in the social studies.* New York: Teachers College.

Evans, R. (2004). *The social studies wars: What should we teach the children?* New York: Teachers College Press.

Finn, C. (2003). Foreword. In J. Leming, L. Ellington & K. Porter (Eds.), *Where did social studies go wrong?* (pp. i–vii). Washington, DC: Thomas B. Fordham Foundation.

Gent, P. (2007). Strange bedfellows: No Child Left Behind and service-learning. *Michigan Journal of Community Service Learning, 13* (2), 65–74.

Gerwin, D., & Zevin, J. (2003). *Teaching US history as mystery.* Portsmouth, NJ: Heinemann.

Giannangelo, D., & Frazee, B. (1977). Map reading proficiency of elementary educators. *Journal of Geography, 76* (2), 63–65.

Gould, P. & White, R. (1986). *Mental maps* (2nd ed). Boston: Allyn & Bacon.

Green, F., & Clark, W. (1983). *Research report on elementary and secondary teachers' competencies in map and globe skills* (Tech. Rep. No. 143). Orlando: University of Central Florida.

Gregg, M. & Leinhardt, G. (1994). Mapping out geography: An example of epistemology and education. *Review of Educational Research, 64* (2), 311–361.

Gregg, M., & Sekeres, D. (2006). My word! Vocabulary and geography learning. *Journal of Geography, 105* (2), 53–58.

Hallden, O. (1998). On reasoning in history. In J. Foss & M. Carretero (Eds.), *International review of history education: Learning and reasoning in history* (Vol. 2, pp. 272–278). London: Woburn Press.

Hanvey, R. G. (1976). *An attainable global perspective.* Denver, CO: The Center for Teaching International Relations, The University of Denver.

Hart, R. (1981). Children's spatial representation of the landscape. In A. H. Patterson & N. Newcombe (Eds.), *Spatial representation and behavior across the life-span: Theory and application.* New York: Academic Press.

Henry, S. (2005). "I can never turn my back on that:" Liminality and the impact of class on service-learning experience. In D. Butin (Ed.), *Service-learning in higher education* (pp. 45–66). New York: Palgrave Macmillan.

Herrenkohl, L. S., & Guerra, M. R. (1998). Participant structures, scientific discourse, and student engagement in fourth grade. *Cognition and Instruction, 16* (4), 431–473.

Hess, R., & Torney, J. (1967). *The development of political attitudes in children.* Chicago: Aldine.

Heyer, K. den (2003). Between every "now" and "then": A role for the study of historical agency in history and citizenship education. *Theory and Research in Social Education, 31* (4), 411–434.

Hinde, E., Popp, S., Dorn, R., Ekiss, G., Mater, M., Smith, C., & Libbee, M. (2007). The integration of literacy and geography: The Arizona GeoLiteracy Program's effect on reading comprehension. *Theory and Research in Social Education, 35* (3), 343–365.

Houser, N. (1995). Social Studies on the back burner: Views from the field. *Theory and Research in Social Education, 23* (2), 147–168.

—— (1999). Critical literature for the social studies. *Social Education, 63* (4), 212–215.

Howerth, I. (1897). A programme for social study. *American Journal of Sociology, 2* (6), 852–872.

Hunt, E., & Metcalf, L. (1955). *Teaching High School Social Studies: Problems in reflective thinking and social understanding.* New York: Harper & Row.

Johnson, A., & Notah, D. (1999). Service learning: History, literature review, and a pilot study of eighth graders. *The Elementary School Journal, 99* (5), 453–467.

Junkel, S., Strong, J., & Hannon, J. (2007). Learning U.S. geography with "The Great Mail Race." *Social Studies and the Young Learner, 20* (2), 19–23.

Kahne, J., & Westheimer, J. (1996). In the service of what? The politics of service learning. *Phi Delta Kappan, 77* (9), 592–599.

Keiper, T. (1999). GIS for elementary students: An inquiry into a new approach to learning geography. *Journal of Geography, 98* (2), 47–59.

Kielsmeier, J. (2000, May). A time to serve, a time to learn. *Phi Delta Kappan, 89* (9), 652–657.

Kirkwood, T. F. (2002). Teaching about Japan: Global perspectives in teacher decision-making, context, and practice. *Theory and Research in Social Education, 30* (1), 88–115.

Kliebard, H. (1986). *The struggle for the American curriculum 1893–1958.* Boston: Routledge, Kegan Paul.

—— (1994). "That evil genius of the negro race": Thomas Jesse Jones and educational reform. *Journal of Curriculum & Supervision 10* (Fall), 5–20.

Kniep, W. M. (1986). Defining a global education by its content. *Social Education, 50,* 437–466.

Kourilsky, M. (1987). Developing economic literacy. *Theory into Practice, 26* (3), 198–205.

Kretzmann, J., & McKnight, J. (1993). *Building communities from the inside out: A path toward finding and mobilizing a community's assets.* Chicago, IL: ACTA Publications.

Laney, J. (1989). Experience- and concept-label-type effects on first-graders' learning, retention of economic concepts. *Journal of Educational Research, 82,* 231–236.

Lee, P., & Ashby, R. (2000). Empathy, perspective taking, and rational understanding. In O. L. Davis, E. Yeager, & S. Foster (Eds.), *Historical empathy and perspective taking in the social studies.* New York: Rowman & Littlefield.

Leming, J. (2003). Ignorant activists: Social change, higher order thinking, and the failure of social studies. In J. Leming, L. Ellington, & K. Porter (Eds.), *Where did social studies go wrong?* (pp. 124–142). Washington, DC: Thomas B. Fordham Foundation.

Leming, J., Ellington, L., & Porter, K. (Eds.) (2003). *Where did social studies go wrong?* Washington, DC: Thomas B. Fordham Foundation.

Levstik, L. (1989). Historical narrative and the young reader. *Theory into Practice, 28* (2), 114–119.

Levstik, L., & Barton, K. (1996). "They still use some of their past": Historical salience in elementary children's chronological thinking. *Journal of Curriculum Studies, 28* (5), 531–576.

—— (2001). *Doing history: Investigating with children in elementary and middle schools* (2nd ed.). Mahwah: NJ: Erlbaum.

Levstik, L., & Pappas, C. (1987). Exploring the development of historical understanding. *Journal of Research and Development in Education, 21* (1), 1–15.

Makler, A. (2004). "Problems of democracy" and the social studies curriculum during the long armistice. In C. Woyshner, J. Watras, and M. Smith Crocco (Eds.), *Social education in the twentieth century* (pp. 20–41). New York: Peter Lang.

McKeown, M., & Beck, I. (1994). Making sense of accounts of history: Why young students don't and how they might. In G. Leinhardt, I. Beck, & C. Stainton (Eds.), *Teaching and learning in history* (pp. 1–26). Hillsdale, NJ: Erlbaum.

McNeal, J. (1999). *The kids market: Myths and realities.* Ithaca, NY: Paramount Publishing.

Merryfield, M. M. (1998). Pedagogy for global perspectives in education: Studies of teacher thinking and practice. *Theory and Research in Social Education, 26* (3), 342–379.

—— (2001). Moving the center of global education: From imperial world views that divide the world to double consciousness, contrapuntal pedagogy, hybridity and cross-cultural competence. In W. B. Stanely (Ed.) *Critical issues in social studies research for the 21st Century* (pp. 179–208). Greenwich, CN: Information Age.

Merryfield, M., Lo, J. T., Po, S. C., & Kasai, M. (2008, January). Worldmindedness: Taking off the blinders. *Journal of Curriculum and Instruction, 2* (1), 6–20.

Meyer, L., Sherman, L., & MaKinster, J. (2006). The effects of the Japan Bridge Project on third graders' cultural sensitivity. *Theory and Research in Social Education, 34* (3), 347–369.

Meyer, S., Billig, S., & Hofschire, L. (2004). The impact of K–12 school-based service learning on academic achievement and student engagement in Michigan. In M. Welch & S. Billig (Eds.), *New perspectives in service learning: Research to advance the field* (pp. 61–85). Greenwich, CT: Information Age Publishing.

Moore, S., Lare, J., & Wagner, K. (1985). *The child's political worlds: A longitudinal perspective.* New York: Praeger.

Morgan, J. (1991). Using Econ and Me to teach economics to children in primary grades. *The Social Studies, 82* (5), 195–197.

Morton, K. (1995). The irony of service: Charity, project and social change in service-learning. *Michigan Journal of Community Service Learning, 2,* 19–32.

National Assessment of Educational Progress. (2001). *The nation's report card: Geography 2001.* Retrieved from http://nces.ed.gov/nationsreportcard/pubs/main2001/

National Center for History in the Schools. (1996). *National standards for history: Basic edition.* Los Angeles: Author.

National Commission on Excellence in Education. (1983). *A nation at risk: The imperatives for educational reform.* Washington, DC: U.S. Department of Education.

National Council for the Social Studies (NCSS). (1989). In search of a scope and sequence for the social studies. *Social Education, 53* (6), 376–385.

—— (1992). *A vision of powerful teaching and learning in the social studies: Building social understanding and civic efficacy.* Washington, DC: Author.

—— (1994). *Expectations for excellence: Curriculum standards for social studies.* Washington, DC: Author.

National Council on Economic Education. (1997). *Voluntary national content standards in economics.* New York: Author.

National Education Association (NEA) (1893). *Report of the Committee of Ten on Secondary School Studies.* Washington, DC: Government Printing Office.

—— (1918). *Cardinal principles of secondary education* (Bureau of Education Bulletin, No. 35). Washington, DC: Government Printing Office.

National Geographic–Roper Public Affairs. (2006). *2006 Geographic Literacy Study.* Washington, DC: National Geographic Education Foundation.

National Service-Learning Cooperative. (1998). *Essential elements of service-learning.* St. Paul, MN: National Youth Leadership Council.

Nelson, M. (1977). The development of the Rugg social studies materials. *Theory and Research in Social Education, 5* (3), 64–83.

Nelson, M. R. (1994). The social contexts of the Committee on Social Studies Report of 1916. In M. R. Nelson (Ed.), *The social studies in secondary education: A reprint of the seminal 1916 Report with annotations and commentaries* (pp. 71–92). Bloomington, IN: ERIC Clearinghouse for Social Studies/Social Science Education.

No Child Left Behind Act of 2001. (2002). Public Law No. 107-110.

Ochoa-Becker, A. (2001). A critique of the NCSS curriculum standards. *Social Education, 65* (3), 165–168.

—— (2007). *Democratic education for social studies: An issues-centered decision making curriculum.* Greenwich, CT: Information Age Publishing.

Oliver, D., & Shaver, J. (1966/1996). Using a jurisprudential framework in the teaching of public issues. In W. Parker (Ed.), *Educating the democratic mind* (pp. 145–169). Albany: SUNY.

Paley, V. (1992). *You can't say you can't play.* Cambridge, MA: Harvard University Press.

Parker, A. (2006, Fall). Visiting and interviewing older adults: Service-learning in the sixth grade. *The Delta Kappa Gamma Bulletin,* 31–35.

Parker, W. (1996). *Educating the democratic mind.* Albany: SUNY.

—— (2003). *Teaching democracy: Unity and diversity in public life.* New York: Teachers College.

Piaget, J., & Inhelder, B., (1956). *The child's conception of space.* London: Routledge & Kegan Paul.

Piaget, J., Inhelder, B., & Szemiska, A.(1960). *The child's conception of geometry.* New York: Basic Books.

Pike, G. & Selby, D. (1995). *Reconnecting from national to global education.* Toronto, International Institute for Global Education, University of Toronto.

Ravitch, D., & Finn, C. E. (1987). *What do our 17-year-olds know?* New York: Harper & Row.

Robinson, T. (2000). Dare the school build a new social order? *Michigan Journal of Community Service Learning 7*, 142–157.

Rochester, J. M. (2003). The training of idiots: Civics education in America's schools. In J. Leming, L. Ellington, & K. Porter (Eds.), *Where did social studies go wrong?* (pp. 6–39). Washington, DC: Thomas B. Fordham Foundation.

Rock, T., Heafner, T., O'Connor, K., Passe, J., Oldendorf, S., Good, A., Byrd, S. (2006). One state closer to a national crisis: A report on elementary social studies education in North Carolina schools. *Theory and Research in Social Education, 34* (4), 455–483.

Rugg. H. O. (1926a). The school curriculum and the drama of American life. In H. Rugg & G. M. Whipple (Eds.), *The twenty-sixth yearbook of the National Society for the Study of Education: The foundations and technique of curriculum-construction, Part I* (pp. 3–16). Bloomington, IL: Public School Publishing Company.

—— (1926b). Curriculum-making: Points of emphasis. In H. Rugg & G. M. Whipple (Eds.), *The twenty-sixth yearbook of the National Society for the Study of Education: The foundations and technique of curriculum-construction, Part II* (pp. 147–162). Bloomington, IL: Public School Publishing Company.

—— (1931). *Culture and education in America.* New York: Harcourt, Brace & Co.

—— (1936). *American life and the school curriculum: Next steps toward schools of living.* Boston: Ginn.

Rugg, H. O., & Mendenhall, J. (1940). *Pupil's workbook of directed study: To accompany Citizenship and Civic Affairs.* Boston: Ginn and Company.

Saxe, D. W. (1991). *Social studies in schools: A history of the early years.* Albany: SUNY.

—— (1992). Framing a theory for social studies foundations. *Review of Educational Research, 62* (3), 259–277.

Scales, P., & Roehlkepartain, E. (2004). *Community service and service-learning in U.S. public schools: Findings from a national survey.* National Youth Leadership Council. Retrieved from www.nylc.org

Schine, J. (1997). School-based service: Reconnecting schools, communities, and youth at the margin. *Theory Into Practice, 36* (3), 170–175.

Schmidt, S. (2008, March). *Tools to negotiate place . . . rethinking what it means to do geography.* Paper presented at the annual meeting of the American Educational Research Association, New York, NY.

Schneider, D. (1976). The performance of elementary teachers and students on a test of map and globe skills. *Journal of Geography, 75* (6), 326–332.

Schor, J. (2004). *Born to buy: The commercialized child and the new consumer culture.* New York: Scribner.

Schug, M. (1993). How children learn economics. *The International Journal of Social Education,* *8* (3), 25–34.

Schug, M., & Hagedorn, E. (2005, March/April). The money savvy pig goes to the big city: Testing the effectiveness of an economics curriculum for young children. *The Social Studies,* 68–71.

Schug, M., & Lephardt, N. (1992, September/October). Development in children's thinking about international trade. *The Social Studies, 83,* 31–42.

Schug, M., & Walstad, W. (1991). Teaching and learning economics. In J. Shaver (Ed.), *Handbook of Research on Social Studies Teaching and Learning* (pp. 411–469). New York: Macmillan.

Schulten, S. (2001). *The geographical imagination in America, 1880–1950.* Chicago: University of Chicago Press.

Shearer, C. (2007). Geography education standards: An overview for teachers. *Social Studies and the Young Learner, 20* (2), 5.

Shin, E. (2007). Using geographic information system (GIS) technology to enhance elementary students' geographic understanding. *Theory and Research in Social Education, 35* (2), 231–255.

Shin, E., & Henning, M. B. (2007, November). *Studying children's thinking about geography concepts.* Paper presented at the annual meeting of the College and University Faculty Assembly of the National Council for the Social Studies, San Diego, CA.

Sosin, K., Dick, J., Reiser, M. L. (1997). Determinants of achievement of economics concepts by elementary students. *The Journal of Economic Education, 28* (2), 100–121.

Soslau, E., & Yost, D. (2007). Urban service-learning: An authentic teaching strategy to deliver a standards-driven curriculum. *Journal of Experiential Education, 30* (1), 36–53.

Spradley, J. P., & McCurdy, D. W. (2003). *Conformity and conflict: Readings in cultural anthropology* (11th ed.). Boston: Allyn & Bacon.

Stevens, O. (1982). *Children talking politics.* Oxford: Martin Robertson.

Stoltman, J. P. (1976). Children's conception of territory: The United States. In J. P. Stoltman (Ed.), *Spatial stages development in children and teacher classroom style in geography: International research in geographic education* (pp. 39–56). Kalamazoo: Western Michigan University Department of Geography.

Suiter, M., & Meszaros, B. (2005). Teaching about saving and investing in the elementary and middle school grades. *Social Education, 69* (2), 92–95.

Task Force on Standards for Teaching and Learning in the Social Studies, (1992). *A vision of powerful teaching and learning in the social studies: Building social understanding and civic efficacy.* Washington, DC: National Council for the Social Studies.

Tobin, K. (1990, April). *Metaphors in the construction of teacher knowledge.* Paper presented at the annual meeting of the American Educational Research Association, Boston, MA.

Tyson, C. (2002). "Get up offa that thing": African American middle-school students respond to literature to develop a framework for understanding social action. *Theory and Research in Social Education, 30* (1), 42–65.

VanFossen, P. (2003). Best practice *economic education* for young children? It's elementary! *Social Education, 67* (2), 90–95.

VanFossen, P. J. (2005). "Reading and math take so much time . . ." An overview of social studies instruction in elementary classrooms in Indiana. *Theory and Research in Social Education, 33* (3), 376–403.

VanSledright, B. (2002). *In search of America's past: learning to read history in the elementary school.* New York: Teachers College.

VanSledright, B., & Frankes, L. (2000). Concept- and strategic-knowledge development in historical study: A comparative exploration in two fourth-grade classrooms. *Cognition and Instruction, 18* (2), 239–283.

Wade, R. (2000). Beyond charity: Service learning for social justice. *Social Studies & the Young Learner, 12* (4), 6–9.

—— (2001). "And justice for all": Community service-learning for social justice. Education Commission of the States. Retrieved from www.ecs.org

—— (2007a). Service-learning for social justice in the elementary classroom: Can we get there from here? *Equity & Excellence in Education, 40* (2), 156–165.

—— (Ed.) (2007b). *Community action rooted in history: The CiviConnections model of service-learning.* Washington, DC: National Council for the Social Studies.

Wade, R., & Yarbrough, D. (2007). Service-learning in the social studies: Civic outcomes of the 3rd–12th grade CiviConnections program. *Theory and Research in Social Education, 35* (3), 366–392.

Westheimer, J., & Kahne, J. (2004). What kind of citizen? The politics of educating for democracy. *American Educational Research Journal, 41* (2), 237–269.

Wiegand, P. (2003). School students understanding of choropleth maps: Evidence from collaborative map making using GIS. *Journal of Geography, 102* (6), 234–242.

Wineburg, S. (2001). *Historical thinking and other unnatural acts.* Philadelphia, PA: Temple University Press.

Winters, E. A. (1967). Man and his changing society: The textbooks of Harold Rugg. *History of Education Quarterly, 7* (4), 493–514.

World Health Organization & UNICEF. (2006). *Meeting the MDG drinking water and sanitation target: The urban and rural challenge of the decade.* Geneva: WHO.

Zarnowski, M. (1998). It's more than dates and places: How nonfiction contributes to understanding social studies. In R. Bamford & J. Kristo (Eds.), *Making facts come alive: Choosing quality nonfiction in literature K–8* (pp. 93–108). Norwood, MA: Christopher-Gordon Publishers.

—— (2006). *Making sense of history: Using high-quality literature and hands-on experiences to build content knowledge.* New York: Scholastic.

Zastrow, C. von, & Janc, H. (2004). *Academic atrophy: The condition of the liberal arts in America's public schools.* Washington, DC: Council for Basic Education.

Teacher Resources

Day, H., & Ballard, D. (2006). *The classroom mini-economy.* Indianapolis, IN: Indiana Department of Education.

Developmental Studies Center. (1996). *Ways we want our class to be.* Embarcadero, CA: author.

Hakim, J. (1993). *The first Americans.* New York: Oxford University Press.

—— (1999). *A history of US* (Vols. 1–10). New York: Oxford University Press.

Kaplan, S., Kaplan, J. A., Madsen, S., & Taylor, B. (1973). *Change for children: Ideas and activities for individualizing learning.* Pacific Palisades, CA: Goodyear Publishing Co.

Kielburger, M., & Kielburger, C. (2002). *Take action! A guide to active citizenship.* Hoboken, NJ: John Wiley & Sons.

Lewis, B. (1995). *The kid's guide to service projects*. Minneapolis, MN: Free Spirit Publishing.

Lindquist, T. (1997). *Ways that work: Putting social studies standards into practice*. Portsmouth, NH: Heinemann.

Parker, W. (2005). *Social studies in elementary education* (12th ed.). Upper Saddle River, NJ: Merrill.

Weitzman, D. (1975). *My backyard history book*. Boston: Little Brown and Company.

Zarnowski, M. (2003). *History makers: A questioning approach to reading and writing biographies*. Portsmouth, NH: Heinemann.

Children's Literature

Collier, J., & Collier, C. (1974). *My brother Sam is dead*. New York: Four Winds Press.

Fleischman, P. (1997). *Seedfolks*. New York: HarperCollins Juvenile books.

Parks, R. (1992). *Rosa Parks: My story*. New York: Puffin Books.

Speare, E. (1958). *The witch of Blackbird Pond*. Boston: Houghton Mifflin.

Films

Carnes, J. (Director). (2002). *Mighty times: The legacy of Rosa Parks* [Film]. (Available from Teaching Tolerance, Southern Poverty Law Center, 400 Washington Avenue, Montgomery, AL 36104)

Pointer, R. (Director). (2004). *Rosa Parks: Modern day heroine* [Film]. (Available from Inkwell Images, 4015 Edenhurst Avenue, Los Angeles, CA 90039-1433)

Songs

Lodge-Rigal, B. (2002). It takes courage. On *Higher Hopes* [compact disk]. Bloomington, IN, 2001.

Index